Sky
Pioneering

Sky Pioneering
ARIZONA IN AVIATION HISTORY

Ruth M. Reinhold

THE UNIVERSITY OF ARIZONA PRESS
TUCSON, ARIZONA

About the Author...

RUTH M. REINHOLD began her research in the history of Arizona aviation in 1970, two years before she retired from commercial flying. She has been a private flight instructor and commercial pilot for several Arizona companies. Reinhold came to Arizona in 1933 after having studied fine arts at Boston University and at the University of California at Los Angeles. She was a member of the Arizona Department of Aeronautics Board and later of the Department of Transportation Board, and belongs to several historical societies.

THE UNIVERSITY OF ARIZONA PRESS

This book was set in 10/11 V-I-P Melior.

Library of Congress Cataloging in Publication Data

Reinhold, Ruth M.
  Sky pioneering.

  1. Aeronautics—Arizona—History. I. Title.
TL522.A6R44   387.7′09791   81-11514

ISBN 0-8165-0737-6   AACR2
ISBN 0-8165-0757-0 (pbk.)

Contents

ILLUSTRATIONS

Maps

Photographs

Foreword

I have known Ruth Reinhold since she first came to Arizona in the 1930s, at about the time she began her long career in flying. Through the middle years of this century, it was my pleasure to fly hundreds of hours with this experienced pilot and remarkable woman.

In our travels around the state, Ruth and I touched on almost every airstrip listed in the *Arizona Airport Directory*, plus eight or nine no longer listed. We touched often also on the topic of Arizona's role in the history of aviation, pondering how this segment of the state's history might be made into a book.

Eight years later, Ruth's manuscript was ready to be a book, following years of research in which she traveled the entire country, engaged in voluminous correspondence, collected photographs, sifted facts for truth, and eventually assembled Arizona's portion of the aviation story.

What Ruth has achieved in this book will, I believe, not only be worthy of emulation by other states but will help a broad range of American readers to appreciate Arizona's place in the ongoing saga of air transportation.

As Arizonans, we can look back on our aviation history with pride: pride in the people involved, in the industry thus brought to Arizona, and in the contribution to the defense of the nation through pilot training in this state. A great deal that many of us did not know about our own state will be found between the covers of this book, thanks to Ruth Reinhold's remarkable diligence and her keen sense of what was both spectacular and significant about Arizona's taking to the air.

BARRY M. GOLDWATER

A Word
From the
Author

I visited Phoenix's Sky Harbor airport for the first time in the spring of 1933. The scene, while far from impressive, was one I will never forget. The airline terminal was deserted, six small airplanes sat in lonely splendor in the middle of the one hangar, and the only activity was the dodging and darting of several dust devils playing tag on the bare dirt field.

Suppressing my doubts, I hunted up the airport manager and made arrangements to begin flying lessons. Several weeks later I made my first solo flight, an event that marked the beginning of my lifelong love affair with airplanes and flying.

Not long after that first solo, I went to work at the airport. My duties were bookkeeping, letter writing, and answering the telephone, but I was allowed to do some minor work on the aircraft under close supervision. For this I received the standard wages then paid to "apprentices": $7.50 a week plus two hours of flying time until I obtained my private and commercial pilot's licenses.

After earning the commercial ticket I was able to forsake office work and fly for a living. For the next thirty-five years I taught students, demonstrated and sold aircraft, and did charter and executive flying which took me from coast to coast and from Mexico to Canada. I also served on the Phoenix Aviation Advisory Board, the Arizona Department of Aeronautics Board, and the Arizona Department of Transportation Board.

During the late sixties and early seventies, my husband Bob and I made a number of flights to some of Arizona's older and more remote airports. We renewed old acquaintances, asked questions of the "whatever became of so and so" variety, and swapped tales about the early days of Arizona flying. After a few of these sessions, Bob suggested that I take notes on some of the stories we had heard. Many of the airport raconteurs were growing old and when they died, their memories of aviation's pioneer era would die with them.

Slowly my stack of notes grew. Jim Vercellino, then the director of the Arizona Department of Aeronautics, offered his encouragement, and suggested that Arizona should join the group of states that had already compiled aviation histories. Following my retirement from commercial flying in 1972, I was able to devote more time to corresponding with veteran pilots and airport people, and to make research trips to various libraries and museums. When Senator Barry Goldwater learned of the project his response was immediate and enthusiastic: "Write a book—and don't leave anything out!"

This history is the result. It could not possibly have come into existence without the aid and support of Senator Goldwater and the participation and cooperation of hundreds of aviation-minded Arizonans who generously shared old photographs, airport directories, approach charts, timetables, and, most importantly, their personal recollections.

To these individuals and especially to Senator Goldwater, I owe an enormous debt of gratitude. The University of Arizona Press is also to be thanked for bringing about publication.

Ruth M. Reinhold

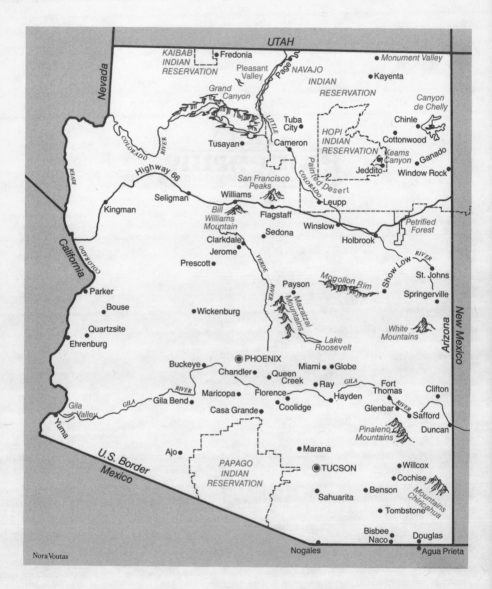

Principal towns and geographical features mentioned in the text.

The Air Age Comes to Arizona

The broad plaza in downtown Prescott, Arizona, was jammed with excited citizens on the afternoon of July 4, 1890. Dogs barked, babies cried, and small boys ran to and fro laughing and shouting. Many of the people in the huge crowd were standing on the tips of their toes, craning their necks to see over the heads of people in front of them. The babble of conversation was loud and a note of suspense and eager expectancy in the hundreds of voices charged the air over the plaza like a midsummer electric storm. This was to be no ordinary Independence Day celebration—the air age was about to be ushered in to Prescott—and the jostling throng was impatiently waiting to witness this thrilling and historic event.

The center of attention, a large canvas balloon, billowed in the middle of the plaza. Eager volunteers held the big bag by its cords while it was inflated, and when it became sufficiently light to rise a few feet a trapeze bar was attached.

Now a sudden, breathless hush fell across the crowd as the daring lady aeronaut, resplendent in spangled tights, stepped forward. She sat down lightly on the trapeze, rearranged her costume, and then called out to her helpers, "Let me go, boys!" The big white sphere, which had seemed so dingy on the ground, became a snowy glistening globe as it rose gently and drifted toward nearby Fort Whipple. In a few minutes the lady released a parachute which blossomed into an enormous red and white flower and, detached from its lifting ballon, let her slowly down to the ground, while the balloon, deprived of its buoyancy by the atmosphere, rolled gently over and descended independently. The crowd cheered as the aeronaut and her balloon were picked up by a Ruffner express wagon.

There were more ascensions during the afternoon, and for each consecutive performance the lady wore a different colored costume—red, then white, and finally blue. All were striking, each topped with a sequined bodice and tiny ballet skirt fluffing out over matching tights. These were the days of sweeping skirts and leg-o'-mutton sleeves, and the glittering costumes and tights created a sensation in the plaza and caused a stampede which cleaned out all the saloons on Whiskey Row. Everyone agreed the exhibitions were wonderful—with the exception of a few matrons who murmured criticism relative to the tights.

The residents of the Mountain City went home happy and satisfied that night, believing that they had seen a spectacular, once-in-a-lifetime performance. They were only partly right. The show had been spectacular, but it was not unique, either to Arizona or the United States as a whole. In fact, ballooning was a relatively common activity, and many Prescott citizens would have been surprised to learn how far back in history such aeronautical activity went.

PRELUDE TO POWER

A new country has no traditions and no legends save those brought from the homelands, and our early settlers struggled first to survive in a raw new world, and then to develop viable communities and industries. None could afford the luxury of dreaming of the old flying myths and folklore, or of dwelling on the new scientific aerial experiments then exciting Europe.

By the latter half of the 17th century, conditions were better. There was a bit of time now to indulge in studies, idle fancy, and gossip. Sailing fleets briskly crossed the oceans between the colonies and their mother countries, carrying goods and news, including scientific writings and political opinions. These voyages continued in spite of governmental differences. It was not a question of whether the colonists would know what was going on in Europe, but how soon.

Isaac Newton's *Principia* was released in 1687 and read; Benjamin Franklin demonstrated the affinity of lightning and electricity, and the lightning rod made him famous; and in 1776 Professor Henry Cavendish recognized "inflammable air" (hydrogen) as being 14½ times lighter than air.

Meanwhile, Joseph Montgolfier and his sons, Etienne and Joseph, successful paper makers at Annonay, France, experimented with heated air trapped in global containers of various materials. On

June 4, 1783, they held a public demonstration in their town square. They released a paper-lined, linen bag with a circumference of over 100 feet. It rose to an altitude of 6,000 feet, and then gently came to earth about a mile distant. This exhibition was followed by a command performance on September 19, using a larger aerostat in which a sheep, a rooster, and a duck were sent aloft to ascertain if life at such dizzying heights above earth was possible. The aerial menagerie gracefully rose, drifted for about a mile, and softly landed in a nearby pasture.

Now, with the blessings of the French Academy of Sciences and King Louis XVI and his queen, the Montgolfiers built a more ambitious aerostatic machine capable of carrying two men to stoke the fire, and extra fuel in the form of chopped wood and straw. On November 21, 1783, Jean François Pilatre de Rosier and the Marquis d'Arlanders, an infantry major, had the honor of being the first men to fly in a human invention. Their historic flight carried them about five miles, and lasted about twenty-five minutes. Man, after centuries of dreaming, hoping and frustrations, had risen above the earth in a machine of his own invention and fabrication.

The spectacular 1783 French balloon ascensions were witnessed by Benjamin Franklin, and thanks to his meticulous observations and precise reporting, American ballooning soon got off to a flying start. It is generally considered that the air age arrived in this country on June 24, 1784, when thirteen-year-old Edward Warren went aloft in a tethered hot-air balloon built by Peter Carnes near Baltimore.

In 1824 a Frenchman, Eugene Robertson, came to New York to give ballooning exhibitions. He attracted large crowds and so impressed young Charles Durant that Durant sailed to France as Robertson's pupil. He returned in 1830 and thus became America's first professional aeronaut. He toured the eastern cities, gave instruction, and finally turned to the manufacture of balloons. By 1840 some were being shipped as far away as California.

BALLOONS AND DIRIGIBLES IN ARIZONA

The first recorded aeronautical activity in Arizona occurred on May 13, 1889. "Professor LeRoy" received almost front page treatment in the Phoenix newspapers for his aerial exploits. The "Flying Cloud," scheduled for an ascension from Patton's Park at three o'clock, caused a traffic jam! "Hundreds of people were there, the streetcars were taxed to capacity," reported the *Phoenix Herald*.

It must have been unseasonably warm, as inflation of the balloon was delayed until a little after five. Meanwhile, impatient spectators found amusement at a shooting gallery until some small boys chopped down a tree which furnished the main support for the stand's back wall which promptly collapsed. The disappointed marksmen then tried to cool off in the swings, but more small boys had broken these. As a last resort the crowd flocked to the "ices" and cool drink concessions.

About 5:30 p.m. the "Flying Cloud" and the Professor ascended. "He jumped from about 3,000 feet," wrote the *Phoenix Herald,* "and fell with terrific speed," opened his parachute and floated down for a soft landing in a nearby field.

Another balloon ascension occurred in September 1892. The *Arizona Gazette* announced that "on the 25th Mlle B. Ozola assisted by the world renowned aeronaut Prof. F. Getzher will endeavor to please the public by making a leap of between 4,000 and 5,000 feet, [after] ascending from a vacant lot on Montezuma St. between Washington and Adams." Mademoiselle Ozola was well known as an aeronaut and parachute jumper.

In December 1894 the citizens of Yuma enjoyed an act by Miss Hazel Keys. The lady took up a small dog which she sent down with a parachute strapped to its back, and she descended in another. The balloon was recovered nearby.

In August 1904 the first practical dirigible, the "California Arrow," was flight-tested over San Francisco Bay. The development of the dirigible marked the beginning of the decline in the free hot-air balloons' popularity. By 1910, except for the Zeppelin-type, all ballooning was losing ground to powered flight. They were still present at larger air meets, but gradually they passed on to the smaller county fairs, traveling with chautauquas, medicine shows and circuses which often timed their performances to coincide with important rural celebrations.

It was just such a celebration that brought the first dirigible to Arizona in 1908. The exciting news broke early in October of that year—the Territorial Fair Commission had engaged the famous Roy Knabenshue and his huge passenger-carrying airship to perform in Phoenix during Fair Week. The October 17 *Jerome Mining News* expounded on the subject, stating that the ship was 112 feet long, 17 feet in diameter, and required 20,000 cubic feet of gas to be inflated. On this same day the *Phoenix Gazette* headlined: "Airship People Have Arrived."

The Arizona Territorial Fair opened on the morning of November 9, 1908, with the successful ascension of the big, white silk bag, skillfully piloted by Knabenshue and his engineer, George Duesler. Two autos, one carrying the *Gazette* representative, followed the shining airship to record its speed as it soared over the city. Thousands rushed from their offices and homes to see the dirigible and cheer. It had been announced that the first flight would be over the capitol building; the change in plans was made—though not announced by the Fair Commission—to give the downtown office workers a pleasant surprise.

The first dirigible in Arizona aloft after taking off from the Territorial Fairgrounds on the morning of November 9, 1908. Roy Knabenshue was the pilot and George Duesler the engineer. Vertical control of the craft was managed by the crew's traveling back and forth on the girders. They were, of course, careful to watch their step.

On this bright morning there was a west wind of about ten miles per hour. As the big dirigible soared from the Fair Grounds and headed eastward along McDowell Road, the *Gazette* car really had to "step on it" to catch up with it near Seventh Avenue. The dirigible's speed was recorded as a little more than thirty miles an hour when it veered south to fly over the *Gazette* office. Crowds lined Central Avenue, waving and cheering the airborne crew. Then the huge, shining white bag turned west, heading for the Fair Grounds.

At Second Avenue the *Gazette* car was right under the dirigible and the crews waved to each other. Going into the wind the airship's speed was reduced to "about twenty miles an hour," judging from the car's speedometer. This gradually diminished and altitude was lost from "about 200 feet" until the ship reached the Fair Grounds where a small cable was dropped, caught by a ground crew, and the airship stopped no more than fifty feet from its takeoff spot. It had been a wonderful and thrilling performance, and the reporter counted himself one of the luckiest men in Phoenix to have engaged in the chase.

Later that day L. H. Landis, general agent for the Southern Pacific Railroad, approached the big dirigible lugging 200 S. P. "dodgers" to scatter over town. He would defy gravity, drop his paper shower on Phoenix, and be Knabenshue's first Arizona passenger—whether paid or free the records do not state. Landis's remarks to the press following his flight indicated ambivalence. He was offered a khaki suit but told he could wear his business clothes if he wished. Believing one should be properly dressed for any occasion, he opted for the khaki outfit. He also scraped a bit of dirt under his fingernails and wore a hat for additional disguise. Unfortunately, his advertising matter was not released. He was "too busy holding on with both hands." After almost an hour's flight and a safe return, he reported feeling a little wobbly, but "who would not have strange sensations after walking on air for almost an hour?" In later conversations with the press he was variously quoted as saying he would "pay $100 to go up any time;" and he would "not get into one of those things again for $10,000." He asked the reporters to be sure to mention his Southern Pacific advertising. He indicated he had no intention of making another trip; after all, he did not wish to be selfish, and others might want to ride, too.

Two weeks after Knabenshue's spectacular exhibition at Phoenix, a balloon again made news in Arizona. "Aeronauts on Colorado Desert," read a headline in the *Arizona Gazette* Wednesday evening, November 25, 1908. The big balloon "America" with her crew, Captain A. E. Fuller, and a Los Angeles reporter from the *Record* had landed on the 23rd on the rough desert about twenty miles east of Ehrenburg, but not from choice. That morning the

"America" with another big balloon had commenced a race from Los Angeles to Milwaukee—or as near to that city as they could get. About six hours out, the bag of the "America" had sprung a leak and the ship gently descended. The men, hanging onto its basket, bumped and scraped along the rough, spiny desert for a little over a mile before the outfit came to a grating halt. The *Gazette* reporter wrote in his story that the pair "escaped from a horrible death in many forms." Neither man was injured.

The aeronauts had no idea where they were—Arizona, California or Mexico—but after spending the night in an abandoned Indian wickieup, they started walking west, lugging their emergency provisions. About noon they met a party of men returning to Phoenix from the Blythe estate. The aerialists learned they were about twenty miles east of Ehrenburg, and calculated the "America" had averaged roughly forty miles an hour before misfortune overtook her. Everyone returned to the grounded ship for pictures (unfortunately, none have been located) and, as the Phoenicians were in a hurry to reach Parker, the balloonists were left at Ehrenburg while the touring group headed for Bouse, Parker and, ultimately, home.

The *Record* reporter was concerned about contacting his paper and extracted a promise from the Phoenix group not to mention their encounter with the balloon travelers until there was time for him to reach a phone and call Los Angeles. The request was honored; hence, no news reached Phoenix until Wednesday. The collapsed "America" was later retrieved.

Following the exciting November of 1908, Arizona would see few lighter-than-air vehicles until 1924, when the "Shenandoah" made her historic voyage and crossed the state twice. All interest was now in powered heavier-than-air flight and its intriguing possibilities.

BOX PLANES AND BIRDMEN

Four hesitant, wavering flights from a standing start, the longest lasting fifty-nine seconds and covering a distance of 852 feet, marked the beginning of powered flight with wings. The December 17, 1903, achievements of the Wright brothers were followed by disappointments and failures, but their experiments continued in spite of Patent Office problems and difficulties with a skeptical press.

In 1908 the brothers overcame the U. S. government's aeronautical apathy, and Orville signed a contract with the army for an airplane to be delivered that fall. Wilbur, then in France with another machine, charmed European flying enthusiasts with his expertise and modesty and sold French patent rights to a syndicate for $100,000. After seeing Wilbur Wright's flying skills and his

small craft's abilities, an intuitive witness, the English Major
B. F. S. Baden-Powell, declared with considerable insight that the
brothers were "in possession of a power that would control the
fate of nations."

At home, more people decided that flying was here to stay and
joined with established groups of the aeronautically interested,
thereby swelling the exchange of new knowledge and ideas. Activity
blossomed along the Pacific coast and the eastern seaboard. In
Chicago a nucleus formed which would influence the midwest-
ern plains and, gradually, the entire United States and Canada.
Chicago's Cicero Field became an important hub for flight schools
and a haven for airplane builders. Glenn Curtiss' factory at
Hammondsport was busy, the Wrights' plant near Dayton, Ohio,
hummed, and a few small parts houses cautiously opened.

Arizona, because of its scant and scattered population, a few
reports of "hostile Indians" lurking in the hinterlands, and geographical barriers of mountains and treacherous deserts, lagged behind some more hospitable sections of the country. However, these
obstacles were not insurmountable to the United States Mails, and
some parts houses did mail order business in the Territory as early as
1907 or 1908. It was only a matter of time before the flying bug
would bite Arizona, and bite hard.

The Douglas Glider

Early in 1908 a group of aspiring young Douglas birdmen was
building a small, single-place glider. By summer the machine was
making several flights a week along a mile stretch of dirt road northeast of town. Ted Bowden, son of the local livery stable proprietor,
rode the racehorse "Pancho" while driving a pair of fast buggy
horses which hauled the glider aloft. Crowds came to witness this
spectacular two-horsepower rig make its mile-long dash, and found
the show worth every penny that was deposited in the hat passed
following each exhibition. As long as the "kitty" was sufficiently
fed, a fresh team was brought in and another breathtaking performance staged.

Creation of this horse-drawn missile seems to have been a sort
of small community enterprise involving at least eight or nine men,
mostly members of the younger sporting element. Judge Forte was
frequently present, and his son Carlos was an active participant. Dr.
A. R. Hickman, a mining company physician, felt a responsibility
should there be an accident, and thus witnessed most of the flights.
Pancho's two owners, A. M. Williams and Sparks Y. Faucet, both
clerk-salesmen for the Douglas Grocery Store, were active members.
Felipe Mazon, who assisted with Pancho's training and the school-
ing of other horses, was often present with his brothers.

It appears that John C. Wright and Ben Goodsell were the principals in charge of the glider's engineering and design. It is likely that they sent away for mail order plans and specifications to aid them with its construction. Wright, a photo enlarger and artisan, was Arizona's first glider pilot. Goodsell worked for the Douglas Traction and Light Company as engineer and draftsman; thus, he made most of the drawings for the glider project and he and Wright collaborated on numerous later design changes that would motorize the small bird.

Unknown to the Douglas group, they had competition in the glider field. Unknown, that is, unless they happened to see an item in the November 16, 1909, issue of the *Arizona Gazette*. On an inner page was the modest caption "Gates Fowler Makes Another Flight at the Phoenix Fair Grounds." The reporter seemed unable to decide whether the vehicle was an airplane or a glider, but it was certainly not lighter-than-air. It was probably the state's second heavier-than-air flying machine. No other records of its activities can be found. For this particular sortie the owner had removed the ball-bearing wheels and installed skids. The tow car, burdened with the additional drag of the wooden runners, "could only attain a speed of about 12 miles an hour with Fowler on board." This was insufficient for lift. Gates got out, and "at 18 miles an hour the machine rose up about 10 or 12 feet and flew or sailed for about 200 feet."

Following its solo adventure, the little glider "landed gracefully and with no damage," which spoke well for its stability, and the gratified Gates said that he was going to buy it an engine. Unfortunately, no record of subsequent flights has been found.

By the fall of 1909, all Arizona was becoming aviation-minded. The *Arizona Gazette* wrote that toy airships were the "Kings of Toyland," indicating that any child who did not have one was underprivileged. Some were very expensive. For $10 an indulgent parent could purchase an airborne plaything with an alcohol-burning motor; another model carried and could drop small exploding bombs. Either would create a sensation at any party. The smaller Scout models sold for as little as $1.50, and because they operated with rubber bands and carried no live ammunition, seemed a saner choice.

At the end of 1909 Arizona's aeronautical complement appears to have consisted of two glider pilots, John Wright and Gates Fowler, the latter planning to buy an engine for his wee bird. Several old-time residents of Douglas believe that that community's one-place glider had been strengthened and motorized and had made a few cautious aerial excursions with Felipe Mazon at its controls. If this is correct, Arizona would have had two glider pilots and one airplane pilot, one glider and a powered airplane. The Army Signal Corps had one Wright flying machine.

EARLY AIR SHOWS

Los Angeles sponsored the First International Air Meet in the United States during January 1910. The event was held at Domín-guez Field, which just a few weeks before had been a cow pasture. The *Arizona Republican* broke the news on January 3 in a small item buried several pages back, noting that sufficient money had been raised by advertising to attract famous participants. The reporter appeared to doubt the sanity of all concerned—promoters, advertisers, contestants and any spectators who might be foolish enough to attend.

A few days later the dates were made firm as January 10–20, and participants included Louis Paulhan, the famous French pilot, Charles K. Hamilton, and Glenn Curtiss, as well as other, lesser lights, making a total of twenty aviators, balloonists, and disciples. "Arizona Day" would be on January 20.

The show was an outstanding success in spite of two rainy, blustery days. Curtiss set a new speed record of fifty-five miles per hour, and Paulhan's altitude registered 4,165 feet, setting another record. Spectators reacted according to their temperaments. Some prayed, others bit their fingernails, still others cried, and a few ladies fainted during the harrowing ordeal. The attendance was variously estimated as from 20,000 to 40,000 persons.

The First Phoenix Air Show—1910

On January 18, Nat Reiss, who had attended the first aviation meet in Los Angeles, announced plans to hold what was billed as the "Second Aviation Meet in the United States" in Phoenix the follow-ing month. He could get the performers, including Glenn Curtiss, for a guarantee of $12,000, which was less than Los Angeles had put up. Great crowds were anticipated, and he emphasized that it would be beneficial to the merchants and the entire state to have the show in town. Planned admission was $1 for adults and 50 cents for children. He returned to Phoenix and immediately contacted Dr. J. W. Foss, president of the Board of Trade. A meeting was called and attended by about twenty-eight interested citizens including Baron Goldwa-ter, Sims Ely, and Charles Korrick. Reiss explained that $12,000 plus 25 percent of the gate receipts had to be pledged; furthermore, all subscribers were warned to expect no return for their investment. There had been Tucson representatives in Los Angeles who were trying to land the show, and the principal flyer, Glenn Curtiss, could appear only once in any state that year.

By January 22 the Phoenix Aero Club had been duly incorpo-rated, the first subscriptions of $25 per share sold, and $12,870 de-posited in the bank. The event was originally planned for February 3, 4, and 5, but was later changed to February 10, 11, and 12.

The Phoenix Aero Club planned well and worked hard. Headquarters were established next to the Phoenix National Bank. The advertising program began—dodgers were posted as far away as Prescott and Jerome—and the show houses presented slides of numerous airmen with their machines. The railroads announced excursion fares to the meet from Yuma, El Paso, and Guaymas, Mexico. The *Republican* wrote that "it was the civic duty of Phoenix to be prepared to sleep 10,000." Citizens were asked to assist in providing rooms and a registration desk was set up at headquarters to help with this.

On February 2, a train carrying a Curtiss biplane steamed into the Phoenix depot under custody of Wells Fargo. Glenn Curtiss sent word that he would be unable to come because of a patent infringement case with the Wrights against the Curtiss-Herring Company. This did not prevent him from sending his two top pilots, Charles F. Willard and Charles K. Hamilton, with their two Curtiss machines. On February 5 regrets came from the Wrights. They were unable to attend or send any airplanes due to military commitments.

The big meet opened February 10 to a capacity crowd. The *Republican* carried a headline the next day that read: "Arizona Atmosphere Split to Fragments," and on February 12 "Genius and Gasolene [sic] Triumphantly Soar." There were plane and auto races, with the airplanes holding a slight edge. Hamilton beat a Studebaker in a five-mile race, given a thirty-second head start. Without the handicap he won by 2 1/5 seconds. These were flights of considerable duration for those days, and Hamilton's eight-cylinder biplane and Willard's four-cylinder machine were in the air simultaneously. Both pilots gave outstanding exhibitions.

The following day things went wrong. A propeller broke. Hamilton's plane caught fire in the air; he managed to extinguish the blaze but burned his thumb. He lost three of his silk upper panels and, because of this, decided to omit his celebrated show-stopper, the steep glide with engine off—a very hazardous maneuver under the best of circumstances.

The performers were requested to remain over for another day, and the following afternoon did their best flying although the crowd was not so large.

Financially, the show was a success. The crowds were well managed, the weather perfect, and the sometimes reluctant press unstinting in its praise.

The First Tucson Air Show—1910

The first successful Phoenix Air Show was a pleasant memory. Money was in the bank to meet all bills and the happy Phoenix Aero Club bid the gratified birdmen good-bye. Charles K. Hamilton was whizzing to Tucson on the Southern Pacific and his biplane was

Courtesy of the Arizona Historical Society

Charles K. Hamilton takes off in his Curtiss biplane from Tucson's Elysian Grove on February 19, 1910. This was the first heavier-than-air flight in Tucson.

making the trip by rail under custody of Wells Fargo. Little Patagonia had guaranteed him $4,000 for an exhibition, but he had elected to accept Tucson's offer of $2,000 plus 50 percent of the gate.

On February 19, 1910, Tucsonians saw their first airplane fly. The arrangements for the show were made by George F. Kitt, president of the Chamber of Commerce, Emanuel Drachman, owner of Drachman's Amusement Park, and other businessmen. To control the paid admissions, the exhibitions were held inside a high-fenced enclosure. Unfortunately, the property outside was neither protected nor properly policed. Hamilton made flights on both the 19th and 20th, but the fence caused minor accidents—snagged wings—on both days. In spite of precautions taken, the paid admission was disappointing—$802—and the Chamber had to pony up $1,200 to meet their guarantees. Too many spectators had elected to stay outside the fence.

Hamilton and his golden-winged biplane next visited El Paso for exhibitions on February 22, 23, and 24. There were problems caused by the high altitude of the city—3,950 feet, which accounted for its rarefied air—and one annoyed spectator remarked that he "could fly better with his shirttail." Additional airfoil space was added to the machine's wings and subsequent performances were complimented; however, all steep banks were omitted, again because of the rarefied air.

The First Douglas Air Show—1910

Before the dust and prop wash from the First Phoenix Air Meet settled, Douglas had commenced negotiations with Hamilton to give a performance. Whether the overtures were agitated by the owner-builders of the rather notorious two-horse glider hitch, now transformed into a Buick-powered airplane, is not known. At least one of the group, A. M. Williams, had seen the Phoenix Air Show as evidenced by a postcard sent to his family, then living in Morenci. On the back he wrote, "Believe I have the best machine. Am going to try it when I get home." Local opinions are that by this time the glider was motorized and had even made a few cautious flights.

Hamilton and show manager Nat Reiss wanted a $2,000 guarantee for the famous pilots' exhibitions. By February 14 only $1,000 had been pledged; however, two days later everything was in high gear and both Hamilton and Charles Willard were scheduled to give performances. The El Paso and Southern Railroad offered a round-trip ride for the price of a one-way ticket from Tombstone, Bisbee, and Cochise. On February 21, the *Bisbee Miner* ran a full-page ad promoting the exciting event and, as a further inducement, an excursion package was offered for only $2. It included a round-trip fare, admission to the meet, and a month's subscription to the paper—all representing a savings of 75 cents.

Hamilton, his mechanics, and the 50-horsepower Curtiss pulled into the Douglas station on the afternoon of February 25. The night was spent assembling the airplane. Charles Willard, with his smaller four-cylinder 25-horsepower engine, had wisely decided to pass on both El Paso and Douglas. Hamilton's experience with the half-mile Tucson field surrounded by the fence and trees and his first disappointing day at El Paso indicated that the higher country was no spot for an airplane packing half the power of his machine; thus, Willard's Phoenix performance was his only show in the state.

Southern Arizona weather on the day of the show was clear but gusty. Crowds began entering the fairgrounds about one o'clock, and a few minutes before three the golden-winged airplane was pushed in front of the grandstand for exhibition. This was followed by a few announcements and explanations, and then the machine was pushed to the southeast corner of the field. Men held the impatient craft while the engine was being started and Hamilton scrambled on board. Within minutes, following a perfect takeoff, he was high above the crowds, both inside the enclosure and out. He swung to the left, passing over sections of Douglas and possibly over Mexico, and then eastward down the valley. Next came a gentle left turn and a sweeping flight over the grandstand before another circle and a perfect landing.

The announcer called it a "cross-country flight" and estimates were that the machine's speed was about 35 miles an hour and its altitude between 300 and 500 feet. The flight lasted 12 minutes. The little airplane was fueled, some minor adjustments made, and the skillful pilot took off for another flawless exhibition.

An enthusiastic reporter from the *Douglas Daily Dispatch* wrote that never had there been two more perfect flights: "Both were away at the first attempt, and his landings executed with such remarkable precision that the aeroplane was never in the remotest danger from running into any obstacle." He added that everyone was satisfied with the performance, but many remarked that "it looked so simple." On a gusty afternoon that statement was a compliment to a good pilot.

The show had been a financial as well as esthetic success. Over 750 people from Bisbee had attended and spent $3,000; in addition, hundreds from other communities and many from Douglas attended. Bisbee was now going to plan its own air show.

A Second Air Show for Phoenix—1910

Arizona closed the year with a second air show in Phoenix. Early in December, Whipple Hall, advance man for show pilot Captain Baldwin, was in town to make the arrangements. Dates were set for December 9 and 10, and both Baldwin and J. C. Mars would perform. The latter had a new design Curtiss with a 75-horsepower motor, making it capable of putting on a real show. No guarantee was asked, just a percentage of the gate and a few minor improvements at the Fair Grounds.

Just after the contract was signed, a wire came announcing that Baldwin had smashed his machine, several days would be required for repairs, and the entire show would be put on by Mars. This was the first of a series of misadventures that plagued the event, but as the Phoenix Board of Trade was committed, it decided to stick with the agreement.

Both the public and the press agreed that Mars gave the best show ever seen in Phoenix. His graceful takeoff was followed by at least a dozen circles of the field at about 200 feet. These were followed by a landing, another takeoff, and more circles at 1,000 feet with his second perfect arrival made just at sundown.

He had been late arriving and the performance did not start until four o'clock, which accounted for the poor attendance. The cause of the tardy show was a defective radiator which a mechanic had discovered just a day before Mars' departure for Phoenix. His machine and mechanics had arrived by train a few days earlier.

Wires flew back and forth, and it was decided that Mars would bring a replacement with him. However, the supply in Los Angeles was exhausted. He might have been able to borrow one from his friend Willard's airplane, but Willard could not be located. It was nearing train time and the desperate Mars simply swiped the necessary part from Charlie's parked machine and, with some misgivings as to the owner's reaction, boarded the train with the radiator.

Again on the 10th the crowd was small, this time due to lack of publicity. Mars was hoping for an altitude record in the smooth winter air, but his engine was fouling plugs and sputtering. The auto-airplane race was won by the plane in spite of its fretful engine, but one reporter intimated that "maybe the car driver was not trying too hard."

Financially the show was a failure because of the poor patronage; however, Mars did not seem to be disgruntled, remarking that he had always "wanted to try one without a guarantee." The *Republican* stated that "Phoenix was the first city to have two aviation meets." Presumably it meant in one year.

The First Bisbee Air Show—1911

Following Charles K. Hamilton's outstanding performance at Douglas, the air show contagion hit Bisbee, and negotiations were begun with west coast agents and G. E. Clements, representative for International Aviators, Inc. This $500,000 corporation managed six pilots, including Roland Garos, Charles Hamilton, and the newly famous "only flying cowboy," Rene Simon, who had soared to fame at Fort Worth as the first birdman to herd cattle with an airplane. In spite of Clements' approval of the Warren Country Club as an airport, the city fathers and the Board of Trade turned down his offer, possibly fearing the costs of his flyers and the shipping charges to the Arizona hustings.

A few weeks later negotiations opened with Didier Masson, who had come to the United States with Louis Paulhen and two or three other aspiring young French pilots for the January 1910 Domínguez Air Meet. He was the only member of the French group who performed in Arizona, and his aeronautical escapades in the state make a fat file of accomplishments and failures—both within and without the law.

He agreed to bring his machine, the "Pegasus," and mechanics to Bisbee as long as the town could guarantee him the sale of $1,500 worth of admissions. This was not a guarantee but a gentlemen's agreement, and it looked good to the Board of Trade. Masson had recently distinguished himself as the first aerial carrier of a major newspaper by hauling 500 pounds of *Los Angeles Times* the 75 miles from Los Angeles to San Bernardino at an altitude of 5,000 feet, a noteworthy accomplishment.

The Bisbee event was scheduled for February 12. Several days before the show, Masson, his mechanics, and the "Pegasus," accompanied by the usual boxes of spare parts, arrived by train. The entire assembly was unloaded and hauled to the Warren Country Club where, several senior citizens recollect, a knot-holed fence had been hastily thrown up around the performance area.

On February 11, Captain John Greenway and Masson drove around the valley to select a course over which the valiant "Pegasus" would race. Masson may have had second thoughts about the entire venture when he saw the terrain over which he was to fly. The Country Club was at an altitude of almost 5,000 feet and surrounded by low foothills. The site was plagued by turbulence and gusts, and the fence built around the performance area further complicated matters. In 1911 little was known about gusty air or its causes, but everyone was acquainted with kids and adult freeloaders; hence, thirty cowboys and thirty cavalrymen were to police the hills and knotholes. This would be a well-run meet.

On February 12, Arizona weather staged its own air show, one that grounded both birds and birdmen. Flying was impossible, and "Pegasus" shuddered in its frail, improvised hangar while a typical, mean Arizona cold front zipped across the territory. There were no weather forecasts then, and the Bisbee press restricted its comments to "torrential rains, tornado-like winds, and blinding snows."

On the afternoon of February 15, Masson and "Pegasus" took off from the Warren Country Club—one assumes not very gracefully. The plane reached an altitude of about 100 feet with considerable weaving and fluttering. It appeared to be straining unsuccessfully for altitude during the erratic flight and in a few minutes Masson, in desperation, headed for the sanctuary of a golf course fairway. On the approach the propeller hit a bunker, starting a chain of unhappy, splintering results. Shattered pieces hit the fuel tank, tore into the rear center section of the upper wing, and split the engine mount.

"Pegasus" was hauled to the hangar, where the crates were opened, a new prop installed, and other repairs made. It was explained that the high Bisbee altitude, figured at 5,000 feet, produced "rarefied air." To overcome this inconvenience, three and a half feet were added to the top wing tips, using spruce, bamboo, and muslin from the precious supplies. Masson's mechanic offered another explanation. He said "Pegasus" had a "colicky engine." Mr. Adossides, Masson's manager, told the immense, disappointed crowd that there would be another flight on Washington's Birthday. The airplane would be repaired by then—and admission would be free.

On that day a still-larger mob of eager spectators invaded Bisbee. "Pegasus" was repaired by 3:30 P.M. and some twenty min-

The "Pegasus" after crash landing on the Bisbee-Warren golf course on
February 15, 1911.

utes later it was rolled from its improvised hangar and dragged
to the racetrack while a crowd of about 500 trailed behind it. The
majority of the spectators, remembering its previous erratic ascension, played it safe and remained near the clubhouse or hangar.
Shortly after 4:00 P.M. Masson and the reluctant "Pegasus" were in
the air—but not very high (according to the reporter, about 100 feet).
The mini-hop was terminated on the far side of an irrigation canal.
No specific information on the second failure was announced by
Masson or Adossides. The people waited and shivered in the pene-
trating cold for another hour. Many missed the 4:30 P.M. train and
trolley schedules. The two mechanics were the only ones giving any
information relative to the machine's limited performance. One said
the motor failed to develop sufficient power at the high altitudes,
and the other that the engine was out of order.

The lame "Pegasus," with her owner and mechanics, left the
city in the same manner as it arrived—by train. Both the *Bisbee
Review* and the Board of Trade members were somewhat bitter
after the event and turned their attentions to a more reliable form
of transportation, the automobile, by beginning a campaign urging
motorists to use the Borderland Route for all transcontinental
car journeys.

ARIZONA'S FIRST TWO AIRCRAFT CORPORATIONS

The year 1910 had been a good one for aviation in Arizona, and more progress was indicated as the Territory gained its first two airplane companies by the year's end. The Phoenix Aero Club was a nonprofit organization, but these two were seriously in the flying machine business. Little information is available on the first, the Continental Aircraft and Transportation Company, formed by two Chicagoans on April 10, 1910. A stock certificate issued for 500 shares is extant, as are some very incomplete and blurry Corporation Commission microfilms. The company held various aircraft patents, but no records of aircraft ownership or operations are in the files. Annual reports were filed from 1912 through 1952, when the Commission revoked Continental's certificate.

More tantalizing but still incomplete information is available for the second corporation, the Arizona Airmobile Company. The president, designer and builder was Norwegian-born Olaf S. Emblem. Plans for marketing the Airmobile was progressing by the summer of 1910. Parts had been ordered and intentions were that it would be flying by Fair Week. The *Arizona Republican* noted that "the Curtiss machines weighed 950 pounds and had a carrying surface of 230 square feet which required a speed of 40 miles an hour to produce flight, while Emblem's design only weighed 600 pounds, had 500 square feet of lifting surface and should leave the ground at seventeen miles an hour."

By mid-October the framework was completed, guy wires were in place, the tail had been tacked on, and the plane's two eight-foot propellers were in town. It would be simple to operate—if anyone could drive a car he could fly the Airmobile, as no particular skill or training was necessary. The awkward levers or sticks used by the Wrights were abandoned; the pilot "drove" it with a single sensible control—a wheel.

One of the main features of the machine was a lead pendulum weight balancing the wing tip controls (presumably ailerons), which prevented the craft from tipping over. As this device was to be patented, the reporter stated that it was a closely guarded secret and no information would be released. Another unique feature was the simple "vee" tail connected to a universal which activated elevators and rudders. (Who said the modern Model 35 Bonanza was the first to use the distinctive and efficient "vee" tail?)

The little airplane was not ready in time to fly at the fair but it ventured into its element the following year with considerable publicity.

The Territory's aeronautical progress at the end of 1910 now included two nebulous airplane companies (one with a partially-completed machine), Gates Fowler and his mysterious glider, and the little Douglas machine, which according to gossip was motorized and flying, between minor mishaps, under guidance of the Douglas pilots A. M. Williams, Carlos Forte, and Felipe Mazon. The report from the First Signal Officer lists the U.S. Army as owning one Wright airplane, three captive ballons and a small practice dirigible as its total inventory of objects aeronautical at the close of 1910. It seems that the isolated Territory of Arizona showed reasonable progress considering its scanty population of some 204,354.

ARIZONA AND THE FIRST TRANSCONTINENTAL AIR RACE

The first air meets featured local flights with distance and altitude records as added attractions. As these began to pall, various organizations and publications offered cash prizes for longer distance or endurance flights. The trend was towards the transportation phase rather than exhibitions.

In the summer of 1911, William Randolph Hearst's *American* offered $50,000 to the first man who could fly across the American continent within thirty consecutive days and complete the journey by October 10, 1911. Contestants could choose their own routes and direction of flight.

Of the several entrants only two completed the trip. Both made Arizona aviation history, piloting the first aircraft to fly into the state on their own power, one from the west and the other from the east. Their only meeting was a short visit in Tucson on the University of Arizona campus. Considering their varied aerial misfortunes across the United States, they were blessed with reasonably good weather in Arizona and rare good luck. The pair, like many early birdmen, were former race-car drivers and motorcycle enthusiasts. They liked speed and things mechanical, and certainly deserved credit for doggedness and their abilities to absorb punishment and keep going.

The favorite contestant, at least with the press, was Calbraith Perry Rodgers, great-grandson of Commodore Matthew Perry. Cal's great-uncle was Commodore Oliver Hazard Perry, and his father, Captain C. P. Rodgers, had been killed in the early Arizona Indian Wars. Denied military service for physical reasons, Cal took up flying early in 1911, and following approximately an hour-and-a-half of dual instruction, soloed at the Wright School. Orville considered him an apt pupil and invited him to start exhibition flying with the Wright team.

At the nine-day International Air meet in Chicago during the summer of 1911, various cash prizes were given for specific events. The sponsors also guaranteed $2 for each minute the contestants were in the air during official hours. The Wrights, the Moissants, and Glenn Curtiss sent their star teams, and numerous independent performers competed. The purse for total duration in the air went to

Cal Rodgers, who up to that time was comparatively unknown. His total time was 27 hours, 16 seconds, out of a possible 31½ hours. His total winnings for all events he entered were an impressive $11,285.

This windfall gave Cal sufficient money to buy an airplane for Hearst's big transcontinental race, but not enough to finance the trip. The Wrights built him a special Model EX biplane with a four-cylinder, water-cooled engine, rated at between 35 and 40 horsepower with a cruise of about 55 miles an hour. Armour and Company, as part of an advertising campaign for their new grape soft

Richard A. Epstein Collection

Calbraith Perry Rodgers' Wright Model EX biplane, the "Vin Fiz." Rodgers flew this frail craft across the continent in the fall of 1911.

drink "Vin Fiz," provided a three-car special train to carry Rodgers's wife Mabel and his mother, the Armour Company representative, an advance publicity man, as well as parts and supplies for the Wright. The train also hauled a racing car to reach the pilot quickly in case of an accident. Cal was to be paid $5 a mile while showing Vin Fiz advertising on both the train and airplane, and Armour paid all expenses except fuel, oil repairs, and parts.

Little is known about Robert G. "Bob" Fowler, the other main contestant in the transcontinental air race. He was fond of athletics, fast cars, and if the opportunity allowed, probably fast horses. He won the Los Angeles to San Francisco Road Race in a roaring runabout built by C. C. Cole, and also raced the car at the Domínguez Field Air Meet in 1910. This is where the aviation bug must have bitten him and also where he learned about Hearst's $50,000 prize.

Cole's head salesman offered to pay him $7,500 if he would learn to fly a Wright pusher and enter it in the race as the "Cole Flyer." Bob promptly took a train to Dayton, had some three hours of dual instruction from Al Welch, Wrights' chief pilot-instructor, ordered a Model B biplane shipped to San Francisco, and hurried home to meet it and get started on the big adventure.

The September 7, 1911, issue of the *Arizona Gazette* showed a good picture of Fowler but gave meager information on his background and experience. According to the article, he was planning to "follow the railroad to Jacksonville, Florida."

On the 12th he took off from the Golden Gate Race Track in San Francisco on the longest initial solo flight in history. A minor incident followed. He and his mechanic had reversed the elevator cables. Up was down and down was up. Bob detected the error, eased back to earth, and the deficiency was corrected. He was off again to land at Sacramento, shake hands with the governor, and be airborne to Auburn for a fuel stop. When he left Auburn the wind was gusting and picking up. This meant speed, and speed was what he wanted. No one knew then or cared about the air currents of the Sierra Wave except the birds, and the intrepid pilot putt-putted along, shivering on his windy perch, trying to climb over the ridges while correcting for the vicious turbulence and still keeping the friendly railroad in sight. No one had taught him how to enter or recover from a spin and one slight misuse of the controls dumped the Cole Flyer spinning down to the ground. The fall was broken by a friendly pine tree and, although groggy and dazed, Bob was not seriously injured. The Cole Flyer was a mess. This unplanned incident occurred near Colfax, California.

New tail surfaces were required. There are stories of confused phone conversations and garbled telegrams regarding these and some of the other required parts, but when the order finally arrived the good citizens of Colfax pitched in and helped with the repairs. The work was done in an improvised hangar—a boxcar—and completed on September 22. The *Yuma Morning Sun*, published on September 21, with a Colfax dateline of the 20th, showed Bob's itinerary. He would make stops at Fallon and Winnemucca, Nevada. This optimistic plan for his first day measured 274 miles via the railroad tracks and would require the little airplane to wheeze up to at least 8,000 feet.

The morning of September 23 was clear and quiet, the Sierra Wave was dormant, and Fowler sailed smoothly towards Emigrant Pass, Donner Lake, and points east. Near the Gap, at about 8,200 feet, the engine quit. Fowler successfully glided down to Donner Lake and landed in the snow. There seem to have been subsequent attempts to take off, but because of the altitude (about 5,225 feet) the tiny machine was unable to get airborne.

The Flyer was loaded on board a train and shipped to Los Angeles. If Bob could not get over the Sierras he would go around them, follow the faithful Southern Pacific Railroad, and stick to the low country. The deadline for winning the prize money had already passed, but he might still be first across the country and beat Cal Rodgers.

Rodgers had taken off from Sheepshead Bay, New York, in his new Wright Model EX (sometimes referred to simply as a Model X) on September 17, the same day Fowler was repairing the Cole Flyer and eating crow at Colfax, California. Cal had crossed Manhattan to the Jersey side, spotted his special Vin Fiz train and checked the white streamers marking the proper track to follow through the maze of railroad yards. An earlier contestant had become lost in the network of steel fanning from the city. Cal had a good day; the 104 miles to Middleton, New York, were covered in 105 minutes.

His departure from Middleton on September 18th was a prologue of things to come. On takeoff he snagged a tree top, tumbled into a chicken yard, killed six birds, and was himself badly cut. The airplane had to be rebuilt. An unfortunate episode at Red House caused two more days delay. Cal landed to change a spark plug, hit a fence on takeoff, damaged a skid, and demolished a propeller. Between engine failures, weather delays, and accidents caused by pilot errors and structural complications, he was three weeks reaching Chicago.

Hearst's $50,000 was safe. Rodgers could not possibly get to the Pacific by October 10, and Fowler at that time was in Los Angeles conferring with his business manager and other associates and planning a new itinerary via the Southern Pacific through Arizona, Texas and the low country. He must have found a sympathetic banker or sponsor, or both, as he organized a retinue to go along with him in a converted baggage car. His mother, four mechanics from the racetracks to watch over the Cole Flyer's health, and, according to some accounts, a publicity agent or advance man made up the party. They were billed as "Fowler's Flying Circus" to get a special discount fare, but there still must have been a bit of money problem as on numerous occasions en route he staged small exhibitions for a fee.

Now that both contestants were on their various but unscheduled ways, the press notices moved from the inner pages of the communities' newspapers towards the front.

Estimated takeoff for Bob Fowler from Ascot Park in Los Angeles was October 10, as announced by the *Yuma Morning Sun*. He did not leave that day. During a test flight two wheels were

broken. There was another day's delay because of the Los Angeles
fog, and on October 19 the Cole Flyer wheezed into the air and
Bob made his first night landing at the Tournament of Roses Park
in Pasadena. Two days later he was in Banning with a "blown-up
engine." The day's delay, and possibly the motor's ailments, were
due to a severe dust storm closing Black Pass (San Gorgonio) and
causing a night's stop at Riverside.

By October 24 all repairs were completed (some records mention a new engine) and the busy gremlins that had been deviling
Fowler and his airplane moved to other localities. That afternoon he
made the first below sea level landing on record, at Mecca, and
remained there for the night.

Courtesy Yuma County Historical Society

Robert G. Fowler (right) and an admirer stand in front of the Cole Flyer in
the Yuma ball park during the last week of October 1911. This was the first
airplane to enter Arizona under its own power.

October 25 was a banner day for Bob, the Cole Flyer, and
Arizona. Takeoff from Mecca was at 8:25 A.M. and, by previous arrangement, when he roared over Imperial Junction, all the whistles
at the waterworks blasted off to alert the citizens of Yuma and vicinity. Soon a small speck was seen over Pilot Knob; it grew to the size
of a bird and then a full-sized airplane while over 2,000 breathless
spectators sitting on the mesa and in the Yuma ball park watched the
wonderful object circle the enclosure and make a graceful landing
almost on home plate.

The smooth, 107-mile flight had been made in two hours and thirty minutes. Bob was the first birdman to visit Yuma; the Cole Flyer was the first flying machine in the city, and the first airplane to enter Arizona under its own power and not riding a boxcar. "Everyone from all over the valley was there," wrote Madeline Spain, who witnessed the great event. "We had been waiting for days, and the birdman's arrival was real exciting." She failed to mention, but the *Yuma Sun* did not, that Fowler almost hit the fence on his roll out. The old ball park airport was at the end of Fourth Avenue and rather short — some 400 feet.

The next morning, willing hands pushed the little machine over to Third Avenue. Bob started the engine following some minor adjustments, eager friends pushed, and the slight downgrade assisted in the first takeoff of a heavier-than-air machine in Yuma. It was windy and rainy there on the following day, and Bob remained until October 29, giving exhibitions of "Over the Waves, Dutch Rolls, and the Death Dive," thereby picking up some $250 to sweeten his depleted kitty.

Fowler clattered into Maricopa on October 29 and landed alongside the railroad tracks across the street from the main post office. It had been a nonstop flight from Yuma — four hours and twenty-six minutes — and the 165-mile trip won him a world's record for duration and distance covered.

Mr. Cooper, Bob's advance man, told the Tucson *Star* on October 27 that he did not know if Fowler would attempt the flight from Yuma to Tucson in one day, but thanks to an efficient Western Union and the somewhat indifferent telephone system, Cooper had the landing spot marked with a white sheet, and an eager crowd assembled at the University of Arizona campus on October 30, when Bob made his splintering arrival. The culprit was a dust devil which hit him as the Flyer was about to set down, resulting in Bob's impalement on a chicken-wire fence with his feet sticking through. Some records mention damage to the skids and an upright, while others write of a broken spar. Several days were required for repairs.

Meanwhile Cal Rodgers and the Wright "Vin Fiz" had entered Texas. Cal's erratic journey through that state included twenty-eight stops — many unscheduled. At Waco the Wright's flying wires were replaced; near Kyle the engine crystallized and had to be changed; on October 22 it chugged into San Antonio for a magnificent welcome. The "Vin Fiz" had a wreck at Spofford, broken skids at Sanderson, and a water pump seizure near Fort Hancock, resulting in a frozen motor. Between that community and Sierra Blanca the overhead auxiliary tank came unglued and bumped Cal on the head, causing a small cut and some grogginess.

On October 30 when the news came that Cal had left Sierra Blanca, throngs started gathering at El Paso's Washington Park. He flew over the cheering crowd and spotted a suitable airport near the railroad tracks and a cemetery where he successfully landed at 3:07 P.M. In ten minutes he was on board his faithful train, dressing for the bullfight, following a short delay caused by his valet misplacing his trousers.

Takeoff from El Paso was planned for about 6:00 A.M. on October 31, but engine troubles delayed Cal until 10:41 A.M. Finally, he got the Wright into the air and flew across New Mexico, stopping at Deming and Lordsburg, before entering Arizona. At 4:45 P.M. he soared over Willcox and set the "Vin Fiz" down in a vacant lot. Another cheering crowd assembled to greet him.

Telephone conversations from Willcox that evening verified that Cal's advance man had selected a fitting Tucson landing spot— the same site that had been picked for Fowler.

The EX was sighted over Tucson, a speck in the distant southeast, shortly after 1:00 P.M. An enormous crowd at the university campus cheered as the now full-sized airplane performed dips, dives, glides, shooting up and diving down while making turns. Too many were gathered at the chosen location for safety and Cal set the "Vin Fiz" down without incident at 1:52 P.M. on the corner of Ninth and Fairmount. One of the first to welcome him was Bob Fowler, who rushed up with congratulations; the two birdmen exchanged greetings and good wishes. It would be their first and only meeting. Following a light lunch Rodgers was off for Maricopa, where he again gracefully landed across from the post office on the spot Fowler had used. The time was 5:00 P.M., and the party remained for the night. This sudden influx of air traffic was almost more than the tiny community could bear.

The next hop, to Phoenix, was made on November 2. Again the huge crowds precluded a safe landing at the planned location near the Churchill School in a pasture sometimes referred to as the "circus grounds." Time en route was thirty-seven minutes. A satisfactory field was spotted near the Fair Grounds and a landing made. The first two Phoenicians to meet him were J. Gordon Shackelford and a friend, both on ponies. Close on their heels came the *Gazette* car followed by Armour's representative. Gordon and his friend were presented with a battered helmet and a pair of goggles with one broken lens, treasures which considerably enhanced their prestige with the younger fry.

In about thirty minutes the Vin Fiz train arrived with mechanics and supplies, the necessary "adjustments" and fueling were completed, and at about 1:30 P.M. Cal was off for Yuma with plans to remain overnight at Gila Bend if darkness overcame him.

Rodgers flew straight south, avoiding Tempe. He apparently swung westward prior to reaching Maricopa, did not find his train but picked up the railroad, and whether or not he recognized Gila Bend is not clear. At Stoval Siding he was almost out of both fuel and daylight so a landing was in order. The train, tied to its tracks, chugged to Maricopa, switched to the main line for Yuma and, as its crew had been unable to locate the still airborne "Vin Fiz," continued on to Yuma. At Stoval Siding, Cal located his errant supply line by telephone and it came chuffing back from the river city with the crew and shelter for the party that night.

It had been a harried, frustrating day, albeit accident-free, and all because of a silly dream Cal had indicating he would be killed in a place named Tempe. Until entering Arizona he had never heard of the town, then learned that all Tucson-Phoenix trains stopped there. Thus the Phoenix landing was almost scrubbed, but after consulting his maps he decided to pay the capital a short visit by merely passing to the west of the ill-omened settlement. His wife Mabel was so agitated she held the train south of Tempe until she was sure he was over Phoenix, thus causing its tardiness. The uncontrolled mob at the "circus grounds" had been upsetting and brought more confusion. The long wait at the siding was a climax.

Rodgers' takeoff from Stoval Siding the next morning followed the usual procedure, refueling and "adjustments," and when aloft things were going so smoothly that he omitted the planned Yuma landing, continuing towards Imperial Junction. Just 133 miles and 125 minutes after being airborne the engine decided it was through and announced the fact by "blowing up." The #1 cylinder blew off, damaging the crankshaft. The resulting debris of hot oil, hot metal splinters, and hot water speared Cal's right arm. Fortunately, he was over Imperial Junction and glided successfully to a vacant lot across the tracks from the depot. This required "vol-planing (gliding) from 4,000 feet" and resulted in a down-wind arrival.

The damaged engine removed at Kyle, Texas, and now repaired, was installed, and on November 5 he flew to Pasadena. By November 7 he was talking to school children about flying and planning his final dash to the Pacific. On November 12 he was off to Long Beach and the Pacific, but at Compton the engine again quit and the resulting accident was Cal's worst. Both his legs were broken and minor cuts and bruises added to his injuries. He was discharged from the hospital three days later and that afternoon flew the seven miles remaining from Compton to Long Beach and the Pacific Ocean. Hearst's prize was lost, but he was still the first to fly across the continent from ocean to ocean.

While Rodgers was struggling toward the Pacific, Bob Fowler was flying east. On November 2 he took off from Tucson for Benson, Bisbee, and Douglas, and flew right into one of Arizona's fast-moving dry cold fronts. His time to cover the approximately fifty miles to Benson was two hours and five minutes, and the bruised pilot and battered Cole Flyer put down at Benson for the night. His airport was a vacant lot (now downtown) west of the river and just north of the highway. Following the always required "adjustments" next morning, the Cole Flyer was airborne for the Warren Country Club. En route Bob missed his guiding railroad and decided he was lost. A landing was made and five or six rather amazed cowboys gave him directions to the Bisbee-Warren area some fifteen miles west. No records divulge any reactions exhibited by the horses to this huge, noisy, oily-smelling bird. At 4:30 P.M. Bob landed at the Warren County Club.

On November 4 Bob's successful flight from Bisbee to Douglas was made in the rain. Opinions vary as to just where he came to earth at 12:52 P.M. on this memorable day. Some records mention behind the YMCA buildings, others that it was the road north of town leading to the Copper Queen smelter; but wherever, an excellent census of the city's population, including kids, dogs, horses, and motor cars, could have been quickly compiled on the spot. The crowd was well controlled and remained clear of the improvised runway. Bob's leather coat, leggins, gloves and helmet, and enormous pair of goggles were properly admired, and the brave airman was driven to town by city dignitaries.

Early on November 7 Bob took off to the accompaniment of all the town whistles, supported by the auto horns and church bells. His flight to Hachita was smooth and happy and, following a short fuel stop, he was airborne for El Paso. Some thirty minutes and twenty miles from his destination the engine coughed and quit. Fowler and the Flyer hit the soft shifty sands near Mastodon, New Mexico, an isolated section house and siding manned by a Mexican crew. Unfortunately, Bob hooked a wing on an inconvenient cactus and damaged a skid. Our traveler was unhurt but disgusted, and philosophically flagged down and climbed on board the next eastbound freight to collect his repair crew and necessary parts in El Paso.

The small section crew and Fowler's team were unable to build a runway in the wind blown sands that was acceptable to the Cole Flyer. Someone suggested perching the little airplane on a convenient handcar and heading the combination downgrade right towards the city in the pass. A derailer or "bug" located a safe distance down-track would attend to the launching vehicle. When the notice came that the Flyer had a clear track ahead, its engine was started, carefully revved up and Bob, the tiny airplane and the handcar simultaneously commenced moving southeast. There were no whistles but the section gang cheered as the strange contraption picked up speed. At about forty-five miles an hour the airplane took to the air like a frightened quail, and with room to spare before hitting the "bug." Bob was safely on his way again; the handcar catapult assist was so successful, it was used several times during the balance of his trip.

Depending on numerous reporters' varied statements, Bob clattered, fluttered, or roared at tremendous speeds through Texas, Louisiana and the flat eastern country, stampeding cattle, scaring wildlife, and giving impromptu exhibitions to gather in a few extra dollars. He plopped down on the 50-yard line at a Texas A & M football game, and made a "mercy flight with serum in the Louisiana swamplands." He survived the Texas winds, a few playful shots from some cowboys, the coastal fogs and rains, and constant problems with his temperamental engine and frail aircraft.

On February 22, 1912, he happily circled over the surf at Pablo Beach, Florida, landed on the smooth, friendly sand and shut down the tired Cole Flyer. The first "transcontinental air race" was over.

During an air meet in St. Louis, not long after the race, the maestro, Orville Wright, called a press conference and sharply criticized the two contestants for their rash excursions. He opined, "The aeroplane is not yet ready for such an undertaking."

2

Bombs
Over the
Border

During the first week of May, 1913, Charles Ford of Douglas, Arizona, flew a small homemade airplane twenty-five miles into Mexico and dropped several high-explosive bombs on a railroad trestle outside the town of Agua Prieta, in the state of Sonora. Although unrecognized by America's military historians, this would appear to be the first aggressive bombing mission flown in the western hemisphere. The damage inflicted was minimal, but the very fact that such an attack could be mounted was indicative of the progress aviation had made, both in Arizona and the nation as a whole.

The death of Wilbur Wright on May 20, 1912, marked the end of one aeronautical era and the beginning of another, characterized by change and innovation. The Wright brothers and Glenn Curtiss had tenaciously held to their original concept, the pusher box plane, but now Curtiss, in spite of a still-threatening patent suit, commenced experimentation with the more efficient tractor type.* This, coupled with the Wright Company's temporary inactivity, gave him the bulk of meager military orders and a greater portion of the few civilian sales between 1912 and 1915.

New, progressive airplane manufacturers emerged, and competition grew. In the west the Christofferson brothers and Glenn L. Martin toyed with the modern tractors, covered fuselages, and the controversial ailerons mounted between the wings. The home

---

*Airplanes with the propeller(s) mounted at the front, thus exerting pull.

builders proliferated and tried combinations of various established designs with individual touches added. The parts houses did a brisk business.

Despite steady progress in both design and construction, the flutterings of the underpowered box planes were far from spectacular —and occasionally an absolute flop. Staying airborne was still something of an accomplishment and acrobatics were impossible.

In Arizona, high altitudes and intense heat posed major problems, and reports of "hostile Indians" in the high country acted as a further deterrent. Consequently, aeronautical activity during these early years was confined to the lower, more populated southern part of the state, and even in this region interest tended to be hesitant and lukewarm.

In direct contrast, Arizona's southern neighbor, Sonora, threw caution to the winds and enthusiastically adopted the box planes and adapted them to military usage. Having no pilots of their own, both the Mexican revolutionists and de facto government forces furnished employment to numerous American birdmen who wanted adventure, money, or both, and their purchases, both legal and illegal, of American aircraft aided small, struggling factories

George Z. Rogers Collection

Members of the Douglas flying club in front of their partially converted glider. From left to right: Judge Forte, Ben Goodsell, Felipe Mazon, Ted Bowden, Charles M. Ford, and Sparks Y. Faucet. The tow rope attachment (far right) indicates that horses were still needed to get the craft airborne.

in the United States. During 1914 and 1915 more flying was done by American mercenary pilots in Mexico than in all of Arizona, and their activities may actually have exceeded those of the Army Signal Corps Aeronautical Division.

Among the first American birdmen to venture into Mexico to participate in combat operations were the members of the informal Douglas, Arizona, flying club, who planned and executed the Agua Prieta bombing. Their airplane was none other than the original, celebrated horse-drawn glider, which had undergone a remarkable metamorphosis to emerge, in its final stage, as a motorized bomber.

THE DOUGLAS BOMBER: 1909–1913

The notorious converted Douglas glider first left the ground under its own power during late 1909. Information on its early adventures, mostly meager press reports, indicates that it led a normal life for any aircraft of its era, experiencing incidents, accidents, and redesigning followed by numerous rebuildings.

Felipe Mazon and Charles Ford, charter members of the informal Douglas aeronautical group, did all the flying after its first engine was installed. A. M. Williams, another of the original glider enthusiasts, practiced "grass cutting" in it at a field near 15th Street. This was the then accepted method of learning to fly, either for those lacking an instructor or those with a single-place machine; that is, taxiing back and forth, gradually increasing speed and learning the control responses and feel until one day, when everything was right, the pilot would venture a modest ascension of five or six feet. Art Curlee, an old-time Douglas resident, remembers that he saw Williams fly the plane several times from the 15th Street field. None of the excursions was very high, nor did the pilot venture far from his takeoff site.

Curlee tells a story from his youth which may account for the first attempted airplane theft in Arizona. He and Danny Forte, A. M. Williams' nephew, were school chums. One afternoon while they were admiring the small airplane tied down on the 15th Street pasture-airport, Danny, impulsively attempting to be a hero, stated "sure I can fly it, so let's go for a ride." It seemed like a wonderful idea. The ship was untied and pushed out onto the field. Somehow Danny got the often-balky engine started, but Curlee is not specific as to whether they both managed to scramble into the single-place seat or just hang on. The plane got away and slammed into a telephone pole, causing considerable damage to one wing. The terrified boys made a fast getaway. That night a stiff breeze came up and the following morning everyone blamed the wind for the mishap. Neither Art nor Danny corrected the error.

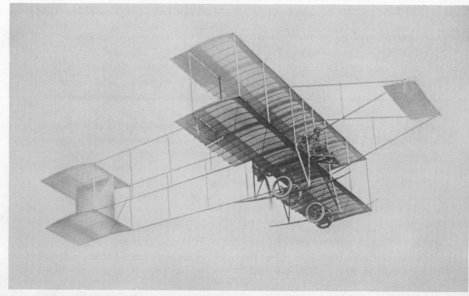

The Douglas Bomber in flight with Charles M. Ford at the controls, fall of 1910. The tow rope attachment is gone and the craft has been outfitted with dual landing gear wheels.

On April 11, 1911, the *Cochise County Prospector* wrote that the airplane had flown at the old quarterhorse race-track near Douglas. The analogy so confused or enthused the reporter that he credited the machine with "a 50-mile an hour gait," and added that A. M. Williams remained aloft for a mile and a half before an admiring crowd of forty or fifty spectators. The little airplane had gracefully left the earth after a run of about 125 feet and reached an altitude of over 100 feet and possibly more.

On November 18, 1911, the *Douglas Daily Dispatch* and the *Arizona Gazette* reported that "A. M. Williams is resting at home with minor cuts and bruises after his aeroplane fell about eighty feet." One source reported a side came off, another that one side collapsed, and a third that a wing fell off. Williams was thrown clear and fortunately escaped any entanglements with the motor.

The plane underwent a major design change and rebuilding following this mishap. From Al Williams, A. M.'s son, comes one of his father's old letterheads advertising that "Al (A. M.) Williams, The Arizona Pilot, is now Touring the West in his Arizona Aeroplane, and Available for Bookings." Terms and a contract would be sent by request, and "all flights were subject to accidents." Whether any business was generated is not known. One is never a hero in his own hometown, and exhibitions could have been given in nearby communities such as Deming or Hachita, New Mexico, or others not too great a distance away to preclude flying, thus avoiding expensive shipping charges.

The next press release mentioning the little machine appeared in the *Holbrook News*, June 7, 1912. It stated that "A. M. Williams of Douglas has invented a new type of aeroplane."

This may have been the final conversion of the notorious Douglas two-horse glider. Now it was a fuselage tractor with a snug cockpit, and any tractor in 1912, while not exactly a new type, was a *rara avis* in Arizona. A new motor had been obtained, the frame had been strengthened, and prior to installing the fabric wing covering, light-weight fine-mesh poultry wire had been tacked onto the four panels. It gave the final assembly a sort of quilted effect and provided quite a bit of reinforcement.

This gave Douglas more aeronautical firsts—home of the first powered machine designed and built in Arizona, the first tractor type, and the first operating flying club, although the close-knit Douglas group did not use that term.

THE FIRST BOMBING RANGE

The chain of events that led to the Douglas birdmen flying off to war, began in 1911. Mexico, torn by factional politics and seething with discontent, was on the verge of revolution. The United States Army had begun to take precautionary measures along the border. Camp Stephen B. Little, north of Nogales, and Camp Harry J. Jones, near Douglas had been established and garrisoned, and in addition, troops were thinly dispersed along the sparsely settled boundary.

In May 1911, Mexico's unpopular president, Porfirio Díaz, fled to France, and several months later Francisco Madero was elected to the office. Madero had neither the ability nor the political support to govern the explosive country, and Victoriano Huerta and his followers began a movement to oust him. The movement was successful. In February 1913, Madero was shot and Huerta became President.

The United States refused to recognize Huerta, and another revolutionary movement with Venustiano Carranza at its head, attracted sympathizers and support. Carranza's revolution was initially financed by the wealthy and powerful state of Sonora. Other factions soon joined, and as the movement grew, assistance came from American border states and from states as far away as the eastern seaboard. American companies which had been encouraged by Díaz to acquire holdings in Mexico felt obligated to protect their investments and sided with the insurrectionists. The declaration of an American arms embargo on May 4, 1912, slowed some supply shipments to the rebels temporarily, but soon the illicit cargo was again rolling across the line at strategic points in Texas, New Mexico, and Arizona. Douglas was one of these strategic points.

By 1913, Sonora, Mexico's most influential state, was firmly in the hands of the revolutionaries, with the exception of a small section near Hermosillo and the port of Guaymas. A Federal army was dispatched from this area to lay siege to Agua Prieta, a scabby, adobe-and-wood border town, closely tied to Douglas by business and family connections. The army camped south of the town, effectively cutting off the flow of arms and supplies being smuggled across the border to the rebels. This threat to the local economy galvanized the close-knit Douglas flying group. Everyone knew about the bombing experiments at the Los Angeles and San Francisco Air Meets in 1910, and also that Bulgarian aviators had dropped small hand-held missiles over Turkish-controlled Adrianople in 1912. Douglas had an airplane and three pilots. Now all that was required were a few bombs; the railroad tracks would be destroyed, General Huerta's supply trains put out of business, and the troublesome de facto soldiers forced to leave their entrenchments.

George Z. Rogers, then employed by the Douglas Hardware Company, was willing to fabricate the bombs, using empty five-pound lard pails stuffed with dynamite, scrap metal, and rough concrete. He also offered the would-be bombardiers a practice range on his ranch a few miles northeast of town.

Following the first trial bombing runs flown by Felipe Mazon and Charles Ford, both the pilots and the few vitally interested spectators learned that the bombs tumbled as they fell, making them miss the targets. Before the second production run, Rogers took the empty pails to a sympathetic local tinsmith who gladly soldered four fins to each missile. The contact explosions were satisfactory and now, when the pilots released the pails, they fell straight. Next, the bombardiers needed some practice targets that would simulate a railroad track, so a collection of old bed sheets was brought to the range and spread in lines to represent the steel ribbons.

In early March 1913, Lt. Col. George Bell, Jr. from Camp Jones visited the practice range and watched Mazon and Ford drop their homemade missiles on the improvised targets. Colonel Bell was a career Army man, a troubleshooter, who had performed numerous special duty assignments both in the United States and abroad. He was on another such assignment now, carrying a special order signed by President Woodrow Wilson instructing him to aid the anti-Huerta rebels in such a manner that it would not be publicly known that the United States was violating its own declaration of neutrality and its embargo act.

Bell was impressed by the Douglas pilots' plans for aerial warfare, but not by their lard-pail type of ammunition or the bed sheet targets. He now took over the supply department and also made arrangements to have another airplane fly to Douglas to round out the bombing squadron. George Rogers remembers waiting with the Colonel in a vacant lot behind the old YMCA building to meet the new pilot, Charlie Mayse, when he flew in from Texas where he had been giving exhibitions.

Both the Douglas airplane and Mayse's ship were kept under guard at Camp Jones when not flying. The bed sheet targets were replaced with old wagon tarps laid down several hundred feet apart in mile or so rows. Amateur armorer Rogers and the cooperative tinsmith bowed out, and real, "store-bought" bombs appeared for practice use. These varied in weight from ten to thirty pounds, the latter considered a little heavy for the machines to carry.

By present appearance of the practice range, it must have seen considerable use with accurate results. A few miles northeast of Douglas, lines of old bomb craters can still be seen, running in an east-west direction for several miles. Diameters are from fifteen to twenty feet across and depths vary from three to over ten feet. Surrounding the rims of these craters is a collection of hundreds of pounds of large metal snap fasteners used on wagon tarps, buckles (some with canvas shreds and bits of webbing attached), and assorted pieces of old cavalry horse hardware. Added to this debris are chunks of rough concrete imbedded with scrap metal, and more scrap lying free. The collection includes large nuts, bolts, rivets, broken springs, small lengths of pipe, sections of valve handles, and occasionally an ancient spark plug—all the wicked debris from the exploded bombs. The most conspicuous articles are the missile casings—burned, broken and twisted metal—and several tall cones almost intact, with fins easily recognizable.

TWO INTERNATIONAL BOMBERS OFF TO MEXICO

Ford and Mazon were considered the most proficient of the local self-taught pilots, and they had actively participated in the two-horse glider's various rebuildings and transitions to a powered barnstormer-exhibition machine. Now the small changeling was to be an international bomber destined for rather important missions, but certainly with questionable status and rank.

As George Rogers remembers, Charles Ford took off on his first bombing expedition on May 7 or May 8, 1913, and safely returned the same day. Distance flown could not have been much more than twenty-five or thirty miles, and rumors were that he damaged a piece of track outside Agua Prieta and surprised the opposition.

Following this successful first mission, Ford and Mazon alternated their attacks in the Douglas plane, and Mayse later joined them in his machine. The harrassment of their bombing sorties may have been one of the factors causing the Federal army to evacuate Agua Prieta and head south for Hermosillo and Guaymas. As the Federal troops moved southwest the two small airplanes continued their attacks on tracks, small bridges, and baggage trains, before returning to Douglas each afternoon. As the army progressed, the pilots landed and camped in Mexico, but always at a safe distance from the rear guards.

Mazon replaced Ford in the Douglas "bomber" for the big adventure deep into Mexico. Rogers believes their support material was furnished by the United States but probably transported by Mexican sympathizers. Neither airplane ever returned to Douglas, but evidence suggests that Mayse reached Hermosillo, and "another machine" was reported at Nogales and Ortiz, while a third, flown by an American pilot variously known as King or Bishop, was also at Hermosillo.

Mazon and Mayse later returned to Douglas but, as was the custom then, did not talk about their Mexican adventures, nor were they questioned. The ultimate disposition of the Mayse and King machines and that of the converted horse-drawn glider is unknown; but, considering the fragility of flying machines and their power plants then, the lack of spare parts and maintenance facilities, and the conditions of the landing areas, their remains are doubtless somewhere below the border.

THE SAGA OF THE "SONORA"

The "Sonora," the first tactical bomber designed, produced, and sold by a United States factory, took off on her first sortie flying the colors of the Sonoran Revolutionists with a French pilot and a Yankee bombardier-crew chief. Furthermore, she was the first airplane known to be seized as a smuggled munition of war, then "kidnapped" along with her crew and custodian, shuffled on board waiting vehicles, and hauled off to Mexico to drop her bombs in anger.

By early 1913 the anti-Huerta movement was doing well. Sonora was controlled by the rebels, with the exception of small areas near Agua Prieta and Nogales, and the important port of Guaymas. At Guaymas, the gunboats "Guerrero," "Tampico," and "Morelos" were berthed, as well as some other odds and ends of the Mexican Navy.

The occasional potshots the gunboat "Morelos" lobbed into the rebel encampments near Batamotal were a constant irritant to the rebel commander, Col. Alvaro Obregón. He wanted the shelling stopped and decided that since the rebels had no ships, aerial bombardment was the solution. The colonel, fully aware of the U. S. arms embargo declared on May 4, 1912, cautiously commenced negotiations for the plans, purchase, and passage of a specially-designed war airplane capable of sinking the pesky Federal fleet, or at least of forcing it to leave.

Because of the annoying embargo on all war materials, the bomber would have to be smuggled into Mexico. This did not present insurmountable problems as the long, thinly-populated border allowed American filibusters to supply their adopted faction with vital goods. Principal headquarters for these clandestine smuggling intrigues were Los Angeles, San Diego, the Douglas-Agua Prieta area, and San Antonio—or near whatever spot action happened to be brewing. Except for those directly involved, no one in the United States considered the revolution to be of much consequence, and efforts to staunch the flow of weapons and supplies into Mexico were spotty and generally ineffective.

The pilot that Colonel Obregón's representatives contacted about flying the new bomber was Didier Masson. After his adventure with the balky "Pegasus" in Bisbee in 1911, he had returned to the West Coast, where he engaged in various flying assignments. When Masson met with Obregón's elegant Mexican officers he was a flight instructor for Glenn Martin, which recommended his aeronautical abilities. Van Griffith, president of the Aero Club of California, made the introductions, and the two colonels, Santiago Camberos and Bouche Alcalde, offered Masson an attractive proposition. He would get $300 a month base pay, $50 for each reconnaissance flight, and $250 for each bombing expedition while flying in Obregón's service. Masson immediately accepted. Thomas J. Dean signed on as mechanic to take care of the proposed new airplane and also to act as bombardier; later he would be responsible for the development of a release mechanism for the missiles.

Masson was given $5,000 to purchase a new Martin pusher with a 75-horsepower engine capable of hauling the pilot, the bombardier, and about 150 pounds of bombs 100 miles. However, at the time Masson "could not find all of the money" and went to work in Martin's factory. Subsequently the funds was found. Later evidence indicates that $5,700 changed hands, and one might assume that the extra money was to defray shipping costs and to purchase spare parts as then no experienced pilot would consider such an adventure without these vital accessories.

The new little airplane, christened the "Sonora," was crated in five boxes and loaded on a Southern Pacific train on May 8, 1913. She was consigned to T. Dean at Tucson, but destined for Sahuarita Station and ultimately Nogales, Sonora. She traveled under custody of Wells Fargo Company. Dean accompanied the shipment; Masson may also have been on board. The records merely indicate the two men met at Tucson. The train carrying the crates chuffed into the

Old Pueblo Station at 5:50 on the afternoon of May 7, and the "Sonora's" troubles began. The rebels' security system suffered a short but complete failure. Wells Fargo agent Hutchinson received a phone call from the United States Marshal's office in Phoenix to hold the shipment. At about 7:30 P.M. an unidentified caller assured Hutchinson that it was all right to release the crates, and by midnight the boxes, weighing approximately 900 pounds, were loaded on a flatbed wagon pulled by four animals and, with Masson, Dean, and a driver, were off for Nogales.

That same day the Mexican charge d'affaires in Washington received news of the transgression. He immediately sent a memorandum to the acting Secretary of State of the United States requesting that this officer prevent the exportation to Mexico of an airplane now at Tucson, on its way to Sahuarita Station, and eventually to Mexico, where it would be used by the "enemies of the Government of Mexico in Sonora." Copies of this plea journeyed through the bureaucratic maze, causing a flurry of communications asking for the machine's seizure, and the arrest and punishment of her custodians for violating American neutrality laws, because the adjutant general had declared the airplane to be "a munition of war."

On the morning of May 8, a phone call from U. S. Attorney Joseph Morrison in Phoenix to the Tucson Marshal's office countermanded the mysterious and erroneous release of the night before. That day at noon, Marshal Johnson and a party left Tucson to find the missing airplane and her attendants.

Both the *Arizona Republican* and the *New York Times* announced on May 7 and 8, respectively, that the U.S. Cavalry had joined the search and was combing the rugged desert south of Tucson looking for the smuggled craft and her custodians, who would be subject to arrest and punishment for violating American neutrality. In addition, both papers noted that "two aeroplanes had been shipped from the factory; one had disappeared between San Diego and Tucson," and the other was somewhere between Tucson and the border, the object of the soldiers' search. To further clutter the facts, the revolutionists released a statement to the effect that they already had one airplane at Ortiz. It had crossed the border in a single crate without problems. No records of this machine have been found, and it may have been mentioned by the rebels as a diversionary tactic to aid the acquisition of the "Sonora."

On the afternoon of May 8, Marshal Johnson and his posse finally caught up to the "Sonora" and her retinue, stuck on a hill near the Chesterfield Mine not far from Sahuarita, some thirty miles south of Tucson. The crates and men were taken to Pike's Ranch and arrived there about 3:00 P.M. A one-legged deputy, Reuben Hawkins, was left to guard the valuable boxes and the rest of the group returned to Tucson. Masson and Dean were released. The local authorities had no grounds for holding them as both declared the airplane was merely to be used for "testing."

While Deputy Hawkins waited apprehensively at Pike's Ranch, rumors about the fate of the little airplane flew. A smart *Tucson Star* reporter opined on May 14 that the airplane in the crates might be a fake. He believed the real machine was in Mexico or very close to the border, and that the off-loaded crates on the wagon at Pike's Ranch were the spare parts — even though deputies had opened two of the boxes at Pike's and identified portions of an airplane. The following day the same publication announced that both Masson and Dean were in Nogales, Sonora, claiming that their airplane carried "secret test equipment and was of a new design" — both truthful to some extent.

On May 20, newspapers across the country reported exciting news: the "war plane," her crew, her one-legged guard, and some ammunition had been "kidnapped from Pike's Ranch!" All this was reported to have been spirited away in various types of equipment: "three autos," "two pick-ups," and "a passenger car and some pick-ups," according to the various papers. One columnist even had the crates loaded on mules, later attacked by Federal troops, and some of the valuable boxes "lost for weeks." The reporters worried about the fate of Deputy Hawkins. They should not have been concerned as he later surfaced as an officer in the rebel forces. The reading public had a field day considering their latitude of interesting choices.

On May 20, the *Bisbee Daily Citizen* wrote that the airplane crossed the line "yesterday afternoon in daylight in three autos, was accompanied by a high-powered bomb of the gravity contact type" and that the cortege passed right under the noses of American customs officers and soldiers. A Tucson reporter wondered why none of the fifteen or sixteen men based at Pike's Ranch had ridden the mere seventeen miles to a phone to call for help after the "kidnapping." The inference was collusion.

Reliable evidence indicates that the real "Sonora" arrived in Nogales on May 15. This is confirmed by a wire from General Obregón to Col. Santiago Cabral who accepted her, which read "Felicitole por introducción del Pájaro," and a further statement that day from a Mexican customs official in Nogales who told reporters, "It cost us a lot of money but we got her."

No news of welcoming festivities was released from Nogales, but on May 16 Masson and Dean took off in the "Sonora" for Hermosillo. Airline distance between the two airports is about 150 miles, and adding 10 or 15 additional miles to keep in lower country and follow the tracks, it would have been a flight of almost three hours for the little warplane. Gasoline would have been available at Magdalena and Carbo and maybe one or two other settlements along the railroad. Judging only from the total lack of information, the flight must have been uneventful. News releases do mention the enthusiastic welcoming mob at Hermosillo, but all details are omitted.

On May 17, Masson gave two exhibition flights. The first was a success, but during the landing roll following the second, he got into trouble. He had a choice of ramming the uncontrollable crowd or hitting a large horse-drawn cab called a *carruaja* or *Berliner*, handled by an exuberant driver. He chose the latter. Reported damages to the "Sonora" ranged from "very minor" to a "wash out," but all agreed that the *carruaja* emerged unscathed.

Following repairs, the "Sonora" took off and flew south toward Guaymas and Obregón's camp near Batamotal. Dr. Albert Pradeu was a First Captain on Obregón's staff in 1913, and witnessed the "Sonora's" arrival at the camp. "Four bed sheets were placed at the corners of the cleared area," he wrote, "two furnished by Obregón and two by me. Using the railroad track as a guide to the south from Hermosillo, and at tree-top height because of a very strong wind, the aeroplane appeared. Two men were on board, Didier Masson, the French pilot, and a young Mexican, Joaquin Bouche Alcalde. Everyone was extremely happy over the arrival of the *pájaro*. The aeroplane's mechanic (Thomas Dean) and an individual lacking one leg (Reuben Hawkins), both Americans and both involved in the smuggling of the aeroplane, arrived on the next train."

With the "Sonora" safely in camp, Dean, Masson, and Colonel Obregón, a confirmed "do-it-yourself" engineer, began preparing the bombs. The first trial runs over the plains surrounding Batamotal were successful, and with all the "experts" satisfied, Masson and Bouche Alcalde took off to try their luck against the Mexican Navy. Their primary target was the "Morelos," which continued to annoy Obregón's troops by lobbing shots into their camp at inconvenient times.

On May 28, 1913, the "Sonora" flew over the "Morelos," dropped several bombs, but scored no hits. The contact bombs with no fins tumbled. Also, Masson was obliged to fly above the elevation of the ship's guns, and this further spoiled his aim. The missiles splashed into the water; there were no explosions, but the psychological effects of the attack were stunning. News releases told of the terrified Mexican sailors jumping into the bay and bomb pits being hastily dug to protect the federal soldiers from the aerial missiles.

During the period between May 9 and June 27 the battles of Santa Rosa and Santa Maria were in progress, and the "Sonora" was

French pilot Didier Masson preparing to embark on a bombing mission over Guaymas, Mexico.

moved from San Alejandro to Moreno as a precautionary measure. She was kept under a 24-hour guard and few persons were allowed near the valuable airplane. The flights over Guaymas continued with Masson and Alcalde dropping both bombs and propaganda leaflets. Only the paper ammunition scored any hits.

On May 29, Masson made six reconnaissance flights, the last resulting in an unscheduled landing in the middle of a skirmish at Enpalme. Masson flew low over the gunboats, some bombs were dropped, the navy guns retaliated, and a few minutes later the

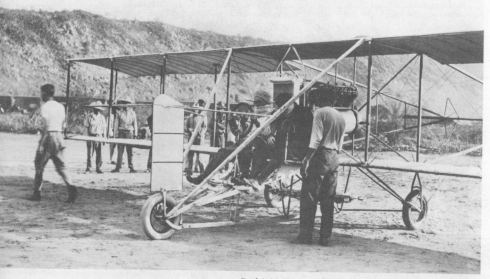

Fred A. McKinney Collection (Courtesy *Brewery Gulch Gazette*)

The "Sonora" ready for takeoff. Pilot Didier Masson grips the controls while bombardier Joaquin Bouche Alcalde checks the bomb sight. The loaded bomb rack is under the lower wing.

"Sonora" emerged from the smoke and confusion at a very low altitude and with a sputtering engine. Masson landed in the center of Enpalme, then deserted because of the fighting, and was rescued by the state cavalrymen, who abandoned their mounts and ran to pull the little machine to safety. The "Sonora's" engine had failed, probably because it was suffering from a bullet hole.

The next dispatch from the strictly-censored rebel press announced that Masson had flown to Hermosillo for new parts and a new propeller. To procure the needed propeller for the "Sonora," Dean reportedly took two secret trips to the United States. Both ended in failure, so he made the necessary part. There were no aircraft supply shops nor any other aircraft in Arizona then, and the time element precluded another journey to southern California. Hints flew that he was trying to locate some of the "Sonora's" accompanying crates which had been left at Pike's Ranch during the hurried "kidnapping."

On June 9 the "Sonora" made her first flight with the new propeller. Now she would be used principally for reconnaissance—the bombings had not been an outstanding success.

Little news about the "Sonora" was available in July, possibly because she was having her engine overhauled and her weapons system reworked. When the airplane first arrived at Obregón's camp she had no bomb sight or racks. The improvised missiles were carried in a wooden box and released by use of an improvised wooden chute. Later photographs showed the plane with a bomb sight, weapons release device, and a rack capable of holding ten missiles.

On August 3, Maj. Reuben Hawkins was interviewed by a *Tucson Star* reporter in Nogales, where the officer was recuperating from an unspecified injury. When questioned about the "kidnapping" at Pike's Ranch, he simply said that he had been "outnumbered and overpowered" and, being a philosophical soul, decided to roll with the punches and make do in a poor situation. He had been well treated, was now a member of General Yturbe's staff, and would soon return to active duty. He reported that the "Sonora" flew every morning when the wind permitted, Masson's flying and bombing accuracy were improving with team practice, and that Bouche Alcalde was usually in the bombardier's seat.

During the last week in August, the federal troops staged three sorties out of Guaymas; they were beaten back each time. The remaining navy ships withdrew to join others at Topolobampo, and the rebels, who were now formally labeled the Constitutionalists, prepared to drive south.

On August 19 the little "Sonora" had a new pilot, Gustavo Salinas, who had graduated from the Moissant School at Garden City, Long Island, in 1911. Jones writes that Masson stayed on long enough to check him out in the "Sonora," and explain the mysteries of her bomb sight and temperamental release.

Extensive desertions by the federal soldiers were reported as the rebels started moving south. The "Sonora" traveled with the troops, and at Ciudad Obregón and Navajoa the famous machine was used for display purposes and flight exhibitions, in addition to performing reconnaissance chores and some bombing.

On April 15, 1914, the "Sonora," piloted by Gustavo Salinas, accomplished the first successful aerial bombardment of a naval ship in this hemisphere when her missiles hit the "Guerrero" at Topolobampo. Seventeen days later, on May 2, the "Sonora" was washed out at Mazatlan. Records say that she landed with two bombs trailing from her rack, but they did not blow, and if Salinas was injured it was unmentioned.

This was the end of the line for the gallant little airplane because there was no one in Mexico capable of doing the major repair work she now required. She was no longer that important to the rebels anyway. On February 14, 1914, the troublesome American arms embargo had been lifted, and there were no longer any delays in procuring airplanes and ammunition.

POST-EMBARGO INCIDENTS

The ending of the vexing embargo resulted in a flurry of small but appreciated orders to America's few airplane factories. It also enabled them to dump some of their near-obsolete pusher box planes, as the U.S. military was flirting with the more modern tractor types.

Francisco Villa, now Carranza's principal general, wasted no time in bolstering his depleted forces and equipment, as this new aerial warfare had attracted his fancy. On February 16, 1914, the *Tucson Star* reported that "General Villa has acquired four new American aeroplanes and intends to use them for his planned attack on Torreon." Señores L. Esquero and A. Salines were to have charge of them, but unfortunately interviews were impossible as both officers had left Nogales for Tucson where they would entrain for El Paso to accept delivery on two of the machines which were coming from the east. "Two others are already in Sonora awaiting orders," the *Star* said, "and these are under the care of Colonel Reuben Hawkins, and were smuggled in during the embargo."

Now, almost overnight, American pilots, lured by the prospects of lucrative flying jobs (there were few at home), and the manufacturers, desperate for sales, were involved in the Mexican situation. The American flyers were offered handsome reimbursements; the rumors that Masson had been shorted some $800 in back pay when he left Obregón's service had little restraining effect, nor did the United States government's directives forbidding U.S. airmen to fly for either faction. No specific figures have been found, but it seems there may have been more United States flyers and flying machines engaged in this quasi-military fracas, both in Mexico and sputtering back and forth over the fence, than the Army Signal Corps could muster.

In the late fall of 1914, two American pilots engaged in the first aerial shoot-out over North America. Phil Radar, flying a Christofferson for Huerta, and Dean Ivan Lamb, representing the Constitutionalists, met over Naco. Both airplanes were reported to be over the Arizona side of the line during their exchange of pistol shots, which lasted about twenty minutes with no hits recorded. It was reported that Lamb loaded from a belt with the gun between his knees and flew with his free hand. When ejecting shells he put the pistol inside his shirt because on one unfortunate occasion an ejected missile had hit his propeller, ruining it and causing a forced landing.

Villa moved south, leaving the border in comparative quiet except for an occasional bandit raid, and during his actions around Torreón and León he was joined by numerous American pilots.

There was George M. Kneightly who arrived in León via train and muleback. His Christofferson may have traveled in the same manner. Kneightly soon decided he did not care for Mexican revolutions and left. He was followed by a chap named Mace who was killed on a takeoff when he hit an adobe wall. The León airport would be classed as substandard; it was reported to be surrounded on three sides by mountains and blocked on the fourth by an adobe wall. Another would-be adventurer was Floyd Smith, Glenn Martin's chief pilot, who escorted a TT pusher to Villa's headquarters at Aguascalientes. Following two weeks in which he made eight flights, Smith returned to San Diego.

President Huerta resigned in July 1914, and the following month Carranza assumed executive powers as dictator of all Mexico. Villa started moving north, and in September he repudiated Carranza, believing that he had placed personal power and ambition above the aims of the revolution, which was to restore the constitution. Now Villa was branded a bandit at large and would be fighting both the de facto troops and the Constitutionalists.

In early February 1915, Villa's brother, Hipolito, became interested in aerial activities when he saw Bill Heath, an employee of air show operator J. S. Berger, fly a Wright at El Paso. Hipolito was so impressed with the little machine's hesitant, fluttering aerial maneuvers that he bought three from Berger, and ordered them shipped to El Paso. The three Wrights (two Model B's and an H S Tractor) arrived in Juarez under the care of Howard Reinhart, one of the factory's most experienced pilots, who would figure prominently at a later date in Phoenix aeronautical activities. One Model B was demolished by a wind gust while being assembled; the other two planes, accompanied by Reinhart, Berger, Heath and a mechanic named Knight, traveled by train to Monterrey where the new fleet was assembled.

The pilots carried messages, did reconnaissance work, and gave endless exhibitions to amuse the soldiers. Both agreed that they were in as much danger from their own troops as from the enemy's. The soldiers crowded dangerously close during takeoffs and landings, and all troops, regardless of faction, amused themselves with playful shots when any machine was flying low.

Leery of this risky activity, the pilots started inventing mechanical troubles and weather problems. The latter was not effective as, in Villa's opinion, adverse meteorological conditions were no excuse for any flight cancellation. Being a simple man, he believed that if he could see well enough to ride a horse any pilot could see well enough to fly. He thoroughly enjoyed any flight exhibition but there seem to be no records of his attempting any personal aerial excursions. He remained faithful to his horses.

Fred A. McKinney Collection (Courtesy *Brewery Gulch Gazette*)

Flying in Mexico could be hazardous. This Christofferson belonging to Gen. Plutarco Calles hit a ditch or prairie dog hole while on its landing roll.

Reinhart, after various adventures, returned to the United States and Dayton, minus some of his due back pay. Heath and Berger were allowed to leave, and Farnum Fish and later William Lambke took over the flying chores, which appear to have been more exhibitions to amuse the troops, message carrying, and reconnaissance.

In the summer of 1915 one of the American planes in Sonora engaged in a new and unusual mission—prohibition enforcement. Demon rum had been laid to rest in Arizona on January 1, 1915. However, along the border the pains of drought were somewhat mitigated by numerous thoughtful saloonkeepers who had made deals with Sonora's Governor Maytorena allowing them to open establishments in Naco, Nogales, Agua Prieta, and other strategic locations in Mexico. Business was excellent and the numerous bistros were jammed during weekends and holidays.

Carranza's commandant for the state was Gen. Plutarco Calles, stationed at Agua Prieta. General Calles, although having the reputation of being a hard drinker himself, assumed the responsibility of cleaning up vice south of the border. The *Nogales Oasis* labeled him as a "prohibitionist of the Carrie Nation type," and all deals made by the tavern-keepers with Governor Maytorena were nullified by the general. No records, either civilian or military, have been found of

Fred A. McKinney Collection (Courtesy *Brewery Gulch Gazette*)

Gen. Plutarco Calles' American pilot, Lawrence W. Brown, holding the type of bomb used to enforce prohibition in Nogales.

Calles' attitude towards what our grandmothers would have called "houses of ill-repute," but he believed in dry enforcement for his subjects. In Agua Prieta the General's soldiers threw all the sinful bottles out on the streets and emptied the contents of any left unbroken in the gutters. Now it was Nogales's turn to be cleaned up.

Press reports indicate the General owned a Christofferson; it is denied by some, but possibly the airplane was rented or, to use a more modern term, leased, and under such conditions would be treated as his and under his orders. On July 31, 1915, the Christofferson with her American pilot, Lawrence W. Brown, and Col. Jesus Maria Aguirre, Calles' chief artillery officer, loaded some bombs and took off to enforce dryness in Nogales. The big noisy bird flew circles over the twin towns, and buildings on both sides emptied as everyone raced to see the show. A few missiles were dropped on the outskirts of the Mexican city but little damage resulted. It appeared that the "bombings" were more to deter the thirsty than to accomplish destruction. Brown then swung back to the American side for another circle of the Arizona city, made a pass over the U.S. Infantry camp where he dropped some leaflets and one bomb, a dummy. The camp's commandant, General Funston, immediately wired the War Department in Washington. This incident made all local newspapers and the *Air Service News Letters*, but no contents of either the telegram, its answer, or the leaflets were ever released.

While Calles was making life difficult for the saloonkeepers of Agua Prieta and Nogales, Pancho Villa, his rabble soldiers, and his airplanes, if he had any left, were heading north to seize Nogales. The fighting started on August 25 and continued through August 28, when Villa captured the city. The battle lines were conveniently arranged at ninety degrees to the border and red flags fluttered to designate the boundary. Barricades were checked on buildings in the critical area and then, so the stories go, the entire population of Ambos Nogales took to rooftops, hills, freight car tops, and other vantage spots to watch the show. It was necessary to fire on a few Mexican troops to prevent their crossing to the American side, but most of the spectators agreed that it was a well-conducted conflict.

The United States recognized Carranza and his government on October 15, 1915, but this did nothing to improve conditions along the border. Villa was now operating in Sonora; bandit raids increased; and in spite of promises from Carranza to control the outlaws, nothing was done. Both Texas and Arizona offered a convenient sanctuary to fleeing marauders, and northern Sonora became a favorite battleground. Stray shots peppered American towns, some American citizens were wounded or killed, and border hotels were forced to advertise their structures as bullet proof, thus assuring guests of some protection. Carranza claimed to be in complete control; it meant little. The bandit leaders were known to both the Mexican and American authorities, but nothing was done to hinder the attacks. The Carranzistas were conveniently absent while the raids were on.

In September 1915 the United States aided Carranza by allowing transportation of his troops over American railroads to reinforce his garrison at Agua Prieta, thus contributing to Villa's defeat. This rout and the recognition of Carranza so embittered Villa that he declared the United States his enemy. He retreated to Rubio and Santa Ysabel, gathered his scattered forces, recruited additional patriots as he traveled, and allowed his American pilots to return home. Then he commenced a campaign of harassment against both the de facto troops and the American border. It was a prologue to the Columbus, New Mexico, raid on March 9, 1916.

Gen. John J. Pershing was ordered into Mexico on March 12, 1916, and requested assistance from the First Aero Squadron. The controversial campaign wore on until the next year when the troops were ordered to return. By February 1917, Columbus, New Mexico was a test station for war materials, including aircraft, and while a few First Aero aircraft entered Arizona, the state did not particularly figure in the conflict.

The days of the frail, fluttering box plane came to an end during 1914 and 1915. Many American aviators who had gone to Mexico to fly for the Federalists or Constitutionalists had sadly learned—as had the airplane and engine manufacturers—that their products could not withstand combat operations, even of the comic-opera type. The attention now focused on the tractors, either of the monoplane or biplane types, some with tricycle gear and others with what is now considered conventional landing gear.

The National Advisory Committee for Aeronautics was formed in March 1915, and two months later news of the first bombardment of London shocked the country into additional action. Massachusetts Institute of Technology graduated its first student with the degree of Science in Aeronautics. Congress appropriated $300,000 for aeronautics and then supplemented this with an additional thirteen million.

The United States declared war on Germany on August 5, 1917. Several weeks before, President Wilson had signed the "$640,000,000 Airplane Bill." Over 20,000 machines would be built and thousands of pilots trained.

A. J. Bidwell, a Phoenix pilot and a member of the LaFayette Escadrille, scored a victory, but other than military flying, little aviation news was released. The papers printed short, censored bits from the various fronts and terse pieces about Arizona men fighting in Europe. Civilian flying was not forgotten, merely pushed aside for the war's duration.

Airports and Airways Along the Borderland and the Santa Fe

The Armistice, which terminated hostilities in World War I, was signed on November 11, 1918. Peacetime activities could now be resumed, and aviation-minded Arizonans happily read that 1,616 JN-4's and 1,100 Standards (all *sans* engines), plus 9,680 Curtiss motors, were to be declared surplus. Soon these modern aircraft and engines would be made available to the public. The days of the box planes were finished.

The glamour branch of the Signal Corps, America's heroic air pilots, found themselves surplus along with the 2,716 airplanes and assorted engines. Both men and aircraft were ill-suited to civilian needs. The Post Office Department acquired a few of the latter for their new Air Mail Service and absorbed a handful of the discharged flyers, but thousands had to find their way into enterprises that were struggling to adjust to peacetime conditions. Military fields were rapidly deactivated, and manufacturers decided that there was no reason to build civilian airplanes when soon there would be no airports, and when all the surplus military equipment was being practically given away.

The Jennys and Standards were only the beginning of the surplus wave. DeHavillands, Thomas Morse Scouts, a variety of flying boats, and other models went on the blocks. The available airplanes were offered new and used, crated with engines, and new or used without power plants. Motors were also for sale in conditions ranging from excellent to derelict. The boxed offerings gave rise to the expression that a pilot "could fly the crates they came in."

As a result of this statement of confidence the surplus airplanes became known as "crates." The term might be affectionate or derogatory, contingent on its qualifying adjective(s) and applied as the occasion demanded.

Hundreds of these surplus machines were bought by the discharged pilots and many more by dealers—both scrupulous and otherwise—and sold or held for fat profits. Tales are told of from $5,000 to $6,000 being paid for Jennys represented as new that had seen considerable use. Others say that a pretty good ship could be found for as little as $200 to $300.

The military pilots from Arizona and elsewhere wanted to continue flying and believed in the future of aviation. The cutback in service personnel had hit their prospects for a career and their pocketbooks; however, they were confident this situation could be remedied. Knowing that thousands of civilians had never seen an airplane, and thousands more had never ridden in one, the veteran pilots set out to oblige.

They bought the surplus offerings and flew home, stopping en route to educate those in the hustings and to put on shows to help defray expenses. They crossed Arizona as they flew west along the Santa Fe Railroad and sputtered along the Borderland Highway. The aerial grapevine got into high gear and word traveled quickly as to the desirability or disadvantages of various towns. Some of these itinerant pilots never made it home. They settled down in attractive communities and started fixed-base operations. A few found berths with the infant airlines, and this lucky group was considered to "have it made," with regular hours and regular paychecks—the latter very desirable. Canvass a group of retired airline captains and it is safe to bet that over 95 percent will admit to a little barnstorming, and a few will confess to 'chute jumping and wing walking when they were young.

These wandering pilots wore tall polished boots with Army-type breeches tucked into them; their leather jackets showed honorable scars, often to the point of being shabby, and soiled leather gloves added a professional touch. They had beautiful beatup leather helmets which they wore around town with the chin straps flapping and with glittering goggles perched above their foreheads. Flowing white silk scarves made from old parachutes completed each ensemble. Sometimes they slept under the wings of their airplanes. Often they had to carry a few paying passengers before they could eat, but small boys followed their steps, offered to clean and polish the Jenny, lug water for its radiator, or pick up rocks from the inadequately cleared fields; anything for a little ride in that shining airplane. Sometimes the boys' families invited these young travelers to dinner, and this was an event which increased one's prestige on the school playgrounds for weeks.

Barnstormers were usually first-class pilots and good mechanics. They had to be both to remain in business. No handy repair shops were in existence to remedy an engine's ills or patch a damaged ship. The only help would come from a friendly local garage or blacksmith shop where the job of adapting used auto parts to a broken or worn airplane engine, straightening bent metal props, or welding fuselages and tail skids was frequently traded for rides. The inevitable result was more interest in aviation, and soon another barnstormer— the garage owner or smithy— was added to the roster.

Generally the barnstormers followed the railroads as their financial existence depended on fair-sized communities. A town would be "looked over," and if a reasonable field were nearby, it would be "worked over" with screaming dives, rolls, and loops to attract the populace. Ten minutes later a 100 percent accurate census of the town's small boys and dogs could be taken near the ship, and the adult count would be about 75 percent of those able to be on their feet. The pilots gave exhibition rides, stunt rides for a little extra, and just safe-and-sane passenger rides. They also taught students, thereby spawning more barnstormers.

These gypsy flyers were criticized by many who considered them a menace to the safe and orderly growth of aviation. Actually, they did much to keep aviation interest alive, and the few struggling aircraft factories realized that they and their numerous students would soon be customers for the new production models.

Already there was a nucleus of pilots and their aircraft in the Los Angeles area. Early in 1919, Cecil B. DeMille, who had taken some flight training during the war, opened an airport at Melrose and Fairfax Streets known as DeMille #1. He opened another nearby and a third in Altadena, and began the first non-subsidized airline in the United States with flights between Los Angeles and the San Joaquin Valley, as well as commuter service to Altadena. These operations included flight training and aircraft sales, in addition to passenger carrying. In spite of adequate financing and good management, the schedules lost money. During 1921 DeMille's company consolidated with the Rodgers flying organization, and an old pasture known as Clover Field became an aerodrome, then the largest in the United States, containing over 100 acres of good sod and a clutch of hangars. It is now Santa Monica's Municipal Airport.

The moving-picture people showed immediate interest. Studio photographers and press representatives often visited the field and their eye-catching pictures were featured in all the major publications. It was wonderful publicity for all concerned. The movie producers became intrigued with the possibilities of aerial spectaculars. The pilots and their stunt men perfected more hair-raising tricks, further refined their acrobatics, and invented new combinations to satisfy the sometimes unreasonable script writers' demands. Pathé and International Studios photographed their antics over the city of Los Angeles, and everyone knew that there was always something doing at Clover Field.

The aviation spectaculars gave the pilots additional work and a more-or-less permanent base. "The Dawn Patrol," "Flywayman," "The Lost Squadron," and Howard Hughes's "Hell's Angels" thrilled movie audiences and increased employment. Teams and associations formed, one of the most famous being the "Thirteen Black Cats of Hollywood."

Six honorary and thirteen active members of this exclusive group, including Jack Frye, Col. Arthur Goebel, Paul Richter, and Ivan "Bugs" Unger, were all well-known and frequent visitors to Arizona. As these interstate friendships proliferated over the years, Arizona benefited.

Aeronautical activity in the state was reasonably brisk in 1919, but not the new production business. There was no reason to invest $6,500 in a shiny new Laird Swallow with a new OX-5 engine when a good surplus J-1 Standard, converted to three-place for barnstorming, could be had for less than half that price. New production airplanes were not in evidence in Arizona at this time, but the quantity of surplus offerings flying about was surprising. The hardy individuals who piloted these "crates" around Arizona were true pioneers. Whether flying for fun, for profit, or for both, they were in large part responsible for the development of a network of airports and airways that continues to serve both the state and the nation to this day.

THE BORDERLAND AIRWAY

Geographically, the Borderland could be considered a poorly delineated strip of troubled real estate south of the 34th parallel from Los Angeles through Arizona, New Mexico, and Texas, with its southern edge the Mexican boundary fence and the Rio Grande River. Aeronautically, it encompassed the routes from San Diego to Phoenix, Tucson, and Douglas, along the international line to El Paso, and south to Brownsville, Texas.

Neither the name "Borderland" nor its routes were new. The original surveyors and users were socially inclined trading aborigines. Then came the Spanish with their missionaries, animals, and *carretas* (carts). They, in turn, were followed by adventurers, pioneers, and the overland stages using routes laid out to avoid the higher mountains while passing the water holes.

The old trails eventually became roads. The new railroads, also dependent on water and gentler grades, followed these traces, connecting established communities and spawning new settlements. By

1908 some of the towns along this old travelway boasted gas pumps and garages, and a few even built auto camps. The route was known as the Borderland, later dignified as the Borderland Highway, which the railroad accompanied.

The new airway, another victim of necessity, hugged the rails. The first two transcontinental flights used the Borderland Airway, and later intrepid pilots toted cooing carrier pigeons over its desolate lands as a positive method of communication—the forerunners of our radios and ELT's (emergency locator transmitters). By 1919 this aerial route was known to the military as a segment of the Army Model Airways from the east coast to the Pacific. To civilians, it was the Borderland Airway, connecting Yuma, Phoenix, Tucson, Douglas, and the towns in between, and was recognized along with the Santa Fe Airway as the focal point of aeronautical activity in Arizona.

PHOENIX: 1918–1926

Less than a month after the Armistice was signed, Phoenix welcomed the first Army transcontinental flight of four JN-4s shepherded by Maj. Albert D. Smith. Five planes had left San Diego on December 3, 1918, and planned to make an overnight stop in the capital city. One suffered bad luck, hitting a power line at El Centro. The collision resulted in a washout but no injuries to the crew. The others had no trouble locating Phoenix, but encountered some difficulty finding the Fairgrounds Airport. The Major's request for markings with white canvas must have been ignored because neither the pilots nor the *Arizona Republican* reporter covering their arrival could find any markers. The pilots finally recognized the location after some circling. All landed safely on the short runway, "but used it all." At the banquet held that evening in their honor, the Major remarked that the airport was a "little small" and recommended a facility a half-mile square, or at least 3,000 by 1,700 feet. It should be smooth, well-drained, level land with no obstructions and good access roads. He said he had noticed several fine locations while searching for the Fairgrounds.

The big JNs got away for Tucson and the east coast the following morning after some cooperative citizens removed a section of the Fairgrounds fence and filled in a ditch.

Several days later another army pilot roared in, also flying a big JN-4. He remained for fifty-five minutes to get gas, oil, and water, and was off to Tucson and El Paso. Five visiting airplanes within less than a week encouraged the Phoenix city fathers to upgrade their municipal airport, and on December 12, 1918, the Chamber of Commerce, fired with enthusiasm, appointed a committee to choose a suitable site for a new municipal field. Meanwhile, the Fairgrounds would be improved.

The first written description of the despised Phoenix Fairgrounds Airport was given to a reporter by one of Major Smith's pilots on December 5. "It [the field] consisted of half the interior of a one-mile race track," the pilot stated. Another report, issued on April 15, 1925, following some improvements, had a sketch showing the eastern half of the track as the airport. Neither description mentioned the tall trees, the wires, and the grandstands, but a few old-timers still tell of them with shudders.

The important news relating to civil aviation in Phoenix in 1919 was the arrival of the Southwest Cotton Company's big new Curtiss, which was Arizona's first executive aircraft. Southwest Cotton was a subsidiary of the Goodyear Tire and Rubber Company of Akron, Ohio. Its plantations at Goodyear, south of Phoenix, grew Egyptian cotton and developed the famous long-staple Pima cotton which was superior to the prized Sea Island variety for airplane covering and other luxurious uses. This crop was spun and woven in Los Angeles, where the parent organization was also proposing a tire factory.

To expedite interoffice communications and some shipments, a scheduled airline to the coast, using dirigibles, was planned. To further improve local efficiency and travel between Phoenix headquarters and the outlying plantations, the company bought an airplane, a modified JN-1. A former ace, Lieut. O. P. Johnson, was chosen to fly it and given the title of "Director of the Aeronautical Department."

"Jenny" was delivered to her new hangar at the Fairgrounds, assembled, and successfully test-flown by Lieutenant Johnson and the company auditor. The two men took off from the Fairgrounds and arrived at Litchfield plantation following a pleasant 15-minute flight—driving time would have been an hour and a half.

The firm later purchased two or three Canadian Jennys and employed several pilots between 1920 and 1921. The planes were based in Phoenix and scooted back and forth between the head offices and the plantations with mail, dispatches, and small supplies.

The average life span of Goodyear's airplanes was short. The unimproved fields, some surrounded by large trees, others populated with agitated horses, cattle, and frightened Duroc hogs, interfered with numerous landings. One by one the Jennys came to earth, but not in a manner that would be approved of by the later Aeronautics Branch of the Department of Commerce. They were washed out. The unhorsed pilots were promoted to cotton buyers or inspectors—very lucrative positions—and soon the rumor started that if one wished to be so employed it was only necessary to become a company pilot.

In the fall of 1919 the "improved" Fairgrounds Airport hosted an air show as part of the state fair activities, featuring a team managed by Burt Barr. This group, billed as Barr's Flying Circus, included Omar Locklear, the highest paid stunt man in the country, and other exciting performers. One of the show's biggest attractions was the Trans-Desert Race—the first "from somewhere in California to Phoenix"—and it was announced that the Governor would ride with the winner following his thrilling arrival.

On November 1 the *Phoenix Gazette* carried pictures and short sketches of the visiting pilots entered in the big Trans-Desert Race. Lieutenant Goldsworthy would fly a Canadian Curtiss as would Burt Barr's entry, "Swede" Meyerhoffer, who had fully recovered from his unfortunate experience with the Lockheed F-1 A at Gila Bend (see Chapter 6). Three other pilots were to "mount American Curtiss'." The race ships took off from Ince Field in Venice, California, and flew to El Centro, where they spent the night. Only one incident was reported. Following takeoff, a pilot became confused and found himself over Mexico. Conditions there were rather delicate, and a few Federalists took potshots at the airplane, "and only his [the pilot's] skill in trick flying avoided a tragedy." He landed safely at the Fairgrounds and the eight bullet holes in his lower panels made for good press notices as well as wonderful conversation. The other contestants had landed at Yuma, and from there followed the Southern Pacific tracks to Gila Bend, with the last leg of the contest flown direct to Phoenix by a compass course—very daring in 1919, and not considered the surest way to get where one wished to go. Howard Patterson won the event—no time was given—and modestly said that it was just by good luck. He had no forced landings, no trouble with his machine, and somehow did not get lost.

Almost every afternoon Omar Locklear put on really hair-raising performances. Phoenix had seen nothing like them before. He swung from the landing gear of a Curtiss by his knees, did a plane change to another Curtiss via a rope ladder, and crawled to the tail of the airplane and stood up. Reports were that some of the ladies could not watch him and covered their eyes. Gossips said two swooned, and advised escorts to always carry smelling salts to hazardous exhibitions like air shows.

Swede Meyerhoffer carried a *Gazette* reporter aloft on November 5, and a couple of days later two sportsmen hired Lieutenant Goldsworthy to fly them down Buckeye-way to investigate likely duck ponds. Several remarked that this was a "first flight for reconnoitering game birds." Their claim was disqualified when another bystander said the Navy pilots in San Diego had been doing it for some time.

On November 11, Burt Barr made some caustic remarks about the city's lack of a suitable municipal airport, mentioning that both Tucson and Yuma had adequate and well-marked fields but that strangers flying in to Phoenix had to make inquiries from pilots who had previously been visitors to the Fairgrounds. He stressed the need for an "all way field," and noted that the two cracked wings which happened during his show had been caused, in part, by the airport being too narrow. His closing statement was that "Phoenix better wake up."

The First Airplane from Blythe to Phoenix

The first aerial survey of the route that would become Green 5 Airway and is now known as Victor 16 began bright and early on the morning of March 12, 1920, when pilot-instructor Randall T. Henderson and his student Ralph Seeley took off from Blythe in Seeley's new JN-4B, and winged toward Phoenix.

In those days, airplanes flying east from southern California came to Phoenix or Tucson by way of San Diego, Imperial, and Yuma. Some of the more adventurous pilots flew through Black Pass (San Gorgonio) then southward along the tracks to Imperial and east to Yuma and Gila Bend. Henderson and Seeley decided to fly directly east. They did not realize they were blazing what would become a well-traveled trail. They were just trying to reach Phoenix and, because of "Jenny's" limited range—and also so as not to get lost—they followed the highway.

They had received a telegram from the Wickenburg Chamber of Commerce advising them of the town's new airport, located near the guiding highway, so they made plans to stop there for fuel.

"Jenny" and her passengers arrived over Wickenburg about two hours and thirty minutes after takeoff, and Henderson circled looking for the new field. He could not find it, and with the fuel uncomfortably low was considering stalling the airplane into the river bed. The landing would be no problem but a takeoff could be tricky. He spied a chap rushing from a building waving a big white cloth, saw him jump into a pickup and roar off in a cloud of dust with the snowy banner streaming. The pickup snorted to a stop north of town at a partially cleared spot, obviously Wickenburg's new municipal airport. Henderson safely landed the Curtiss amid a mass of broken glass and small tree stumps, as a crowd gathered. In honor of the first airplane in town, schools were dismissed, and soon the crowd around the plane was augmented by teachers, children, dogs, and horses. While "Jenny" was being fueled the teachers recruited a gang of youngsters to pick up some of the glass. Helpful Chamber of Commerce members pitched in to grub stumps and fill up the worst holes, and by afternoon the new airport was acceptable for a safe departure. The truck-riding flagman who commandeered Arizona's first "Follow-Me" vehicle was properly introduced and thanked. This perceptive citizen, seeing the circling aircraft, had guessed the problem, rushed into a nearby restaurant, grabbed a tablecloth, and then highjacked the pickup and its owner.

The broken glass on the Wickenburg Airport was explained as a spin-off from a recent local election. Maricopa County had chosen to go dry, but neighboring Yavapai remained wet. An enterprising saloonkeeper who was not litter-conscious opened a bar just across the line. The easiest way to dispose of his discarded bottles was to throw them into the next county, from which he had lately been evicted.

"Jenny" landed at the Phoenix Fairgrounds later that afternoon. When Seeley's business (which included attending a conference to promote a better highway between the Arizona capital and Blythe) was completed, he and Henderson took off for home. Henderson had been concerned about the takeoff—those wires and trees could be a problem—but with the help of a fresh breeze the obstructions were safely missed.

Neither pilot had been happy with the situation at Wickenburg, and Henderson had carefully observed the country during the eastbound flight. He decided that Wenden's main street was preferable to the Wickenburg Municipal as a refueling stop; however, when they arrived over town there was too much traffic to hazard a landing. Maneuvering an airplane with no brakes along the narrow road could end in disaster. "Jenny's" OX-5 motor obligingly sputtered on to Salome.

The citizens of that tiny community gathered near an open field and watched the airplane land, taxi up to a barbed wire fence, take on a charge of gas, and make a successful takeoff. It was the first westbound flight over that route, the future Victor 16 between Phoenix and Blythe.

Another highly unusual flight originated from Phoenix later that year. On November 15, Tucson ran out of Cactus Brand Bacon. Various ways of delivering more bacon were discussed, but all were to slow. E. A. Tovrea, president of the packing company, engaged a pilot in town for fair week to fly a big load to the Old Pueblo. The *Republican* printed a picture of Tovrea and the pilot loading what appears to be a fifty-pound box of bacon into a Standard, or possibly a Jenny. This was surely the first air express shipment of bacon in the state, and worthy of mention.

Central and Roanoke Operations

At about this time operations commenced at a second, impromptu Phoenix airport, Central and Roanoke. There is no definite information available as to who started the facility, but it was probably pilot Joe L. Schmitt. Joe was bitten by the aeronautical bug at an early age. He hung around barnstormer Lincoln Beachey when he was in Kansas City and pestered him for a ride, doubtless in return for "polishing the airplane." It was a fine experience even though his father, Joe Sr., gave him a sound trouncing in the family woodshed following the adventure.

Joe Jr. moved to Phoenix after being stationed at Fort Whipple, near Prescott, in 1918. Before coming to Arizona he had been educated at the LaSalle Military Academy, enlisted in the U.S. Army Signal Corps, and spent fourteen months flying at Kelly Field. He was in Phoenix during 1919 and 1920 and bought two surplus Jennys for $100 each.

Joe's operations in Phoenix must have been intermittent as he returned to LaSalle for a summer session in 1920, and later attended Phoenix College and St. Mary's to accumulate sufficient credits for a degree. What he began at the airport at Central and Roanoke was continued during his absences, however, and he should be honored as Phoenix's first fixed-base operator.

Nationally, aviation was commencing to grow up. President Harding urged the enactment of an Aerial Code, to be followed by the drafting of a bill to regulate the operations of interstate commerce. The Aeronautical Chamber of Commerce was organized. Commercial aviation, struggling with no government assistance or law enforcement, had fared poorly, and this new organization, while having no direct powers, could exert influence and gather and disseminate needed statistics. In 1921 they assumed publication of the *Aircraft Year Book*, a recognized source for authentic annual information.

No federal registration of aircraft was required at this time, and the figures compiled by the Chamber after interviews and correspondence with 125 sound, fixed-base operators considered the "Pioneers," the military, and numerous local Chambers of Commerce, represented a vast amount of work.

Total aircraft population of the United States for 1921 was estimated to be 1,200, an approximate increase of 20% over 1920. Six hundred of these planes were presumed to be in the hands of the gypsy flyers, the balance owned by fixed-base operators and a very few private owners. The 125 "Pioneers" had made 130,736 recorded flights, the average jaunt being 21 minutes long and costing $9. Passengers were usually charged 55¢ per mile for intercity trips. Other listed uses for the aircraft were surprisingly similar to those of today with the exception of fire patrol and insecticide application, which were then military duties. Arizona, having no substantial flight operators, did not report to the first yearbook.

The publication did credit the state with twenty landing fields, three of which were federally owned. These were Tucson Municipal, a joint-use facility, and the Aerial Border Patrol fields at Douglas and Nogales. Arizona's air-minded neighbor, California, had 149, and Texas led the nation with 164.

The yearbook's accident reports were taken from member information and press clips; both may not have been impartial, but were the best available. Unless a fatality or spectacular crash occurred, or the press was on hand, many a major mishap went unreported. Total accidents nationally were 114, resulting in 40 fatalities and 80 injuries; 47 were reported to be the result of "pilot error" and 29 resulted from "stunting." California led the nation with a total of 15.

The First Aerial Wedding in Phoenix, June 11, 1924

The spring and early summer of 1924 was an exciting time for the younger set in Arizona's Verde Valley. Popular Jennie Willard of Cottonwood was getting married. The lucky groom was Ersel Garrison, also from Cottonwood. The really thrilling part of it all, and the principal conversation topic at the many pre-nuptial festivities, was the fact that Ersel owned and flew a Standard C-6, the first airplane based in the Valley, and the ceremony would be the first "aerial wedding" in Phoenix. Jennie and Ersel would fly to the capital for the event, and then all the way to sunny California for their honeymoon.

The happy couple took off from Bridgeport, where Ersel kept the Standard, at 5:00 on the morning of June 11, 1924, and landed an hour and a half later at the Phoenix Fairgrounds, where they were met by a group of friends including Governor Hunt. Following the ceremony, the bride and groom took off. Ersel made a few circles over the waving crowd and then straightened out and, for some unexplained reason, came in for a landing. The touchdown was perfect but then the Standard swerved to the right. Some claim that the pilot turned to avoid hitting people alongside the track; others saw something fly off the landing gear. The *Republican* reporter believed that he attempted another takeoff and "almost made it," but hit a fence post. The ship nosed up; results—a splintered propeller and severely damaged fuselage. The latter was burned on the spot but the engine was salvaged. Jennie was unhurt but Ersel had a cut lip. The shaken honeymooners went to San Diego on the train. It was a disappointing ending for the first aerial wedding in Phoenix.

Joe Schmitt, founder of the Central and Roanoke operation, performed memorably at the state fair later that year. The fair manager had been very blunt and critical. Joe's stunt flying lacked thrills and the sophisticated Phoenix audiences were accustomed to better. They had seen "Daredevil Campbell," the "Cannonball," and the exciting acrobatics of Burt Barr's and the Gates' troupes. In comparison, Joe's cautious performances were tame. "Jazz it up a bit—give them something new," suggested the manager.

Joe did just that when he swooped low and ran his wheels over the roof of the grandstand. Opinions differ regarding the paternity of this trick. The Army Air Service claim they rolled their wheels along the corrugated tin roof of the navy hangar at San Diego to show the boys how good they were—and with luck to unnerve a few sailors, nothing mean or vicious intended. The navy modestly admitted that they were the first to rattle the tin-clad army hangars, believing the army birdmen needed a demonstration of real precision flying. In any event, the maneuver is guaranteed to clean out any metal-topped structure—which Joe easily did during his initial performance on the grandstand roof. As the fair manager neither wanted his customers scared to death nor scared away, it was a one-time exhibition.

This roof-rumbling performance was augmented by Joe's smoke writing exhibition—the first such in Phoenix. His initial practice attempt was a choking failure as he got thoroughly smoked himself when the vapor escaped into the cockpit, but by Fair Day this inconvenience was corrected and an enthusiastic crowd cheered him on.

The next year Joe gave up flying and gradually phased out his airplane business. He was getting married, school was completed, and other interests subordinated aviation except for an occasional pleasure hop. Operations at Central and Roanoke continued, however, under temporary tenants.

The year 1924 was summarized in the *Aircraft Year Book* (1925 edition) as being "significant." The United States had maintained undisputed leadership in the air. The wonderful Around-the-World Flight by the Air Service, and the winning of thirty-two new world records out of a possible fifty-nine by American pilots flying American ships, was a worthy accomplishment. Significant also was the decline of commercial aviation and the closing of about 50 percent of the reporting "Pioneer" fixed-base operators. The 124 who had completed returns for 1923 had shrunk to a sad 60 for 1924. Aircraft in operation and number of passengers carried also withered as the wave of enthusiasm receded. There was a lack of good airports, airways, and financial backing, which would never be available until a sound national policy was formulated. Henry Ford's plans for an airline and the formation of the National Air Transport had little effect on Arizona, while the "suicidal practices of the gypsy flyers" caused continued prophesying of doom to the entire country. All Phoenix could boast was the haphazard group at Central and Roanoke, half a dozen "landing patches," and the fairgrounds which a few transients favored and the military used under protest.

The year 1925 opened with a cartoon and an article in the always crusading *Phoenix Gazette*, criticizing the depleted Air Force. This was followed by a series of editorials on the sad state of the aeronautical industry, which the paper said was "on the point of collapse." Foreign markets were being neglected, government control was needed, and the gypsy flyers had to be curbed. Bills to aid commercial aviation languished in Congress, and if conditions remained static, all progress would be sacrificed. The passive City of Phoenix received another blasting for not providing an adequate and safe airport.

Howard Reinhart and Bernard Whelan, pilots and fixed-base operators from Dayton, Ohio, came to Phoenix that fall and leased the Central and Roanoke site. Old tenants were welcomed as were new ship owners and transients. On January 14, 1925, Phoenix could claim one more stable operator who would conduct a flight school for the winter. J. G. "Tex" Rankin and C. P. Quinn came roaring in from Walla Walla, Washington. They were reported to be the first to fly the inland route from the northwest to either California or Arizona. Tex had flown his Lincoln Page south via Bend and Lakeview, Oregon; Alturas, Reno, Yerington, Tonopah, Furnance Creek, Las Vegas, Needles, Kingman, Seligman, Clarkdale and thence direct to Phoenix. It had been a long, cold, dreary ride over isolated country and he was happy to be in Arizona. At that time, pilots from the northwest usually reached the state by flying down the coast to San Diego and then east, so this journey had been a real adventure.

A New Municipal Airport for Phoenix

As the local pilots continued to use almost any large open space for their operations, complaints and ridicule plagued the Phoenix Municipal Airport, variously referred to as the Race Track Airport, Phoenix Municipal, or "that Fairgrounds field." The horses approved of the track but pilots had few good things to say about the joint use facility.

Encouraged by the passage of the first Air Mail Act (Kelly Bill) on February 1, 1925, and by additional nagging from army representatives who were now brutally blunt about the lagging airport plans (some stated that if a suitable facility was not provided, Phoenix would lose all opportunity for airmail service and be removed from the government's list of prospective terminals), the city fathers went to work on the project. What led this body to select a dairy ranch on the outskirts of Phoenix and ignore more convenient locations is unknown. By 1925 airport standards the property was too far from town and accessible by an indifferent road.

Following the property's purchase by the City of Phoenix, Ira Pirtle, who had worked for the Street Department since 1917, was persuaded to move into the old brick farmhouse with his family to supervise the land clearing and development of the new airport. In addition to his regular duties in the city, Ira was now an airport construction supervisor and bossed the grading and the removal of brush and a few of the taller cottonwood trees bordering the property.

This brick farmhouse on Christy Road and 59th Avenue was the first airport terminal building in Phoenix.

At first there was little aerial traffic at the new field and no regular attendant during the hours when Ira was in the city, but any stray transient landing there would be serviced by a fuel truck from the bulk plant, providing he had made two or three circles over their yard. If these had been omitted, he was welcome to use the telephone. There are no records of any specific accommodations for these drop-in travelers, but Mrs. Pirtle was a friendly and hospitable soul, and it is unlikely that anyone flew away hungry.

Big plans were made for the new field's dedication on November 9, and ships and parachute jumpers from Fort Bliss were promised, along with machines from the military installations at San Pedro and Coronado. Fifteen planes had already arrived in town by November 7, as the coming celebration would coincide with the opening of the State Fair.

Dedication Day, November 9, 1925, was an unqualified success. The ceremonies were at noon, and afterwards the military aircraft flew in formation over the home of World War I hero Frank Luke as a tribute to the gallant officer. A fine air show completed the flying program.

Phoenix was praised by the press for its timely acquisition and the new municipal field received the endorsement of the military amid assurances that within two years aerial mail service would be established to serve the community.

But despite the favorable publicity, the new Phoenix Municipal Airport generated little business or interest. Most action remained at Central and Roanoke and one or two other open fields in the downtown area. There is no mention of Tex Rankin using the new facility, and when Howard Reinhart decided to spend the following winter in Phoenix he indicated interest in locations closer to downtown. Municipal was "too far out, not near anything" and failed to lure prospective passengers — the bread-and-butter business for all airplane owners. A few military visitors used the new airport and soon complained about the tall, protective cottonwoods. Others claimed they could not find it and resorted to the Fairgrounds. All of this gave the new facility a shady reputation, and optimism about Phoenix's aeronautical future began to wear thin at city hall.

The Closing of the Central and Roanoke Airport

Phoenix's residential section was spreading north during the mid-1920s, and although Howard Reinhart and Bernard Whelan had enjoyed prosperity during the winter of 1925–26, it would be their last season at Central and Roanoke; however, other aircraft remained at the popular spot. Central Avenue was then shaded by palms, ash trees, and cottonwoods. It was a favorite route to the desert for an outing, or for a pleasant drive. The autos had not completely replaced horses, and on fine afternoons many rigs trotted up and down the road, and there were numerous riders heading for the bridle paths that began at Camelback Road. Much of this traffic passed the airport at Central and Roanoke. Also scattered in the vicinity were numerous spinoffs from prohibition, discreetly called "clubs," and installed in attractive former residences. These were quite respectable, appropriate spots to take one's mother, wife, or girl friend, meet other friends, and have a drink or two. As two of the nicer establishments were handy to the Central and Roanoke field, mutual benefit resulted. A few drinks at a favorite club would remove any inhibitions about riding in one of those dangerous flying machines. Others, returning from the introductory aerial excursion, felt an immediate need for a bit of a bracer.

As the local population increased and some law and order came to the flying business, more complaints were filed against the popular little airport. None are recollected against the "clubs" but, as remembered, the spring of 1927 saw the last of any aviation activity at Central and Roanoke. During spring vacation my husband and I visited my family who lived at the northwest corner of 3rd Street and McDowell Road. The house was on the east half of the lot, and the west two acres belonged to an aged, half-blind horse named Laddy. East of the house was a large clear lawn and in its center grew a very tall and conspicuous cottonwood tree which fascinated the nearby pilots. They made frequent swoops at its tall top, coming near enough to rustle the leaves and stir up the neighborhood, but never sufficiently low to hit it.

One afternoon mother and some friends were having tea in the yard and a red biplane came screaming over to make the customary salute to the tree. The ladies squealed and scattered as the pilot circled to make another pass. This time his depth perception failed or he misjudged his airplane's capabilities, as when he pulled up the red tail hit the tree's top. A shower of leaves, birds' nests, broken limbs, and dirt made a shambles of the tea table and the yard. All this racket startled Laddy who commenced running in circles and fell into an irrigation ditch which held some two feet of water. The poor, feeble, disoriented animal was unable to get up, and the Fire Department had to be summoned to rescue him.

Mother was in a fine rage. She began by phoning the governor, worked her way down through the legislature to the police department, voicing complaints to all and finished with a thank you call to the fire department, dispatching two cases of beer to that worthy organization as a more concrete expression of her gratitude.

The following day, when things were almost back to normal, my husband and I visited the airport, planning to take a ride in one of the ships. The place was deserted and all that remained of the busy little operation were a couple of sawhorses and a few empty oil cans neatly stacked under a tree. The red airplane's spectacular buzz job had been a farewell salute to the Central and Roanoke Airport. It also marked the beginning of the end of the several other sandlot aviation operations in what is now the inner city.

THE GILA VALLEY

While Phoenix was developing into a busy aeronautical center, other towns along the Borderland route were also experiencing an upsurge in aviation interest.

The small town of Clifton in the Gila Valley was the scene of interesting aerial activity in the summer of 1917. The August 27, 1917, edition of the weekly *Courtland Arizonian* reported the following:

Clifton, August 21. The invention of an aeroplane which if carried to a successful consummation will revolutionize the flying game the world over has been made by an Arizona man named Fowler, recently of Miami, according to a statement made by W. A. Pitt who arrived in Clifton from his farm in the lower valley.

Mr. Pitt states that a company in which he is interested has been formed in the valley for the purpose of securing funds for the construction of a working model. Several business men have taken blocks of stock ... to show faith in the new venture which has been patented, and the plans are now in the hands of authorities in Washington. It is thought that if these are feasible the government may purchase the rights to manufacture. Negotiations have been carried on for some time between the company and governmental authorities as well as Senator Ashurst.

One of the principal features of the machine is that it does not require a running start for ascent, and does not require a cleared space for landing. According to the inventor the airship will rise straight up ... and descend in a corresponding manner. Another innovation claimed by Fowler is that the machine will remain stationary in the air as long as the motor is running.

The new and radical little flying machine was a sort of community enterprise. The townsfolk assisted in covering the wings with flimsy cloth fabric and helped with other chores. Basically the contraption was a conventional tractor biplane with motive power furnished by a Model T Ford engine. Abrupt vertical lift was generated by a second Model T power plant attached to a gyro mounted above the craft's upper wing.

On flight-test day the whole town turned out to watch Fowler's first ascension. The number two engine was started and revved up. The intrepid pilot pulled a lever and the tiny airplane leaped into the air above its board fence enclosure. It wavered and hesitated a second or two, then fell straight down with a resounding crash. The pilot-inventor was uninjured physically, but his pride and dignity were so shattered that he and his family left town shortly thereafter. It would be six years before a helicopter managed to sustain powered flight.

On April 18, 1919, the *Graham County Guardian* published the exciting news that Safford would witness a balloon ascension and a parachute jump by aeronaut Charles Hawley. Hawley had just left Miami, Arizona, where a great crowd had observed his successful ascension and thrilling leap from 2,500 feet.

The ascension in Safford took place in a vacant lot bordered by cottonwood trees. A large crowd assembled and nearby housetops, porch roofs, and trees were burdened with small boys hoping for a good view of the performance. When finally released, the big balloon rose sluggishly to about treetop level. It was hit by a gust of wind and took off toward the southeast, dragging the basket and Hawley through the foliage, scattering debris, and dislodging a few birds and boys. The big bag sank below the cottonwoods, slowly rose again, and drifted to a safe landing in a nearby wash. No serious injuries resulted to the spectators, the pilot, or his equipment, but the parachute jump was omitted from the program—Hawley never got high enough.

Safford was blessed with several natural airfields which required a minimum of work, and visiting pilots took advantage of all of them in the early 1920s. There was the balloon ascension location, sometimes referred to as the fairgrounds, which was almost right downtown. Another natural airport was a piece of land south of the present Safford Packing Plant. It was favored by some birdmen but disliked by the barnstormers as it was almost impossible to control the crowds, and too many freeloaders could find vantage spots close by. Consequently, the itinerant passenger-carrying pilots used Robinson's Ranch, which is near the present municipal golf course. They flew riders from this site for $10 each. In addition, there were 'chute jumps, wing-walking acts, and acrobatics—all undertaken with one thought in mind—to attract large crowds of paying passengers.

The town of Willcox, forty-five miles south of Safford, was the trading center for the Sulphur Springs Valley. It was situated at the junction of the paved roads from Safford and Douglas and the newer but unpaved Borderland Highway. Because of its location, it played host to pilots following the railroad and Borderland Highway from El Paso to Tucson, a route that had been pioneered by Cal Rogers and the "Vin Fiz" in 1911.

By the early 1920s Willcox decided it needed a municipal field. Air traffic was increasing, what with the military using the Borderland route and the civilians tagging along after them. When the brisk west winds were blowing, many Tucson-bound airplanes needed to stop for fuel. Contributions were solicited from local merchants, and the facility was constructed.

The new field was soon recognized as one of the best in the state, but for some reason the Willcox city fathers never listed it in the *Aircraft Year Books* or other early flying publications. There was a charge for inclusion in the *Year Books*, and this may be the reason for omission, the community figuring that they could depend on the "grapevine" and save a few dollars. Lack of advertising notwithstanding, by the mid-1920s Willcox was hosting a steady stream of passing aviators. It was the place to stop between El Paso and Tucson, and its status was maintained by gradual additions and improvements to the runways.

DOUGLAS, NOGALES, AND YUMA: 1916–1926

For years, horses in the city of Douglas had been "broke" to the rumblings, whistles, and bells of trains. During the period between 1909 and 1915 the animals (perhaps with a hint or two from the sophisticated Pancho, hauler of the famous Douglas glider), had also learned to accept the raucous clattering of airplanes. But on the morning of September 14, 1916, the horses were astounded, and the entire town thrown into an uproar when a huge, low-flying airplane with a big star on its tail swooped low over the city and landed on the parade ground at nearby Camp Jones. Everyone headed for the field, and a few got there in time to greet Lieuts. Carl Spatz and T. H. Bowen when they happily climbed out of what must have been the biggest airplane in the country—a beautiful Curtiss R-2. It was the first airplane to travel from Columbus, New Mexico, to Douglas, and the first United States military aircraft to fly into Arizona. The pilots remained in town until September 18, and told interested citizens that the trip was for experimental and testing purposes.

Following this exciting encounter, aerial activity in Douglas tapered off until after World War I. In July 1919, Colonel James Prentice arrived from Washington to select a site for the First Aerial Border Patrol Station. He met with the Chamber of Commerce and Mines and told them that the city was to assume no expense for either the planned new airport or the proposed hangar, which would be as high as the Gadsden Hotel. The site selected for the big aerial facility was about 1.5 miles northeast of the city. It was described in the U. S. Touring Bureau's Touring Guide for 1922 as "2,000 feet square, elevation 4,000 feet and a Border Patrol Aerodrome."*

When the Border Patrol was organized and installed at the new Camp Jones Airdrome, the citizens of Douglas enjoyed an almost-daily air show. Besides flying regular patrols, the Border Patrol pilots engaged in various aerial maneuvers to improve their proficiency, and many of these could be witnessed by the townspeople. The massive DH-4s flew with a good, solid bark coming from their big Liberty engines. They did not flutter and sputter as had the old-fashioned box planes, but were husky, efficient fighting machines mounting guns and bombs; a few even carried radios.

During the Patrol's active days, the Camp Jones Airport was improved and enlarged. The airport property was purchased by the Chamber of Commerce and Mines for $1,000 and leased to the government for $1 a year. Shops, servicing, stores, and helium were available for the military, and two good hangars kept all aircraft snug during inclement weather.

By late 1923 the Aerial Border Patrol had been deactivated and the airport reduced to servicing status, but military traffic continued to use the field for practice and cross-country flights. Occasionally a

---

*The Touring Guide, one of the first, if not the very first, civilian directories of airplane landing fields was originally published in 1923. It included descriptions of airports and their facilities and a road map showing airport locations. The information presented in the Touring Guide was often incomplete and sometimes misleading, but the publication was of great help to itinerant pilots nonetheless.

Barnstormer Charlie Mayse brings Santa Claus to Douglas in December 1923. The Shell Oil Company provided candy for the local children in exchange for advertising on the lower wing of Mayse's Hisso Standard.

civilian transient dropped in, but as aircraft grew more dependable and their range increased, many pilots took the more direct route to Tucson and Phoenix via Deming, Lordsburg, and Willcox.

During the winter of 1923–24, Charlie Mayse, a well-known local barnstormer, brought Santa Claus to Douglas. Several days before Christmas, people watched a roaring, snorting airplane circle town, and when it taxied up to the waiting crowd a real live Santa Claus in fur boots, toting a pack full of goodies, climbed out of its front seat. He was just like the Santas in the big city stores and asked the same embarrassing questions such as whether one had been a good boy (or girl) during the year. It was a long ride from the North Pole to southern Arizona, Santa would say. His reindeer were tired and resting in Tucson, so Mr. Mayse had flown him to the border. They had already stopped at Ajo and Bisbee, and when they took off they would visit the kids in Willcox, Benson, Cochise, and Safford before returning to Tucson.

The Aerial Border Patrol airdromes were formally closed in May 1926, but Douglas continued to host a scattering of civilian and military transients and the always-dependable Charlie Mayse, who dropped in to offer passenger rides or make occasional border crossings to the mines at Cananea and Nacozari, in Sonora. When the general economic and aviation surge came in the late '20s and was further stimulated by Lindbergh's famous trans-Atlantic flight, the Border City was ready for Arizona's first scheduled air carrier with a new, lighted field, the first truly international airport in North America.

Like Douglas, the city of Nogales acquired its first airport courtesy of the Aerial Border Patrol. A site was selected in July 1919, and by late summer the Patrol had settled in at the new field, called the Camp Stephen B. Little Airdrome.

Some local residents took airplane rides with the officers at Camp Little, but little else is remembered about early flying in Nogales. During the Christmas season of 1923–24, Charlie Mayse brought Santa Claus to town. There was practically no other flight activity at this time, the First Aerial Border Patrol had disbanded, and military traffic had shrunk to a handful of ships which stopped for fuel.

In 1925 the garrison at Camp Little made some interesting "improvements" to the seldom-used airfield. There was nothing for the cavalry to do and they were bored. A good polo field would have a therapeutic effect so it was decided that one would be built on the airdrome. However, the goal-posts had to be planned to accommodate any aerial traffic—that is, made quickly removable. If equestrian activities were in progress when an airplane circled, the posts were hastily taken down and the joint-use facility reverted to an airdrome until the visitor had parked his ship or refueled and taken off.

Later that year the Camp Little Airdrome was officially deactivated along with the other Aerial Border Patrol airports, but the landing field stayed open for civilian use and the few stray military pilots who dropped in. The polo-playing cavalry remained, but suffered little inconvenience from transient airmen.

Yuma held the distinction of being the first Arizona city to host Bob Fowler on his transcontinental journey in 1911, but since that exciting occasion air traffic over the town had been sparse. This was perplexing to most Yumans as they believed their community to be the natural gateway city between Arizona and southern California. There were intermittent reports of a proposed airmail route to the coast that would include Yuma as a stopping point, but no action was taken until late 1918.

On December 8 that year, Maj. Theodore McCauley swooped down in his JN-4B. He was on "speed dash" from Waco, Texas, to San Diego and stayed only long enough to get gasoline, oil, and a bit of water. He said he would be back soon with five heavier aircraft, all ballasted to simulate mail loads, and requested that the town prepare a 400-acre airport.

The city promised to build a suitable landing strip on a nearby mesa and to mark it with a 100-foot diameter circle with a stripe in the center. This was the start of Yuma's continuing airport program. On December 10, the *Yuma Sun* wrote that five airmail stops were planned in the west: El Centro, Yuma, Tucson, Columbus, New Mexico, and El Paso. When this report was followed by the Army's recommendation of the southern or "fair weather route" for the mail, Yumans felt assured of their position as a gateway city to the southwest from the Pacific coast.

The long-awaited airmail service failed to materialize, however, and the Yuma airport remained quiet. In April 1920, four big DH-4s, assigned to the army engineers for photographic work, flew in. On April 22 one of the pilots was drowned following a forced landing in the swift Colorado River. It was the third accident in Yuma in a short period of time.

One of the problems with the Yuma field, as with many early landing fields, was excessive joint use. An airfield was usually combined with a fairgrounds, rodeo grounds, or ball park (including bleachers), a golf course, or almost any reasonably level site cleared in the interest of another activity. This idea had originated with the early pilots who, because there were no established landing fields, selected these desirable locations. Even though the airplanes were now larger and more numerous, it seemed to many city governments a wicked waste of land to devote several hundred acres to the exclusive use of perhaps a dozen ships a year.

In April 1923 this craze for efficient land use caused another accident in Yuma. Four great Martin bombers belonging to the Marines had departed from San Diego for Washington, D. C., with Yuma as their first scheduled halt. As the bombers touched down at the airport they had to swerve to avoid a corral that had been constructed near the runway intersections. One of the planes attempting to avoid this obstruction hit a touring car filled with interested and enthusiastic Mexicans who had driven out onto the field. The Mexicans all ducked; there were no injuries except to the unlucky airplane and the auto. The four bombers were off the following morning.

Yuma was spreading to the south, and by early 1928 it was evident that a new and larger airport would be needed. Already the municipal field was considered a bit small for the newer, heavier, faster military models, and with the inevitable passage of federal legislation governing both aircraft and pilots, it was hoped that the airmail and general aviation boom would finally arrive in Yuma.

THE FIRST MUNICIPAL AIRPORT IN THE
UNITED STATES—TUCSON

The four JN-4Bs under Major Smith, which visited Phoenix in December 1918, also stopped in Tucson. By the following year, the Old Pueblo, because of its strategic location on the developing Army

Model Airway and its proximity to the newly-organized Aerial Border Patrol, hosted numerous traveling airmen. The Chamber of Commerce had an Aviation Committee but no local airplanes or airport; however, all transient pilots were met when they landed at the Fairgrounds, entertained by committee members, and usually put up as guests at the Old Pueblo Club. News of this gracious treatment spread fast and more birdmen visited Tucson.

In 1919 various Air Service acrobatic teams, often referred to as "flying circuses," were touring the country, putting on Liberty Bond Air Shows. A group was scheduled to visit Tucson and for this occasion a proper airport was required. Time was short but a tract of land owned by Judge Sawtelle on Oracle Road where the Amphitheater High School now stands, was hastily cleared for the performers and named Sawtelle Field. The name was then changed to McCauley Field, and when the Flying Circus staged their show on May 8, a huge and enthusiastic crowd watched the fine precision flying.

On May 9, 1919, Mayor O. C. Parker received a letter from the U.S. Air Service asking the city to build a proper airport. The request was transferred to the chamber of commerce, and, at a joint meeting of this body and the city council on July 21, Councilman Randolph E. Fishburn convinced the gathering that Tucson should build an aerial field. The site selected, with the approval of the army's representative, was four miles south of town on the Nogales Highway.

Tucson was the first city in the United States to spend municipal funds on land for, and improvement of, an airport. The new project was named McCauley Field, then changed to Fishburn Field, and when that councilman moved to El Paso in 1920, it became the Tucson Municipal Flying Field.

Tucson scored a second "first" that fall when the Arizona Aviation Company was incorporated— the first company in the state having aviation as a primary interest. In September the directors met to formulate a program. California entrepreneur Syd Chaplin was selling Curtiss Orioles like hot cakes in Los Angeles, so the Tucson company acquired a distributorship for them in Arizona. Other planned activities included flight instruction, passenger and freight transportation, maintenance, storage, and sales, in both Arizona and New Mexico. On October 8 the company rented the new airport from the chamber of commerce for $50 a month and began building a hangar.

The Tucson airport was officially a joint-use facility, and when the Arizona Aviation Company opened, their operations service and mechanical assistance were available to all. The company flew Senator Ralph Cameron on his political campaign in 1919 and covered the state. This was the first time that an airplane had been used by a political candidate in Arizona. The company continued to oper-

Bert Fireman Collection (Courtesy Arizona Historical Foundation)

Tucson Municipal Flying Field in the early 1920s. This was the first municipally owned airport in the United States.

ate for about eighteen months, sadly discovered that "there was not sufficient business to maintain an economical level," and liquidated in 1920. The *Arizona Year Book* stated that "the company was ahead of the times."

Early in 1921 the Air Service's recruiting was cut and its budget allotment reduced. Further economy measures caused another cut in 1922. As the agitation for expenditure reductions continued, there was a decline in military traffic in spite of Tucson's advantageous position on the slowly developing Army Model Airway. As the border became quiet, the activities of the Aerial Border Patrol were reduced, and a few of the pilots were dispatched to perform fire patrol over the nearby forests. A little business was generated for Tucson by these observation flights, but because of insufficient funding Nogales remained their base. The Aerial Border Patrol used Tucson only for emergency services, but the extensive mapping done by the engineers brought some business to the new airport.

There was little civilian traffic. Figures up to 1923 indicate military movements constituted 90 percent of all activity. Between the time when the Arizona Aviation Company closed and the Army Air Service sent three soldiers to Tucson to service military ships, there seems to have been no one in attendance at the airport. However, any transient making the two or three customary circles over town and the Standard Oil bulk plant would have started a parade of curious people, including the active aviation committee, as well as the fuel truck driver hurrying to the airfield in his vehicle.

Business picked up during 1924, and when barnstormer and flight instructor Charlie Mayse arrived it received another boost. Lola Mayse says that Charlie established the first flying school in the state, which is technically incorrect as it overlooks the activities of the Arizona Aviation Company and Phoenix's Joe Schmitt. However, Charlie did open the first fixed-base operation and school that remained in business.

With his nose for sniffing out passengers, Charlie explored the Gila Valley, and was the first to fly into Cochise, Duncan, Globe, Safford, and Fort Thomas, where he met Walter Ballard who took some instruction from him. Walt suggested using a field on his uncle's ranch near Glenbar, and there Charlie met Lola Carter, Walt's cousin. His flights to Glenbar became more frequent, and one Sunday, as Lola tells it, she was "all gussied up in a navy blue georgette dress and white leghorn hat" when Mayse dropped in. They started for a little airplane ride, and ended up flying to El Paso where they were married. Old rumors said that Charlie kidnapped her. Lola denies this but does not deny that theirs was the first aerial elopement in the state.

Mayse was always very tight-lipped about his adventures with the Douglas bombing group in Mexico during the revolution, and told his wife and anyone else who asked that he had learned to fly in Oklahoma in 1919. Wherever he learned, he was a skillful, tireless pilot with a yen for exploration. He became a fixture in the towns along the Borderland Airway, and a frequent visitor to other parts of Arizona as well.

Several times between 1923 and 1925 Ivan Unger, who had a considerable reputation in Los Angeles as an aerial acrobat and stunt man, joined Charlie for weekend shows. Crowds flocked to the airport to see the exciting performances and take rides. Young Gilbert Sykes of Tucson took up 'chute jumping more for sport than remuneration as he exchanged his exhibition earnings for flying lessons. He should be classed as Arizona's first native skydiver because the other performers came from out of state.

The outstanding event of the year 1924 for Tucson was the overnight stop of the Air Service's famous Around-the-World Flyers. They were on their way home from the east coast, and Tucson would be their only Arizona stop. On November 21, 1924, practically the entire population of the city watched the three small specks in formation over the Rincons grow into three huge Douglas World Cruisers, make two circles of the airport, and then come in to land. Following entertainment and gifts from the city, they were off the next morning for Santa Monica and Seattle.

A Double Celebration for Tucson

Publicity for the Borderland Highway began as early as 1911, and now that the Army Model Airway had inched westward, the military installations at El Paso, Columbus, Douglas, Nogales, and Tucson were designated as Borderland Airdromes, and the route along the fence became known as the Borderland Airway. Since 1918 or earlier everyone knowledgeable about aviation had recognized this southern route as the most feasible for transcontinental flights. It was the low-level, fair weather way to fly, and also the safest and most efficient.

Tucsonans believed that there would soon be transcontinental aerial mail service and that it should be promoted along this desirable flyway. Toward this end, the Aviation Committee of the Chamber of Commerce decided in 1925 to rededicate their municipal airport. A new airport name, chosen by the Aviation Committee, would be kept a secret until the ceremony. The air show, which was to be all military, would feature competing acrobatic teams from Kelly Field, Rockwell Field, and Fort Bliss. The service fliers would entertain the crowds with formation flying, 'chute jumping, and there would also be a 300-mile relay race.

Arizona furnished her best fall weather for the big two-day celebration. By noon at least fifty airmen had arrived in thirty-five military airplanes. The relay racers were off early to allow a mid-afternoon finish; the event was won by a pair of Army officers with a time of 2:05:41 for the approximately 300-mile trip. There were also parachuting and message dropping contests, as well as acrobatic acts. Copper trophies were given the proud winners, and afterwards the municipal field was dedicated as Davis-Monthan Airport before a crowd numbering over 5,000.

Reports certifying this field as the first municipal airport in the United States indicate that the name Davis-Monthan was bestowed although it was not used. The same name was reserved for another facility, the present Davis-Monthan Air Force Base. The field honored in 1925 was called "Tucson Municipal," the "Army Field," or "Charlie Mayse's Airport," depending on the user. The latter name caused unhappiness at city hall a year or so later when some painters, declaring that "Tucson Municipal Flying Field" was too much lettering for any one hangar roof, simply applied "Mayse Field" in large white characters on the building's top. Charlie denied any responsibility. He said he was "away and, shucks, busy flying."

Another Airport for Tucson

During 1923 and 1924 the far-sighted Aviation Committee of the Tucson Chamber of Commerce realized that their new municipal airport, though still only partially developed, was becoming inadequate for the new, larger, and faster military ships. They began investigating promising sites. In 1925 two pilots, D. P. Knight and John Harrison, filed claim on several land parcels southeast of the city. One particular section was ideal for an airfield—level, not too brushy, adjacent to the railroad, and not too far from town. On the recommendation of Moss Ruthrauff, Pima County Engineer, City Councilman Pete Waggoner asked the pilots if they would relinquish their claim on this piece so that it might be used as a future municipal airport. Knight and Harrison gladly agreed, and the council asked Kirke T. Moore and Gilbert Sykes to go to Phoenix to acquire the property. Sykes remembers that the city gave them a check for $19.50 to cover filing fees and the two set off to the capital to buy a new municipal airport for Tucson. While consummating the transaction, an intuitive clerk strongly advised them to also acquire a second, adjacent section. This was a knotty problem. They were only authorized to obtain one section. What would the council say if they returned with two and no authorization for the additional purchase? Would there be criticism for squandering the taxpayers' money, or compliments for their perception and faith in aviation? The men took off for lunch and consultation; sound judgment whispered that the extra parcel should be secured. Moore had $10 and Gilbert admits to having $9.50. Following lunch their $19.50 assets were pooled and the additional section acquired. Though they did not know it at the time, they had just bought Tucson the largest airport in the United States, 1,280 acres. Now this progressive community owned two municipal flying fields, one a couple of sections of virgin desert and the other not completed. Sykes remembers that the council was less than enthusiastic about the second section, but both he and Moore were eventually reimbursed for their extravagant advance.

Civilian flying activity remained static in Tucson in the later months of 1925 and throughout 1926. Charlie Mayse was now the only flight operator left in the Old Pueblo. He continued with his students, his plane sales, his air shows to attract passengers, and his barnstorming around the state, but it was a struggle to stay in business.

THE SANTA FE AIRWAY

On February 9, 1880, the Santa Fe Railroad, struggling towards the Pacific, reached the city for which it was named, but only by a spur line. The main tracks bypassed the old town and led to the newer and booming city of Albuquerque. The last stagecoach was stabled and the huge freight wagons abandoned as the rails worked westward at a rate of about two miles a day. On September 24, 1881, the tracks reached Horse Head Crossing which was renamed Holbrook in honor of William Randolph Holbrook, an engineer who had supervised construction of this section.

As the tracks stretched west, new towns mushroomed, many by virtue of being the temporary end of the line. Others came into being to serve as water stops for the thirsty steam locomotives or as convenient shipping points for huge cattle ranches which were forming in central Arizona. A few, such as a raw lumber camp called Flagstaff, had been there before the coming of the railroad.

While the Santa Fe Railroad came across Arizona from the east, the corresponding airway which developed after World War I came from the west, using the tracks and the Old Trails Highway (later Route 66) as a guide. The town of Kingman on the western edge of the state was the first link in a chain of communities along the railroad and highway that became resting and refueling points on the new airway.

Kingman had its first encounter with airplanes on February 22, 1919, when four army DeHavillands swooped down over the city and landed. It was the same group that had visited Phoenix earlier that month before flying on to the West Coast. Now the planes were winging homeward to Ellington Air Base by way of Albuquerque.

On July 4 another DH arrived over the city. The pilot came unannounced from the Independence Day festivities in Prescott. He took on some gas, oil, and water, and left immediately for San Diego. He, as had his predecessors, complimented the city on their makeshift airport and the quick service from a nearby filling station.

Williams, 113 miles east of Kingman, also had a place where an airplane could be landed. The field, like so many of that era, was an impromptu one selected by an inquisitive gypsy flier in search of gas, oil, and something to eat.

The arrival of the first birdman occurred in the spring of 1919. One day the Santa Fe agent at Bellemont phoned Williams' Superintendent of Schools and told him that an airplane, flying low and following the railroad tracks, was heading for his town. As this was the first ship to come this way, the thoughtful agent believed the superintendent might wish to dismiss classes so the pupils could watch it pass over from the safety of the playground. Classes were let out and the students congregated in the yard where they were admonished "not to leave the spot and to report back to classes as soon as the plane passes." The tiny speck was seen weaving along the track and it soon grew into a full-sized JN4D-2 which, instead of continuing west, began circling town. It became obvious that the pilot intended to land in a pasture on the northwest side of town. The ranks of orderly students broke in a wild dash for the field, led by the superintendent and other teachers, all with coattails flying. The pilot was Lieutenant Moltan, late of the Army Air Service. He had purchased the surplus Jenny and was flying it home to California where he hoped to do a bit of barnstorming. "Jenny" was refueled, but not completely filled as the pilot expected some difficulty with the high-altitude takeoff.

The following morning the first takeoff attempt had to be aborted. Moltan took a longer run on the second attempt and he and "Jenny" were over the pasture's fence with a few inches to spare. When airborne the lieutenant remembered he had neglected to pay his hotel bill. As he had gained insufficient altitude in which to turn around, he landed in another pasture straight ahead, then taxied back to the fence and the watching crowd, which included the hotel owner.

The bill was paid, "Jenny" swung around into the wind, and another takeoff begun. On the third attempt Moltan and the plane hit a tree. The honest pilot was uninjured, but the airplane was badly damaged. The remainder of the day and half that night were spent dismantling the battered ship, and trucking it to the railroad depot where it was put on board a flatcar for travel to a more forgiving altitude.

During 1921, Lieutenant Alexander Pearson landed his big De-Havilland at the Williams fairground. Brush was cleared away from the east side of the oval race track and this was the Lieutenant's airport while he studied air conditions over the Grand Canyon. This remained the official facility until Weber Field was built in 1925.

In nearby Flagstaff the available landing strips were even poorer than the Williams fairground track. They were small, guarded by tall trees, and often muddy. The dismal field conditions, the 7000-foot altitude, and the capricious weather, caused pilots to avoid Flagstaff landings whenever possible.

Airplanes were putting down in the town of Winslow as early as 1919, using a dry lake bed north of town called Tucker Flats. Early in September 1923 Lieut. John A. Macready and Lieutenant Stephens arrived in their big Fokker. They had been taking aerial photographs of the Colorado River and were stopping in Winslow to leave their exposed photographic plates for shipment and to pick up more film. After a short visit they departed to continue their photographic work over the Canyon territory.

On September 14, 1923, the Holbrook Tribune reported that the pair were expected to land for additional supplies on September 17 or 18. Holbrook did not have an airfield so the chamber of commerce hastily cleared a spot south of town. Unfortunately for Macready and Stephens the monsoon season arrived, spawning unusually violent storms. The hard rains continued, delaying the pilots until September 21, by which time the lower portions of Holbrook were a muddy, flooded mess. Macready chose a mesa about two miles northeast of the community. His choice became, a year or so later, the Holbrook Airport.

Winslow had no formally listed airport in 1924. Aerial visitors continued to use Tucker Flats or the ball park, which also served as a racetrack and fairgrounds. Aviation interest was picking up, however. The remarkable Around-the-World-Flight by the army flyers increased enthusiasm. Babbitt Brothers' Trading Post displayed a large world map in their window, and four small red airplanes were moved along to show the army fliers' positions as the dispatches came in.

During August, Charlie Mayse, W. B. Bill Atwell, and their mechanic sailed in from Tucson to give the people of Winslow an opportunity to fly. Their two J-1 Standards would remain in town for four days. According to the local paper, both planes were "new, well built, and entirely safe ... and the acrobatic exhibitions given by the experienced pilots displayed such skill that confidence would be felt by even the most timid."

All this aerial activity and the arrival of one Bob Housler convinced the City of Winslow that a safe, well-marked municipal airport was a necessity. Housler was an ex-army photographer and pilot. Northern Arizona papers referred to him as "the unofficial representative of the Army Air Service," and whatever his status he had the ear of influential officers in Washington. He exercised this influence to promote a string of improved landing fields from Los Angeles to Albuquerque, Santa Fe, and eastward. Whether he received government compensation is not known; however, he was instrumental in accelerating the development of what would soon become Airway Green 4. Today he would be called an airway-airport planner, have a modest staff, and receive attractive compensation.

Late in 1924 Housler was in Winslow supervising construction of that city's new municipal airport. By December 12 it was leveled, dragged, and marked in accordance with military specifications and plans were being made for the all-important dedication. At that time the press evaluated a new airport by the "massive crowds" attending and the "swarms of aircraft" that came for the dedication. Favorable publicity was vital; an airport's financial well-being depended upon its having a good reputation. The community was also trying to satisfy official Washington and win the much-desired airmail service.

The dedication of Winslow's Barrigan field was scheduled for Saturday and Sunday, May 16 and 17, 1925. Saturday afternoon was disappointing. Arizona uncorked one of her stiff spring winds and all flying had to be canceled until late afternoon, when the blow subsided somewhat and pilot Frank Clark put on a thrilling acrobatic performance. Sunday was perfect and the eleven visiting airplanes staged snappy, well-organized exhibitions.

Winslow now had a fine airport named for its progressive, air-minded mayor, John A. Barrigan, and the townspeople hoped that an airmail contract would be awarded to Tri State Airways, a newly incorporated California-based company that, with Bob Housler, was promoting the airway from Los Angeles to Albuquerque.

In addition, it was hoped that Winslow's new facility would generate an influx of passengers to take scenic rides to the Grand Canyon and other lovely but remote spots such as Monument Valley.

Williams, like so many other towns along Highway 66, was caught up in Bob Housler's infectious airport improvement/building urge. The town dedicated its new facility on June 10, 1925.

The Weber Field dedication ceremonies, while not as elaborate as the Winslow event, were something for which Williams could be proud. In addition to the seven military aircraft that attended, Charlie Mayse and Tex Rankin were on hand to carry passengers. A happy *Williams News* reporter wrote that the new airport was adequate for the large military DeHavillands and also for the larger commercial ships.

Bob Housler was also scheduled to be present, but for some reason he failed to appear. After this date both he and Tri State Airways dropped from sight and comment along Route 66. Housler's contribution to the communities of northern Arizona would not be forgotten, however. Thanks in large part to his efforts, the aerial traffic that had begun so modestly at the end of World War I continued to increase along the Santa Fe Airway, as it was coming to be known.

During the summer of 1926 activity was quite heavy. In June, Charlie Mayse revisited Williams with another pilot. They were barnstorming and took three of their passengers on the first commercial sightseeing flight over the Grand Canyon.

On August 6 several contestants in the cross-country Ford Reliability Tour gassed at Winslow's Barrigan Field, and on August 13 another birdman stopped there for fuel, oil, water, and some food. Late in September, Lieutenants Macready and Stephens returned to complete their interrupted photographic work on the Painted Desert and the Petrified Forest. Pages in the airport register began to fill up, and the waiting pilots praised the new field and congratulated the city on their choice of location and the development of the facility.

The year closed along the Santa Fe with feelings of satisfaction and accomplishment. Arizona's central airway was now supplied with a string of good airports. It was photographed, charted, and traveled by both civilian and military airplanes. Now all that was needed was more traffic.

A HIATUS IN PROGRESS: 1919–1926

As 1926 came to a close, the future of civilian aviation in the United States was uncertain. Considerable progress had been made in the development of airports and airways, but flying still remained a haphazard, high-adventure pastime indulged in by a mere handful of people.

Arizona lagged behind other parts of the country in aeronautical growth. The *Aircraft Year Book* credited the state with sixty-four airfields—a miniscule 1.7 percent of the total facilities in the United States. Half of the Arizona fields were designated "emergency," meaning they were of little value to traveling pilots except in the most dire circumstances.

The state had no flying clubs, no airlines, no airmail, and only one permanent, fixed-based flight operator, the energetic Charlie Mayse. Total aircraft population barely exceeded thirty, and traffic along the two principal airways, the Borderland and the Santa Fe, was discouragingly light. Uncertain en route facilities and the unreliable, heavy water-cooled engines of the era were not conducive to extended cross-country flying. For longer trips it was still faster to take the train, and flights of much more than 100 miles were considered unusual.

But all this would soon change. New, more powerful engines that would revolutionize aircraft design and make long-distance flying more practical were being tested, and in Washington, D.C., laws and regulations had been drafted that would do much to promote civilian flying and breathe new life into Arizona aviation.

Civil
Aviation
Takes Off:
the 1920s

Civil aviation came of age legally, politically, and socially with the implementation of the Air Commerce Act on January 1, 1927. The National Advisory Committee for Aeronautics, in its Twelfth Annual Report, wrote that: "This Act provides the legislative corner-stone for the development of commercial aviation in America," and its stipulations became the foundation of the present, volu-minous statutes regulating all airborne vehicles while they are over American lands and waters.

The Air Commerce Act asserted the federal government's responsibility to develop commercial aviation, and to regulate all aerial interstate commerce. Airways would be designated, lighting systems and emergency fields developed, and all existing airways with their appurtenances would become federal property, with the exception of terminal fields and facilities. The old Main Line or Columbia Route, the Army Model Airway, Arizona's Borderland Airway, and the Tri-State or Santa Fe Airway would, in the next few years, become colored and numbered government aerial high-ways. Most postal terminals were to be transferred to their munic-ipalities. In Arizona, the Tucson and Yuma airports would remain as joint-use (military and civilian) facilities, but be administered by their cities. Compulsory licensing of all aircraft, pilots, and main-tenance crews engaged in interstate commerce was made manda-tory, but for intrastate operations only registration of aircraft was necessary. All aircraft, however, were to be marked with an issued number, and all flights on government airways were to abide by the new air traffic rules.

In Arizona as well as other states, the loudest roars of protest came in response to the required licensing of pilots and mechanics, both aircraft and engine (pluralities were permitted). Written and practical exams for all classes were compulsory, as well as a medical examination. Allowance was made for the holders of the previously issued F.A.I. and Joint Cognizance Board licenses, the military and airmail pilots, and "those with known and proven experience." The act included a savings clause allowing continuous operations to July 1, 1927, under a Letter of Authority providing an application had been filed with the secretary of commerce prior to March 1, 1927, and not acted upon. These letters were later extended as the handful of inspectors were unable to contact and examine the flood of applicants, and the total budget of $550,000, with only $250,000 allotted to aircraft in commerce for fiscal year 1927, was not nearly enough to do the job.

Arizona and New Mexico were in the 9th District which also included Southern California where district headquarters was established. California had the majority of impatient pilots and received the most attention. Little was seen of the new inspectors in either Arizona or New Mexico.

All across the nation the inspectors were overwhelmed. An October 31, 1928, report showed 3,650 active pilots. California led the herd with 633; Texas had 176. Of the top nine states these were the only two not in the east. In 1928 aircraft in commerce received a budget of $700,000. In fiscal year 1929 their $702,000 allocation was increased by an emergency addition. Gradually the inspection business in Arizona picked up.

While many of the old-time birdmen resisted the new licensing and inspection procedures, and others bemoaned the "end of all good flying," the passage of the Air Commerce Act was a crucial turning point for civilian flying in the United States. The imposition of law and order in the skies helped win over the conservative businessmen who had strongly disapproved of the gypsy fliers and their freewheeling ways. Another important step was taken to make aviation acceptable to bankers and investors when the new Buhl C-3A aircraft was granted No. 1 ATC (Approved Type Certificate) on March 24, 1927. Henceforth, all aircraft manufactured for commercial use would be required to obtain this badge of respectability, and the coveted ATC with its guarantee of government-approved engineering and workmanship would, in a few years, sound the death knell for the war surplus ships.

On the morning of May 20, 1927, a young, unknown airmail pilot named Charles Lindbergh, flying a Mahoney-Ryan aircraft powered by the new, reliable 220-horsepower Wright Whirlwind engine, took off from New York. Some thirty-three hours later he landed at Le Bourget Field outside Paris, and became the first pilot to successfully fly solo across the Atlantic. Lindbergh was proclaimed a national hero and the wave of publicity that accompanied his return to the United States acted as a powerful stimulus to the already growing aircraft industry.

The legal and financial commitment of the federal government to the development of commercial aviation, coupled with the Lindbergh sensation, had a profound, positive effect on all airplane-related activities. In Arizona this effect was felt in the growing interest in flying and in the continued development of the state's airports.

IMPROVEMENTS FOR PHOENIX MUNICIPAL

Less than four months after the signing of the Air Commerce Act, Ira Pirtle, manager and construction supervisor of the new Phoenix Municipal Airport, started the first airport register in Phoenix.

In this little no-frills register which covered the period between September 1926 and April 1927, Ira noted the arrival of out-of-town aircraft. The information included the date, time, type of aircraft, and the pilot's name, along with the pilot's comments about the airport's condition. The complaints of the visiting birdmen ran to a pattern; the field was "too far from town," "not on the highway," and needed "upkeep." Ira noted that in the eight months he had been keeping the register there had been a total of forty visiting airplanes, not an impressive record, but not too bad for its era, considering that some planes undoubtedly used the Central and Roanoke facility.

Phoenix received its charter for membership in the National Aeronautics Association on July 11. The group promptly met with the army's airport specialist to formulate plans for improvements on the municipal field. During the meeting the mayor, with a very red face, stated that he had received several calls requesting airplane trips over Phoenix and the vicinity, but there was not a single commercial airplane in Phoenix. As flight operators Howard Reinhart, Bernard Whelan, and Tex Rankin were in the city only during the winter months, this was undoubtedly correct.

Aviation enthusiasm picked up with this announcement and the advent of cooler weather. Another representative of the Aero Corporation of California flew into town and told the city officials and members of the Aeronautical Association that the company's plans to commence their line from the coast to El Paso were almost complete. He begged all communities on the route to begin a concerted drive for airmail by submitting petitions to the Postmaster General requesting the service. He further bolstered Phoenix's morale by saying the municipal airport was not too far from town, that its markings were adequate, and its size was sufficient for any

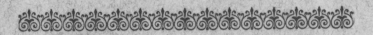

VAN BUREN AIRPORT
Opposite State Hospital   Phone 6424

Free Exhibitions and Parachute Drop
Every Sunday

Aerial Photos - Training - Flying Service

RINEHART-WHELAN CO.
PHOENIX   :-:   ARIZONA

Brochures such as this one were distributed by progressive flight operators in the 1920s. The advertising copy inside explained the mechanics of banking and the causes of turbulence, and told passengers to "relax, trust the pilot, and enjoy the flight."

large aircraft in capable hands. He did tactfully suggest, however, that when extended to its full size and with other improvements completed, it would "be one of the best in the country."

The Pacific Development Company of Los Angeles controlled 28,640 acres of land in a new and promising subdivision of Phoenix, and its president wished to attract California buyers to the site. Flying prospective purchasers to the property appeared to be an attractive solution, and so, on October 15, 1927, twenty-one press and real estate men took off from Los Angeles' Burdett Airport in five aircraft bound for Phoenix. One ship landed at El Centro with engine trouble, and of the four that arrived over the city, only one was able to locate the Phoenix Municipal Airport. Two set down at the old Fairgrounds and the other, after circling for almost an hour, landed at Reinhart and Whelan's field on 24th and Van Buren. Undaunted, the Pacific Development Company's president told reporters he was planning to start an airline to bring prospective property buyers to the valley. One trip a day was anticipated, but he would not consider this until the municipal airport was improved and properly marked.

Later that month the city announced that there were plans to improve the municipal facility with the admission that it was difficult to recognize from the air and had been surrounded by a "square of trees." Some changes had already been made. Most of the trees were gone, the stumps whitewashed, the surface graded, a 100-yard white circle painted in the field's center, and the name "Phoenix Airport" painted over the main gate.

The report on the expenditures required to make the Municipal Airport a Triple A field was presented on November 23. In these days of pre-airport aid, spending vast sums on any landing field's improvements was a touchy matter, but slowly developments continued. Additional land was cleared, more stumps were dynamited and burned, and the Pirtles' house was renovated to become an airport terminal building.

A few tie downs were installed, there was a phone at the house, but no fuel facilities yet—although just a circle over the bulk plant would bring a fuel truck scurrying to the airport. Getting transportation to town was relatively easy. An airplane landing always attracted a crowd and there were many invitations to ride to town. The long return trip presented more problems as the unlucky traveler who could not promote a lift was likely to feel that he had "bought the cab" when presented with the bill.

Improvements continued to be made at the municipal airport with the army's blessings. The airport now had two crossed runways of about 3,700 feet each. A few old-timers remember the facility as an "all way field" but only partially developed; others recollect it as having only an east-west runway, and no one recalls any paving or surfacing of any kind. The Aero Corporation of California, now

Passengers pose in front of the first tri-motor to land at Phoenix. A modern fueling system had not yet been installed at Phoenix Municipal and two to three hundred gallons of gasoline had to be pumped to the plane's tanks by hand.

known as Standard Airlines, was using it, as was the fitful Maddux Airlines and numerous transients. No landing fees were charged but gas and oil sales returned some revenue.

Despite the overall success of the improvement plan, there were stormy sessions at city hall regarding the airport. To many council members it seemed that the place was a constant source of expenses which returned little money to the city's coffers. Finally the council announced that the field would be put up for bids — they wished to get out of the airport business — but no one was interested.

Phoenix Municipal attracted little student and passenger business. Most of this patronage went to the new South Central Airport as it was more convenient to downtown and the operation was geared to this type of service. However, after instructor Ralph Carson and his partner Bill Langdon acquired their new American Eagle, a few passengers and trainees furnished some business. On weekends and holidays there was constant visiting between South Central, 24th Street and Van Buren, and "Christy," as the municipal airport was called. When work commenced at Scenic's new and glamorous

Sky Harbor Airport, progress there had to be constantly checked even if the new facility were only an 80-acre patch with unfinished construction along the north side.

These short hops were the most common type of pleasure flying during the 1920s. Pilots then did not set out on cross-country excursions with the nonchalance of today's aviators. Even a trip to Tucson required some planning and forethought. The traveler had to collect a few hand tools and small but vital plane parts; a map had to be located; the Phoenix Weather Bureau had to be phoned for information; and in those pre-flight plan days, specific arrangements had to be made for emergencies. With the exception of a few, scattered communities the country was raw, unforgiving desert. No planning was required for the short hops to a neighboring field since the trip consumed little flying time, but the adventurer might be gone half a day chatting with friends, meeting new acquaintances, and watching itinerant pilots arriving and departing.

During the late 1920s, a great many communities built new airports or improved existing fields, and an airport dedication somewhere was an almost weekly event which any devoted pilot hated to miss. Both Apache Airlines and Copper State Airways got into the air, and those who had lacked the foresight to at least make a small investment in something aeronautical hurried to jump on the bandwagon.

The "improved" Phoenix Municipal hosted the great, the near great, and an unrecorded number of just ordinary flyboys in addition to the added airline schedules. The fuel sales picked up. Bert Balchen gave spectators a thrill when he looped Standard Oil's big tri-motor Ford right over the field, and a military DM-4 bringing in some serum after dark provided more thrills. Christy was not lighted, and shortly before the ship's expected arrival Ira Pirtle and his older children lit bonfires around the airport's perimeter near the cut stumps to guide the visitor. The big 25,000 candlepower flares were also ignited but by the time the pilot recognized the airport he was low on fuel and made an emergency landing in a field just to the east. The ship was damaged but the cargo and pilot were unharmed.

On February 10, 1929, tragedy struck. Louis Gay, a flight student at Christy, had purchase a new OX5 Eaglerock. It was supposed to be delivered on February 10 or 11, so early on the 10th Louis drove to the field for a bit of final practice. Bill Langdon, from whom he had taken some instructions, was making a few minor adjustments on his American Eagle and suggested to Louis that they test hop the plane. At 6000 feet Langdon instructed Louis to stall the ship. The Eagle went into a spin, ordinarily not serious except that after about two turns it "went flat." Contact with the ground was hard and solid, right in the middle of the field. Both men were rushed to the hospital seriously injured. Langdon died that afternoon about the same time as Louis's new Eaglerock arrived in town.

Albert Pirtle Collection

Instructor Bill Langdon was killed and passenger Louis Gay was severely injured in this crash at Phoenix Municipal on February 10, 1929. The accident was the result of a flat spin.

Gay was never sure what went wrong. He just remembered the spin as being "damned flat, like a pancake" with no feel, pressure, or responses to the controls, and the helpless, sickening sensation of the horizontal revolutions as the dirt runway rose up to meet them.

An investigation followed the Langdon-Gay accident. Langdon's partner, Ralph Carson, told the authorities the ship was in good condition and safe, indicating some sort of pilot error as the cause of the tragedy. Instructors preached safe flying to their students, then they went up and broke all the rules in the book. They usually got away with it because they knew how to do acrobatics and recognized the limitations of their ships.

The fatal accident worsened what was already a bitter and discouraging year for the Phoenix City Council and the Aviation Committee. J. Parker VanZandt's Scenic Airways had begun construction of the Phoenix Sky Harbor facility on November 16, 1928, and already much of Phoenix Municipal's business was being siphoned off to Scenic's large, modern, more convenient airport. First to leave Christy was Maddux Airlines which shared both a downtown office with Scenic as well as their Sky Harbor space. Standard moved to the new field, and when Apache Airlines began scheduled flights from Globe and Superior to the valley, the planes landed there to make connections with Standard's flights. The first Powder Puff Derby chose Sky Harbor as an important overnight stop, but the final blow was the elaborate dedication of the new field, attended by some 8,000 persons on Labor Day 1929.

THE FIRST SEAPLANE IN ARIZONA

By the late 1920s, the citizens of Arizona were growing accustomed to aeronautical activities. The sight of an airplane in flight no longer created a major sensation and in some more populated areas sophisticated pedestrians were even able to ignore the roaring little machines flying overhead. There were some types of aircraft that were still unusual, however, and in April 1927, one of these rare birds, a seaplane with an Italian crew, visited Arizona.

Until 1925 Italy had no civil aviation. This situation was remedied by Premier Benito Mussolini who organized an Air Ministry with himself at its head. Also that year, General Francesco de Pinedo won the Federation Aeronautique Gold Medal by accomplishing a flight of over 34,000 miles in a single engine, wooden hull, rag wing hydroplane. Today such a flight would be considered exceptional; in that era it was unbelievable.

Il Duce hoped to achieve mastery of the air and he wished to impress other nations with Italy's aviation progress. Consequently, General de Pinedo was dispatched on an aerial tour of Europe, Africa, South America, and the United States. The itinerary included a stop in Arizona.

De Pinedo's new ship was a dreamboat for its time, a converted seaplane bomber with twin plywood hulls, powered by two Fraschini engines, and outfitted with the latest in navigational equipment. The plane, christened the "Santa Maria," could cruise, depending on the load, at 115–120 miles per hour, and had a top speed of 127 miles per hour.

This combination goodwill-propaganda flight began from Caglia, Sardinia, on February 13, 1927. General de Pinedo, with Capt. Carlo del Prete as copilot, meteorologist, and navigator, and Lieut. Vitale Vacchetti as mechanic, flew down the coast of Africa, made a rough Atlantic crossing to Brazil, and from there flew north to New Orleans and Galveston, Texas. The plan was to circle the United States and return to Italy over the North Atlantic. The Orteig Prize for the first solo flight across the Atlantic was still unclaimed. De Pinedo expressed no interest in it, but the American press was of the opinion that if all went well and the timing was right he would attempt to capture it for the glory of Italy.

From Galveston the Italians flew to Lake Medina near San Antonio, cut across Texas, and followed the shallow, winding Rio Grande to Elephant Butte Dam near Hot Springs, New Mexico. Radiator trouble there caused a day's delay; the over-4,000-foot altitude, the heat, and the still air, caused additional difficulties. More than 700 pounds of luggage, spare parts, and other items were offloaded and all motorboats were called out to stir up the smooth water. At 1:15 P.M. on April 5 the sluggish hydroplane was airborne and headed westward. About twenty-five minutes later the "Santa Maria" returned. It had failed to gain sufficient altitude in the heat.

Takeoff was planned for early the following morning, in hopes that there would be cooler temperatures and a breeze. The short flight had additionally lightened the ship, and with the motorboats again roiling the water, the takeoff in the cooler morning air was easier.

All Arizona was alerted and expectant, eager to see the first seaplane to come to the land of the desert rats. This was worth the dusty, rough, six-hour drive to Roosevelt Lake, and mobs— including many loyal Italians—made the rugged trip. The "Santa Maria" gracefully set down on the lake at 10:16 A.M. Two motorboats towed her to the steep bank and del Prete and Vacchetti supervised the refueling. Fred Paine, manager of the Standard Oil Company from Phoenix, had been notified to bring 200 gallons of aviation gas and was waiting there with his truck. As the big hoses were connected, de Pinedo went ashore to exchange greetings with the crowd and the press. The air was still and the lake glassy. De Pinedo was worried about the takeoff, and became further distressed when he learned that more fuel had been pumped into the tanks than he had requested. Remembering the difficult experience at Hot Springs, he

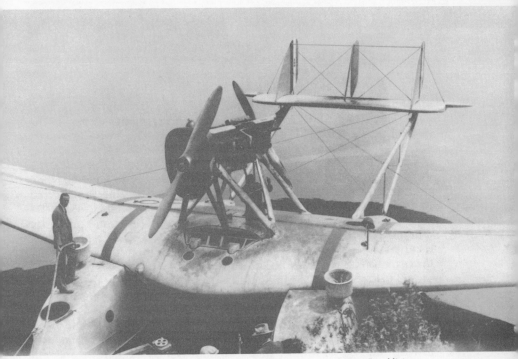

E. D. Newcomer Collection (Courtesy *Arizona Republic*)

The Italian seaplane "Santa Maria" being refueled on Roosevelt Lake, April 5, 1927.

The charred wreckage of the "Santa Maria" salvaged from Roosevelt Lake.

ordered some of the gasoline removed. The commander himself emptied one pailful into the lake; then, after giving directions for the de-fueling, left for a luncheon in his honor. The festivities were almost over when there was a cry of "Fire!" The "Santa Maria" was blazing, and in spite of heroic work with an extinguisher by a by-stander, it was all over in ten minutes. The heavy engines crashed through the burning structure into deep water, leaving the charred remains of the hulls floating idly. De Pinedo wasted no time. He cabled Mussolini for a new airplane and the reply came promptly that one would be shipped to New Orleans and he should go there to receive it. Assistant Navy Secretary Davison offered the Commander the use of a U.S. airplane but he politely refused.

The immediate feeling in Italy and in some parts of this country was that sabotage by expatriates had caused the tragedy. The mys-terious fire threatened to create an international incident, but the efforts of an *Arizona Republican* reporter covering the story, re-vealed the true cause. A young boat dockhand who had assisted in towing the "Santa Maria" to shore, had lighted a cigarette and un-thinkingly tossed the burning match into the fuel-covered waters. It was a relief to learn the truth; de Pinedo shook hands with the culprit and forgave all. The Commander and his crew then rode to Phoenix in one of the official cars.

On April 8 the *Republican* announced that the Italians would go to San Francisco by train, and from there to New Orleans to pick up their new boat, then continue the planned tour of the United States. However, under no circumstances would de Pinedo venture west of the Rockies again. Searching for a lake in the towering rock mountains and dun-colored deserts was worse than trying to spot a tiny island in the ocean. He was a saltwater man, and though no record had been found of his opinion, it is clear that he did not admire the Southwest.

On April 9 the navy sent two planes from San Diego to Phoenix Municipal Airport for de Pinedo and del Prete. The U.S. Navy pilot and the commander reached the Pacific without further incident, but the ship carrying del Prete, flown by Lieut. Cmdr. W. A. Hactor, had engine trouble near Jacomba, California. It was a most inconvenient location. The lieutenant commander picked the best available landing spot—it was short and muddy—and Cmdr. A. E. Montgomery and de Pinedo circled the stricken airplane in their big U-O, watched it make a nice landing but noted that Hactor was unable to stop the roll-out in time. The plane hit a small ditch bank, slowly upended and turned over. Both men were thrown clear and received no injuries though they did get a very disagreeable mud bath. The airplane was a washout. The U-O circled until Montgomery and de Pinedo were sure neither pilot was hurt and then flew on to San Diego where a car was immediately dispatched to bring the unfortunate birdmen to the coast.

De Pinedo and his party continued north to San Francisco (by train) and thence to New York, instead of New Orleans, where they picked up their new S-55 which had come as deck cargo on a liner. Several shakedown flights were made and the party took off for Trepassey Bay, Newfoundland. The commander had made no comments regarding the Orteig Prize, but many felt that he would make a dash for it if the weather were favorable. What reports were available to the commander and del Prete are not known, but Lindbergh's decision was made after receiving a special report from the New York Weather Bureau on the afternoon of May 19. Three days later the second "Santa Maria" was airborne for Italy but there was little press comment. Lindbergh had landed in Paris and the world had a new hero.

De Pinedo's return flight was not without difficulties. Strong winds slowed the "Santa Maria," the fuel was exhausted about 200 miles from the Azores and the aircraft had to be ignominiously towed to port, where it was refueled for the final hop to Rome. De Pinedo was no longer high man on Mussolini's totem pole.

THE LARGEST AIRPORT IN THE UNITED STATES: DAVIS-MONTHAN, 1927

Following the implementation of the Air Commerce Act, aviation commenced a discouragingly slow albeit steady metamorphosis, and as the efforts of the CAA increased when bolstered with more adequate financing, the pace quickened. During the next seven or eight years the industry would undergo a radical change. Soon knowledgeable customers were asking operators if their aircraft and pilots were licensed. The more progressive began advertising this desirable status and a few added the fact that they carried liability insurance.

Tucson was prepared for the new air age with the largest municipal airport in the United States. Public spirit was high and, with the enthusiastic cooperation of the utility companies, the army, and the chamber of commerce, the water, lights, sewers, and other improvements were installed by Dedication Day. The "Lindy Light," a large rotating beacon, paid for by public subscription, was installed and operating. Colonel Lindbergh himself would be present at the ceremonies to throw the switch. The new facility, which was to be joint-use, would be called Davis-Monthan. Tucson would pay 80 percent of all maintenance costs, and the military 20 percent plus a reimbursement of $1 a year for lease privileges. The army would also build its own hangar(s) and service buildings, and install its own fuel system.

Everything was ready for the big dedication on September 23, 1927. A full size replica of the Spirit of St. Louis, made of ocotillos, sahuaro, and other varieties of cacti, perched in a rakish climb near the spot where the ceremonies would be held. Its cylinders were made of barrel cactus and the propeller of prickly pears. Over 600 Lindbergh medallions were struck and sold to help offset the costs of entertaining the visitors, and special airmail "Welcome Lindbergh" cachets were issued.

The meticulously planned program was scheduled to begin at 2:00 P.M.; at 1:46 P.M., 20,000 spectators saw a tiny speck in the heat haze grow into a full-sized Ryan Brougham, circle the city, then taxi to the hangar after a perfect landing. Out climbed the "Lone Eagle" to the thunderous applause of the crowd.

Colonel Lindbergh was taken to Pastime Park, the government hospital north of town where the ceremonies took place. The carefully planned and printed program could not mention the masses of well-mannered spectators lining Lindbergh's parade route, the four bands, the thousands crowded into the university stadium, nor the swarms of out-of-town visitors. It was a day long to be remembered and savored by Tucson.

Buehman Memorial Collection, Arizona Historical Society

Charles Lindbergh (far right) at the dedication of Tucson's Davis-Monthan Airport, November 23, 1927.

Traffic at the new facility was light at first. The January 1927 issue of *Western Flying* listed a total of 215 landings at Davis-Monthan—of these 185 were military. In 1928 the military arrivals totaled 171 and civilian movements 310. By this time the city realized hangars were needed, and by August, eight were erected and three spoken for. Standard and Scenic Airlines, and a new company—D-M's first fixed base operator, Southwest Air Service, had rented them.

A 1929 traffic count for Tucson as tabulated by *Western Flying* totaled 692 aircraft with 404 of them being civilian. The ratio was closing in favor of non-military movements. An administration building was needed to serve the airlines which were stopping there now and to provide for the still-promised airmail.

Later in 1929 a city worker, Bert Cosgrove, was hired as the Davis-Monthan airport manager, the first such position held by a Tucson city employee. Shortly thereafter a $25,000 bond issue was passed which allowed for the construction of the much-needed new administration building. By January the plans for the building, a concrete apron, and other small improvements were progressing. This might be considered the real takeoff point for Davis-Monthan which would become one of the finest joint-use airports in the country and is presently an outstanding military base.

THE ONLY TRULY INTERNATIONAL AIRPORT IN THE AMERICAS: DOUGLAS

Formal deactivation of the Aerial Border Patrol came in April 1926, and Douglas, the Arizona city with a long list of worthy aeronautical "firsts," was left with a small, abandoned flying field. Cochise County leased the property for use as a fairground; technically the airport remained open, but activity there was minimal. Transients used the shorter and more popular Deming-Lordsburg cutoff between El Paso and San Diego and there were no locally based machines.

The implementation of the Air Commerce Act brought official assurances of progress, but these vague promises were offset by the ugly rumor that both Phoenix and Douglas would be omitted from the planned southwest airmail schedules. Interest picked up when two airlines, Standard and Maddux, made surveys of the city, but the first to take any positive action were five local residents who formed an Aero Club in May 1927. They acquired a state land lease for a parcel which would eventually become the first truly international airport in the United States. The property status was changed from a lease to a certificate of purchase providing for payments over a forty-year period, and in September the organization's name was altered to the Burlingame Heights Company. This group, aided by other enthusiastic men, applied for a Douglas Chapter of the National Aeronautics Association, and was accepted on October 12, 1927. The charter carried the names of the thirty-five founding members and was the first granted in the state by that organization.

Both Standard Airlines and Maddux Airlines promised schedules to Douglas if a suitable airport were provided, and a committee began working on site selection. The Burlingame Heights property was most desirable, being close to town; the approaches were excellent and little grading and clearing would be required. Following several spirited meetings, the company agreed to relinquish the land for their invested amount, $1,200, which would be raised by public subscription. Following approximately two hours of brisk telephoning the required sum was pledged and the contract was assigned to the Bank of Douglas as trustee of the city. J. S. Douglas, president of the Douglas Investment Company, donated fourteen acres along the border to connect the new parcel with Mexico which planned a joint facility. In this way the first truly international airport was formed.

In exchange for a ten-year lease, the county appropriated $10,000 in June 1928. This sum was used for clearing, grading the airstrip, digging a well, and building a small brick house for an airport manager. The city allocated $7,500 for lights, and a later sum of $4,000 from the county completed construction. The only thing lacking was a hangar which was a prerequisite for the coveted A1A rating which was desired by both the city and the county.

While efforts were made to acquire the steel framework of the army's abandoned Camp Jones hangar, surveying on the Mexican part of the airport was completed. Sonora's Gov. Fausto Topete and his staff visited the new Douglas field to assess progress. Inquiries made regarding the approximate cost of grading the Mexican property so pleased the governor that the work was begun the following day, surely setting some kind of speed record for slashing governmental red tape.

The Douglas Aviation Committee continued to try to acquire the Camp Jones hangar but the army refused to go along with the scheme. This decision was disappointing but grading and other construction continued at the site. The blueprints for the wonderful new facility arrived in Douglas in August 1928. The giant air complex would be the largest in the United States and was advertised as the only "truly international airport in the continent," being both physically and legally eligible for the distinction. When completed, touring pilots could comply with the new United States border crossing regulations effective February 1, 1929, sedately taxi through the wide gate into Mexico to complete formalities there, and be away with only one landing and takeoff. Aircraft entering the United States executed the requirements in reverse, thus eliminating the hated "pogo stick" performance of two landings and takeoffs at two international airports only a few miles apart.

By late 1928 the new airport was lighted and usable, but there was still no hangar. Standard Airlines commenced connecting schedules with the Texas and Pacific Railroad's "Sunshine Special" on February 4, 1929, the first viable plane-train schedule from the West Coast to Chicago. Local businessmen could now reach Los Angeles in a mere eight hours, and the speed and convenience of this service was said to be worth every penny of the $57.50 fare.

In March, northern Mexico was in the throes of the sad and dreary Escobar Rebellion which brought the new Douglas facility a mix of military and civilian business. The military planes were to protect the American border and the small civilian models passed on into Mexico where they were converted to simple bombers.

All that now stood in the way of the city's desired A1A airport rating was a hangar. In June 1930, the city council and city water department appropriated $15,000 for this necessity. Harold Bean, former FAA Arizona District engineer, remembers Douglas's big new 100 by 120 foot hangar was partly financed by the federal government under a predecessor program of the WPA. The building's huge, smooth-rolling doors opened almost 120 feet wide and had a 20-foot overhead clearance that would accommodate the later big DC-3s. This was the first instance of such federal assistance to a civilian airport in Arizona.

Even prior to the Depression foreign clearances through Douglas's international facility were unimpressive (by present day standards) — possibly a half-dozen per month. Charlie Mayse in his Wacos and later in his new Ryan Brougham cleared customs several times a year en route to Cananea or Nacozari. Sometimes the flights were for the mining companies; others, logged as "short hops," were for local passengers, and some were for barnstorming. In spite of prohibition, the only good Sonoran resort hotels were at Agua Caliente and Ensenada. Pilots en route to these cleared through Nogales and most travelers bound for Mexico City went by way of El Paso. Then the only two communities of any appreciable size with reasonable airports accessible via Douglas were Cananea and Nacozari — both dismal mining towns.

The city of Douglas was justly proud of its new facility and printed a two-page descriptive release listing its size, location, various services and their costs, and also included suggestions for touring pilots entering and leaving Mexico. These suggestions pertained to "touring trips" and not commercial flights. All pilots entering Mexico were required to register their ship and passengers at the American Customs Office and secure a permit from the local Mexican consul. There were no charges for these permits, and following this formality, the pilot got in his ship, taxied through the gate and presented all credentials to the officials at Agua Prieta. When leaving Mexico, telegrams were required to be sent to the Mexican Customs and immigration offices at Agua Prieta and to American Customs at Douglas stating approximate arrival time.

With the uncertainty of Mexican telegraph and telephone service and the unreliability of the aircraft engines of that era there were some unusual incidents. The Mexicans were very understanding, however, and unless there had been a deliberate legal infraction they tended to be lenient. If a pilot became lost and was forced to land south of the fence no serious difficulties ensued. Assistance was offered and the confused and embarrassed birdman given directions back to the States. As the expression went, "It was an illegal entry, so why not follow it with an illegal exit." It was the responsibility of the erring pilot to make his peace with the less forgiving U.S. officials.

It would be mid-1932 before the lighting and emergency fields on the Los Angeles-El Paso Airway (LA-EP) were completed and American Airways could schedule night operations on that segment, but from the beginning the famous Douglas Airport lighting system had prevented accidents and saved lives. The annual monsoons move into Arizona during the summer, and one July evening scattered showers peppered the Douglas area. These were followed by a morning cloudburst directly over the field that left a residue of drizzle and fog which, by late afternoon, mixed with the smelter smoke to produce near zero visibility conditions at the airport. At sundown a pair of bewildered ferry pilots in two Ryan Broughams churned around in the murk looking for the field. In desperation they turned north and continued their circling. A quick-witted airport attendant flipped on all the lights, including the big beacon, and in minutes the two happy, relieved aviators were taxiing through the mud to the fuel pits. They told bystanders the huge light sliced the undercast like a burning Texas oil well, and as there were no oil wells reported in Arizona, the illumination had to come from Douglas International Airport.

The stock market crash in October 1929 had little impact on Douglas aviation activities, but by mid-1930 its effects were being felt in central Arizona. Sprawling Scenic Airlines was liquidating and other flying companies were on the verge of folding or had already closed. Douglas went right on plugging. They won their fight to get the airmail schedules and the new international airport received its A1A rating on December 12, 1931. The aeronautical "goose hung high" in the smelter city, but the successive Depression waves proved almost catastrophic. American Airlines' two daily schedules, supplemented by a mere trickle of transients, constituted the new airport's traffic, but its upgrading never ceased.

FLAGSTAFF'S NEW AIRPORT

Flagstaff City Clerk Clarence "Maggie" Pulliam carefully broke the seals on the big mailing tubes, unrolled their contents, and spread Flagstaff's new municipal airport plans all over his office. B. Russell Shaw, a well-known aero engineer who had designed the new St. Louis Municipal Airport and other outstanding facilities, had prepared them; he had also included specifications for hangars and a small terminal. The buildings would have to wait until later, but even with only the runways completed the city would have one of the finest fields in the Southwest, and certainly along the Santa Fe and Highway 66. The main runway, northeast by southwest, would be 300 feet wide and 6,600 feet long. The other two, northwest by southeast and north-south, would be 200 feet wide and 6,250 and 5,200 long, respectively.

J. Parker VanZandt, Scenic Airways' president, predicted that Flagstaff would soon become an important aviation hub for central Arizona. It would have everything — proximity to the Grand Canyon, and to both the Santa Fe tracks and paved Highway 66 (pilots still desired a back-up system and navigational aids). The city was further blessed with a permanent, natural beacon that classed with Pike's Peak and Mt. Washington — 12,635 foot Mt. Humphrey, which could be spotted from 150 miles away. The San Francisco Peaks' abilities as a "weather factory" were completely ignored by the new airport boosters, but soon recognized by both local and itinerant aviators. The peaks generated and attracted blowing snow, fog, and violent thunderstorms, and as the new airport was eight miles northeast of the city and east of the mountains, the prevailing winds accompanying the violent storms from the west quadrants slashed through the passes, and whirled around the lower cinder hills surrounding the runways. If wind socks had been installed at each corner, it would not have been unusual for all to be standing out and whipping in four different directions.

Despite these drawbacks aviation interest in Flagstaff was in high gear by the end of February 1928. Maggie Pulliam had sparkplugged both the formation of an aero club and the city's interest in and acquisition of the new municipal field. He and the other active participants were justly proud of their almost mile-square facility.

The Flagstaff Aero Club employed a flight instructor and while the field was being readied and the organization's finances assembled, ground school classes were held; the eager members were busy building a three-foot scale model of a Jenny. By June a new Eaglerock had been ordered from the Aero Corporation of Arizona.

The June 7, 1928, dedication festivities were a success. The Sun wrote that "one of the greatest aggregations of aviators and airminded people ever assembled in Arizona was here today ... " Army, Navy, and Marine Corps ships from California and Texas, Arizona aviators, and over 1,000 other visitors helped to make the occasion memorable. At 3 P.M. Mayor I. B. Koch presented the field, which was named in his honor, to the military services and the civilian public. It was graciously accepted, and a flag raising and suitable tunes by the local band made the customary lumps in all attendants throats. Following this, Capt. H. D. Campbell of the Marine Corps said, with a degree of exaggeration normal for such an affair, that it was the "only adequate landing field he had seen on his 500-mile flight from San Diego."

With the dedication out of the way the Flagstaff airport went into operation. Word spread quickly that it was a fine field with good service and was a pleasant place for an overnight stop. During October, the aero club instructor and his prize student took off for Colorado Springs to pick up the club's new ship. Following their return with the Eaglerock, the fifteen active members commenced flying.

On February 1, 1928, a CAA inspector visited town. He was not mentioned as the first such official, but it is reasonable to believe that he may have been. He was from the Los Angeles office and came to inspect Koch Field, the local pilots' papers, and the aero club's Eaglerock. The 180 Hisso had just been overhauled to ready it for spring business and the club wanted it certified for paid passengers. Everything was in good order, and the membership and the instructor were satisfied. Western Air Express was planning its new route. The club members were flying, Scenic flitted in and out, and occasionally a transient dropped from the sky.

The Depression brought an end to this pleasant period. Flagstaff's lumber, railroad, banking, and tourist business suffered and so did the new airfield. The aero club's instructor left in search of greener pastures, Scenic Airways terminated its Arizona operations, and by 1932 the club's Eaglerock was resting, neglected, in a hangar. It was eventually sold and the Flagstaff Aero Club disbanded.

Word soon got around that Koch was deserted. The deer and antelope appreciated the cessation of activity and returned to graze, and then the bean farmers came. The city derived some small income from the land rental and the legumes thrived in the cinder soil. Koch's runways were bordered by the bumper crops, and even without maintenance remained clearly visible and reasonably smooth, although somewhat narrowed by the legumes' encroachment.

Flagstaff's experience was all too common in other Arizona communities during the early years of the Depression. The effort to impose law and order on the airways, Lindbergh's flight, and the resulting aviation boom of 1927–29 had done much to propel flying into the mainstream of American life, but now there would be a period of retrenchment and for those who loved flying and believed in its future, a long and difficult struggle for financial survival.

Making a Living

Flying was an exciting hobby for most pilots in the early days of Arizona aviation, but for others, more deeply bitten by the aviation bug, it was a way of life. Piloting airplanes for pay was an uncertain and sometimes hazardous occupation, but these pioneering professional aviators found the rewards worth the risks.

Military pilots, barnstormers, flight school operators, and airline personnel crisscrossed the state in their aircraft in pursuit of a dollar. They made maps, took aerial photographs, put on air shows, carried passengers, and hauled every type of cargo imaginable— anything to be flying—and making a living.

THE GRAND CANYON PROJECTS

No one knows who discovered the Grand Canyon. Don López de Cardeñas was the first European to see it during the fall of 1540, but it had been known to the Indians for generations.

Beginning in 1869, the river and the main canyon were comprehensively surveyed, mapped and explored by the Powell Expeditions, and again surveyed, charted and sketched by Robert C. Stanton's party—this time for a water-level railroad from Colorado to the Gulf of California.

In July 1901, the Santa Fe tracks reached Grand Canyon Village on the South Rim. Now travelers could see a small bit of the famous gorge in comfort. No more jogging in the dusty stages from Flagstaff or Williams for the better part of two days. The tourist business mushroomed.

Early in 1919 the secretary of the interior asked the air service to make reconnaissance flights over the Grand Canyon to "ascertain the feasibility of carrying passengers commercially, to discover sites for airports," and to generally study conditions in the area. Four DH-4 "bombers" were making a loop tour of the southwest, and on March 1 they flew over and filmed the Grand Canyon; one aircraft explored the gorge as far as Diamond Creek.

In June 1921 another Air Service pilot, Lieut. Alexander Pearson, arrived in Arizona to study air currents in and over the Grand Canyon. He took off from Williams on June 24, flew around the San Francisco Peaks, and then roared north toward the Canyon. After crossing the gorge several times he dipped down below the rim and landed on a little strip that had been cleared for him at Indian Gardens, a halfway rest point on the Bright Angel Trail between the South Rim and the Colorado. One newspaper reporter was so carried away by this feat that he wrote that "soon [air] ships will be crossing the Canyon many times a day, and also going into it and landing. Good-by to the mule trains."

Two years later the U.S. Geological Survey Expedition under Claude M. Birdseye was completed and the aerial photographs made by Lieutenants Macready and Stephens on their flights over the Canyon and territory north of Winslow were released. This marked the virtual end of what could be called the exploratory period of the Grand Canyon. It was now mapped, photographed, painted, sketched, measured and sampled. Various airplanes had clattered over and into it, and all this voluminous information was neatly documented and stored in the Washington archives.

The canyon was ready for the tourists, and Arizona pilots believed it was ready for an airline. Everyone said that thousands would fly to the canyon and those who came by train or car would all wish to fly into it and along it. A combination airline and aerial sightseeing operation would be a gold mine. Unfortunately, "everyone" would prove to be some thirty years premature with these predictions.

During the summer of 1922, Emery and Ellsworth Kolb, river explorers, photographers, and the owners of a popular gift shop on the South Rim, became interested in aviation. Ellsworth mounted a camera on a Lincoln Standard piloted by R. V. Thomas, and took aerial movies of the canyon. He and Thomas landed at Indian Gardens, and then returned to a little field near Tusayan. This field was an open, level space which Emery planned to acquire and develop into an airport. Three years later he applied for and received a U. S. Forest Service permit allowing him to use this location for commercial flights. This was the first official Grand Canyon airport, and was incorporated into the present Grand Canyon air facility during the 1960s.

R. V. Thomas and Ellsworth Kolb following their landing at Indian Gardens in the Grand Canyon. Kolb was taking the first aerial movies of the Canyon; Thomas was the first civilian to land in the Canyon.

SCENIC AIRWAYS

Meanwhile in Detroit, the National Parks Syndicate had formed with J. Parker VanZandt as president. The Syndicate was organized to operate flying services over, in, and between the various national parks and monuments. A Grand Canyon operation would be its initial project with the flight service to be known as Scenic Airways.

During the summer of 1926, VanZandt visited the Canyon to study air conditions and to locate a suitable operational base. When he learned of the Kolbs' aeronautical activities he suggested they pool interests. He and Emery carried on desultory negotiations but failed to come to an agreement on partnership. Emery had acquired the rights to additional land near his Tusayan airfield and this forced VanZandt to look elsewhere for a suitable location.

A year later a lease was signed with the Forest Service for 768 acres on the main highway south of the canyon rim and the El Tovar Hotel. The setting was lovely, the development costs would be minimal, but the new field did have serious limitations. A northeast departure was almost impossible because of rising ground and tall trees; the field could not be seen from either the highway or the railroad, and its distance from El Tovar was twelve miles, two of which were over a rough, often very muddy, dirt road. Nevertheless work went ahead to get "Red Butte," as the new airport was called, ready.

VanZandt hired "Kit" Kintner, former postmaster at the canyon and an ex-rancher, to be general manager and ramrod for Scenic's Arizona projects. Carlyle LaMar Nelson, former secretary to the governor of Utah, and air service colonel, was chosen as chief pilot.

No enterprise could have started with a better foundation, more enthusiasm, and brighter prospects. A motion picture company planned to film the "Romance of the Colorado River," and Scenic was contracted to do the flying "at their own price." The Harvey Company inquired about an aerial mosaic of the Canyon; offers had been received for exclusive aerial photographic rights, and an oil company wanted a survey made. Requests for airmail across the gorge were received—a flight of about twenty minutes to a location which took several days to reach by road—and the potential for air freight was promising. A northwestern railroad inquired about flights to Calgary, Banff, and Lake Louise to transport passengers over this stretch of scenic beauty which was serviced only by an indifferent highway, and applications were in from eleven other American National Parks for air service. Scenic stock was selling well and the company was flying high.

On September 19, 1927, VanZandt and several other Scenic officers took off from Detroit in a Stinson, dubbed Scenic #1, for the canyon. Air travel being what it was then, the flight took twenty hours. There were forced landings at Julesburg and Sterling in Colorado, difficulties at Raton Pass, and a flock of terrified prairie chickens had to be shooed away from the Las Vegas, New Mexico airport before a landing could be made there.

While staying at the Canyon the Scenic party made numerous trips around the Navajo and Hopi reservations. With Indian trader John Wetherill as their guide, they flew to Kayenta and, using that as a base, surveyed Monument Valley, the Hopi villages, Rainbow Bridge, Glenn Canyon, and Navajo Mountain. Scenic #1 was the first airplane to land at Kayenta and at the other nearby spots. Considering the complete lack of all aeronautical aids in that country, these accident-free excursions were a credit to the pilots and their aircraft.

In March 1928, a general letter to all stockholders from Van Zandt announced that the facilities at the South Rim were completed. The hangar, offices, waiting room, and shop were ready, there had been fine cooperation from the park officials, the local Santa Fe people and the Fred Harvey Company which ran the El Tovar Hotel, and both the Santa Fe and Southern Pacific were interested in combination train/plane sightseeing tours.

Mort Moores Collection

A Scenic Airways Ford tri-motor over the Grand Canyon Bridge in 1929.

On June 10, 1928, the Grand Canyon Airport was formally opened. Business that summer was excellent. Chief pilot LaMar Nelson's log book showed more than 500 Scenic passenger flights plus numerous exploratory, photographic, charter, and miscellaneous trips. He took humorist Will Rogers and his young son to the Indian village of Hoteville for the Snake Dances. They landed in a dry wash nearby and on the return flight made a complete aerial tour of the Grand Canyon. The following day Rogers' syndicated column noted that "The Canyon is an ideal place for the disposal of used razor blades."

The stock market continued its rocketing rise and any company connected with aviation appeared a certain winner. The United Aviation Corporation was formed in May 1928, and it immediately approached Scenic with a merger offer.

On October 23, 1928, President VanZandt notified all Scenic stockholders of this opportunity which was contingent on not less than 2/3 approval of the stockholders. The first step was the consolidation of Scenic and Gray Goose Airlines, which was based at Chicago Municipal, and with Interstate Airlines, operators of a new, lucrative airmail route between Chicago and Atlanta. Scenic and the other companies joining the syndicate would keep their identities but enjoy many financial advantages.

The merger was completed early in November and VanZandt, after a whirlwind business tour of the east coast, returned to Phoenix where he planned to establish the headquarters of a state-wide chain of CAA approved flight schools and charter lines.

Scenic Airway's Phoenix Sky Harbor

Work began on Scenic Airways' Phoenix Sky Harbor on November 11, 1928. The location for this $150,000 facility had been selected by "Kit" Kintner and LaMar Nelson with J. Parker Van Zandt's blessing. Initially the site was frowned on by the other Scenic directors as being "too far from town," but as of the 1980s the choice had survived fifty years of justification.

Kintner moved to Phoenix for the winter to supervise construction, and LaMar Nelson had the responsibility of establishing the company's CAA approved "dude flight school." The canyon operations would be open only during summers and the elaborate Phoenix Sky Harbor would be ready for the rush of fall business.

The company now had a complete fixed-based operation in Phoenix, incuding aircraft sales and servicing. It was also flying two state-certified passenger schedules. One was between Fredonia, the Grand Canyon, and Phoenix, the other between Phoenix, Tucson, and Nogales, Arizona. Passengers on their way to Mexico left Phoenix at 4:00 P.M., Tucson at 5:10, and arrived at Nogales about 5:45 in plenty of time for a drink or two and a leisurely dinner. Return flights departed Nogales at 8:00 A.M., were in Tucson some forty minutes later, and arrived at Sky Harbor about 9:45 — early enough for any travelers to appear at their offices before lunch. This run was immediately and inelegantly dubbed the "Drunkards' Special."

On February 23, 1929, the posh Arizona Biltmore Hotel opened with a three-day, never-to-be-forgotten, party. The press reported that it would take ten airplanes to get the Los Angeles guests to Phoenix for the event. Scenic added an extra flourish to the opening celebration. Just at sunset on February 23 one of the company's big airplanes flew low and slow over the hotel's front lawn and dropped a massive golden key inscribed "Opening Arizona Biltmore Feb. 23, 1929." The key was retrieved by a brightly-garbed Indian runner who handed it to Charles B. Harvey, manager of the chain, and its presentation marked the formal opening of the famous hostelry.

Jack Miller Williams and Barbara H. Williams Collection

Scenic Airways' partially completed Phoenix Sky Harbor in late 1928 or early 1929. To the west lies downtown Phoenix.

Scenic had opened its CAA approved ground and flight school in late spring, 1929, at the then unfinished Sky Harbor. It was the first such approved school in Arizona, and by fall business was excellent. The cost of instruction was $300 for thirty hours, paid in advance, and about a dozen new trainees were signed up.

Many other students who had taken flight instruction at South Central came to Sky Harbor when their old field closed, as well as pilots from Christy and the Van Buren Street Field, and winter visitors. As an additional lure for the snowbirds, free instruction was guaranteed any day the sun did not shine.

Scenic employed the first woman instructor in the state, Marie Graham. It was believed then that most women would not endure the rough language used by male pilots while teaching novices, and that a lady instructor would attract the patronage of more females.

There were numerous charter flights, in addition to trips to the Grand Canyon, Monument Valley, and Fredonia for the fall Kaibab deer hunt. The North Rim was overpopulated with deer, and eight horrified fawns were captured by the Forest Service and airlifted to

Red Butte—760 deer passenger miles—to implement a plan to revive their numbers at the South Rim. The transplant was so successful that fifteen years later numbers of their progeny again had to be
relocated, this time back to the North Rim, but this trip was made
by truck.

Scenic's business was reasonably good, except at the Grand
Canyon where the Fred Harvey Company discouraged aerial
tourism. No signs or soliciting were allowed, nor could rides be sold
until the Harvey tour buses were filled. If a customer specifically
requested an air trip, a ticket could be sold, but the Harveys ran a
tight outfit and discretion had to be exercised in drumming up traffic. A further hindrance was Red Butte airport's location—invisible
from both the highway and railroad—and the ban on all advertising.
Scenic's partial solution was to get some of the waitresses and bus-
boys at the El Tovar to "talk up airplane rides." A small commission
was paid and now and then the unofficial sales group was taken for a
hop over the canyon as additional compensation.

W. A. Ordway Collection

A successful hunting party prepares to return to
Phoenix aboard a Scenic Airways Ford.

Scenic advertised extravagantly in eastern publications. The territory it covered was publicized as the Rainbow Route of the Southwest, a rainbow insignia decorated their aircraft, the pilots' uniforms, and the mechanics' natty coveralls, and souvenir cards carrying the date, type of equipment used, and the pilot's signature were given to passengers after each flight.

A favorite flight with patrons of the Biltmore and Ingelside hotels in Phoenix was the trip to Kayenta for an all-night stay. The Scenic plane took off from Sky Harbor late in the afternoon loaded with box dinners and coffee. The guests watched the Yebetchai (Navajo ceremonial dances) all night, then returned the following morning in time for a late breakfast.

Scenic Airways' Phoenix Sky Harbor was dedicated on Labor Day 1929, with a crowd of more than 8,000 spectators to observe the big air show and festivities. *Aero Digest* reported that the company had invested over a million dollars in the state and was operating from seventeen Arizona airports. They had purchased the Chandler Airport, in addition to developing Red Butte and Sky Harbor, and continued to take charters to the canyon, the Indian country and to Rocky Point in Mexico.

Two months later the Stock Market Crash dealt a death blow to Scenic. The company had failed to turn a profit and now the eastern backers announced that they could no longer finance a failing, disconnected Arizona operation with no apparent chance of landing an airmail contract. Word went out that there would be an "orderly liquidation." Scenic's directors offered their lovely new Sky Harbor facility to the city of Phoenix but the city fathers, twice burned by airport ownership and with little money in the municipal coffers, refused.

Scenic's airplanes were sold to eastern buyers. The Grand Canyon facility was simply locked up and abandoned as were many other airports during those unhappy times. Sky Harbor was never left unattended. Standard Airlines continued their schedules and the few transients passing through always found someone "tending the store."

It was a sad ending for this colorful, ambitious company, which was ahead of its time. Scenic did leave Arizona an impressive legacy, however: a string of improved airports, the state's first CAA approved flight and ground school, and the example of a first class aviation operation with an excellent safety record.

APACHE AIRLINES

Ralph G. Vaughn was a Texan endowed with an itchy foot and a liking for wings. After serving in the Aeronautical Division of the Army Signal Corps, he settled with his wife Ruth in Ontario, California, where he opened a flight school.

It was during 1924 or '25 that he and Ruth decided to visit her parents in Rillito, Arizona. On this and subsequent journeys to Rillito, Vaughn found that he could not just sit and visit with his in-laws, so he made barnstorming side-trips to Benson, Springerville, Pleasant Valley, and Payson. Late in 1927 he visited the San Carlos Apaches who, he discovered, really appreciated riding in the "big eagle that makes a loud noise." In addition, the people of Globe and Superior were enthusiastic passengers.

Ralph continued to operate his Ontario school. Students, aerial photography, moving picture flying, and the ever-popular weekend air shows which lured paying passengers kept him busy, but the idea of a flight operation and possibly a small airline in Arizona kept nagging his thoughts.

In the spring of 1929 he moved to Globe where he began a successful campaign to get the town to improve the Midland Airport. He also began teaching students and making plans for a scheduled airline to Phoenix and Superior.

On August 16, 1929, the *Miami Silver Belt* announced in large headlines that the Arizona Corporation Commission had granted permission to Apache Airlines and its president, Ralph G. Vaughn, to begin passenger and express service between Phoenix and the Globe-Miami district. Arizona's first exclusively intra-state carrier was in business.

Ralph Vaughn Collection

An Apache Airlines Kreutzer tri-motor at Globe's Midland Airport in 1929 or 1930.

Vaughn left for the West Coast to order a Tri-Motor Kreutzer. This baby airliner, along with the two Wacos he already owned, would be his fleet. He also hired another pilot to head the Apache Flying School.

The first scheduled flights to Phoenix began on November 23. The morning flight left Globe at 8:10 and arrived at Sky Harbor at 9:00, returning at 9:10 and landing at Globe at 10:00. The afternoon flights departed from Globe each afternoon at 3:10, Phoenix at 4:10, and were back home by 5:00. The one-way fare was $10, a round trip $16.50; these were later cut to $8.75 and $14.85, respectively. Stops were made at Superior if there were passengers to be picked up.

The copper towns were not yet affected by the stock market debacle and the new line's business was good. A local dress shop used the parcel service, the town's florist had fresh flowers flown in, and soon businessmen discovered the convenience of the short fifty-minute flight as compared with the long, dusty drive. Vaughn also continued with his barnstorming trips, charter business, and flight school.

The Depression finally caught up with the bustling little operation in mid-1930. The mines closed, business slowed, and then became nonexistent. The entire complex of communities (Globe, Miami, Superior, Ray and Hayden) was financially dependent on the copper industry. The few nearby ranches could not support the economy. Additionally, many were already heavily mortgaged and facing foreclosure. The banks shut down and people went on relief.

It was a bitter blow to Globe's civic pride to lose its fine airline which had put it in a class with Phoenix, Tucson, Douglas, and Winslow, but airlines needed passengers, passengers had to have money, and there was little of that commodity in the neighborhood. Apache went out of business.

THORNBURGH AND KRAVITZ

In late October 1929, Jack Thornburgh and Irving Kravitz arrived in Phoenix and set up a fixed-base operation at Phoenix Municipal.

Kravitz, who was originally from Ojai, California, had enrolled as a flight student at Air Technological School of Aviation in San Diego. While at Air Tech, he met Jack Thornburgh, an ex-Navy pilot who was a flight and ground school instructor there. Jack had plans to open an operation in Phoenix and suggested that "Kravy" get a transport license and join him. This was immediately after the first collapse of the stock market, and as Kravy wrote, "Because of the Depression, things looked grim and I decided to go along."

The boys flew Jack's OX5 Travel Air to Los Angeles, where Jack bought a new Great Lakes. The transaction included a dealership for Arizona. They then took off for Phoenix, Jack in his new ship and

Kravy tagging along in old "Elephant Ears" as the Travel Airs were called.

Their operation followed the pattern of many similar aviation enterprises then and later. Kravy would help Jack with the building projects, gas their own and any transient aircraft, drag the field and help maintain the airplanes, thereby getting some on-the-job training. In his spare time he would fly. By January 10, 1930, he had accumulated the required 200 hours solo to qualify for his transport license. He passed the flight test and could now carry revenue passengers and cargo as well as instruct in any single-engine land airplane with a gross weight of 3,500 pounds or less.

Phoenix Municipal had few improvements. The partners built a small wooden hangar with an office close by the existing caretaker's house and the gas pits. They were better pilots than carpenters, but they were open for business.

In December they purchased another Great Lakes and on January 28, Kravy's log noted: "Soloed first student, Carl Bailey." Senator-to-be Barry Goldwater was another of their students. Barry spend a good deal of time dragging the field as well as becoming a private pilot.

Thornburgh and Kravitz remained at Phoenix Municipal for part of 1930, and then moved to Sky Harbor. The last official reference to this particular municipal field appeared in the 1930 *Aircraft Year Book*. No services were listed in the tabulation—it was now just a place to land an airplane if the pilot was in trouble.

THE ARIZONA REPUBLICAN'S
AERIAL PICTORIAL SURVEY

During the winter of 1927, Phoenix flight school operators Howard Reinhart and Bernard Whelan were joined by an aerial photographer named E. D. Newcomer. At first Newcomer's business was fairly brisk, but by 1928 he realized that he would soon be out of work unless he could drum up some publicity. Consequently, he went to see W. W. "Wess" Knorpp, the business manager of the *Arizona Republican*, and proposed taking a series of aerial photographs of the state's mines, resorts, industrial plants, and other businesses for the newspaper.

The rapid aviation expansion of 1927 and 1928 had been appreciated by Knorpp. A carefully planned photographic tour would aid the state's aviation progress and benefit the *Republican* too. He and Newcomer began to plan the expedition.

One of the largest crowds ever assembled at the Phoenix Municipal Airport gathered early on May 28, 1928, to witness the start of the *Arizona Republican's* well-publicized Aerial Survey. This was the first time a complete airborne pictorial study of an entire state had been attempted.

Pilot Bill Kingsley (left) and photographer E. D. Newcomer about to take off during the *Arizona Republican* Aerial Pictorial Survey, May 1928.

After a brief ceremony, Newcomer and his pilot, Bill Kingsley, climbed into their R & W Standard and took off. Newcomer took pictures of Phoenix, Gillespie Dam, and other choice locations, and then Kingsley set the plane down at the Gila Bend Municipal Airport at 11:10 A.M.. After lunch the survey flight was airborne for Yuma. Cattle herds, citrus fields, Laguna Dam, and various other items were photographed, and two hours later the Standard landed at the 160-acre Yuma Municipal Field.

The next day the aerial survey covered the territory between Yuma and Ajo. Departure from Ajo was delayed until late in the afternoon so as to allow an after-dark landing at Tucson which had the only municipal airport in the state boasting lights.

At about 8:30 P.M. the silver biplane was picked up by the beams of Tucson's 30-million candlepower Lindbergh Light. Kingsley circled the field while Newcomer took photographs of the waiting crowd using the flashing beams of the powerful beacon as illumination.

From Tucson Newcomer and Kingsley flew on to Nogales, Douglas, Bisbee, Willcox, Safford, and Globe, before returning to Phoenix on June 30. Three days later the flyers took off on the northern and eastern segments of their aerial survey. After photographing Prescott, Jerome, and the Verde Valley, they went on to Flagstaff where they participated in the Koch Field dedication ceremonies.

The big Standard was ill-suited for windy, high-altitude flying so the survey borrowed a Whirlwind Waco from pilot Ernie Wickersham for the remainder of the northern flying. The loop was successfully completed in a week's time, and on June 16, Newcomer and Kingsley landed in Phoenix. They had flown some 3,160 miles and returned with 203 pictures. Included in the collection were views of thirty-five cities, more than twenty mining complexes, fifteen industrial plants, numerous resorts, public buildings, agricultural developments, ranches, dams, and airports. Newcomer, hampered by goggles and shivering in the chill wind as he wrestled with the heavy, unwieldy camera in the bucking front cockpit, had taken photographs of remarkable quality. In addition, the expedition had further stimulated interest in aviation around the state. The *Arizona Republican* was very satisfied with its decision to back the aerial pictorial survey.

AERO CORPORATION OF ARIZONA
AND OLD SOUTH CENTRAL

In mid-1927 a group of young Phoenix businessmen formed the Aero Corporation of Arizona. All were interested in flying and wanted a convenient, non-airline oriented field geared to sport and business activities. They hoped such an operation could make a little money when supplemented with aircraft sales and weekend passenger hops. Its operation might soften the blow of expensive flying lessons and the experience would be interesting and fun.

A plot of level, graded land was found at South Central and Mohave. There were trees and wires at each end, but these obstructions were not considered serious detriments. A row of hangars and a small office were put up. This work along with some grading of the field was accomplished mainly during weekends by the officers and directors, and by chief pilot Charlie Goldtrap who devoted full time to the project.

By the end of November two Eaglerocks were flying from the South Central field, two more were to be delivered in early January, and student enrollment was good. Soon South Central was known as the airport where flying was fun. This did not mean that the students there were inadequately trained by incompetent or unlicensed teachers — it was just a reflection of Goldtrap's philosophy that flying should be approached seriously but not solemnly. It was a rewarding vocation or hobby to be enjoyed.

On March 7, 1928, the Aero Corporation of Arizona was granted a permit by the Corporation Commission for charter, scenic flights, rentals and student instruction. Business continued to be good, and on weekends Sheldon "Shorty" Miller entertained the crowds with delayed parachute jumps from an Eaglerock with Goldtrap doing the flying. Numerous navy pilots on cross-country flights (old buddies of Charlie's) stopped in for fuel. These arrivals always brought a group of cars hurrying to the field; they provided a bonus in passenger hops as well as the desirable profit from the fuel sales to the thirsty military ships.

From the few photographs available of neatly parked airplanes, a row of clean, painted hangars with an attractive sign overhead, and none of the usual airport junk lying around, the Aero Corporation of Arizona looked like a prosperous, well-run establishment. Its neat appearance reflected Goldtrap's navy training.

The national Aeronautical Chamber of Commerce, with authority from the new Aeronautics Branch of the Department of Commerce, had compiled a list of definite standards for both approved ground and flight schools. These were incorporated into the federal body's licensing requirements on February 28, 1929, and became effective the following June.

Approval was not mandatory for flight and ground schools but it was a badge of progressive respectability, and the better operators, like the South Central outfit, endeavored to acquire the certification. Some years later the insurance companies, recognizing the general superiority of the approved group, lowered their rates substantially, and this induced others to upgrade their operations and obtain the desirable designation.

Most schools, whether approved or not, offered good, practical flight instruction. Unfortunately, a few flight operators were unscrupulous. Some school owners simply took their prospective students' cash and flew off, leaving no forwarding address. Others were of the promoter type. These individuals invested heavily in splashy advertising but failed to mention that their planes and instructors were unlicensed. The scarcity of inspection personnel to enforce the regulations, and the flamboyant press notices made it easy for these questionable operators to mislead uninformed customers. If questions were asked they were generally brushed off with the explanation that there was no need for a license unless one wanted to fly for the airlines or carry United States Mail. When the students from these schools eventually did apply for licenses they found, much to their chagrin, that the hours of flying they had done in the promoters' unlicensed ships did not count toward getting the coveted official papers.

In spite of all the Arizona activity, primarily centered in Tucson and Phoenix, no permanent inspector was based in the state. Various men came from the CAA's Los Angeles office when several students were judged qualified by their instructors. These inspectors gave both flight and written examinations at Sky Harbor, and made a serious effort to curb some of the wild flying that was then popular. A two- or three-day visit and some threatening lectures accomplished little. As for the unlicensed pilots and their unlicensed aircraft, there was little the government representative could do.

There was always something doing or something to do at South Central. Most owners then performed the constant servicing chores required to keep their airplanes in flyable condition. After every flight oil and grease had to be wiped off as accumulations caused the fabric to deteriorate. Rocker arms were greased, the drooling engines cleaned, hoses and radiators checked, and other minor adjustments made.

When the pilots flew there were spot landings to practice as protection from the complete motor failure that was certain to occur sometime. Phoenix was getting a few tall buildings, and these along with the old standbys—Camelback, Tempe Buttes and property section lines—made perfect "points" for acrobatic practice. Pilots could also go calling on friends, preferably girls. This did not require a landing but simply locating the correct house and giving it a thorough buzz job. Such a salute was not always appreciated by the older family members, but it usually impressed the girl and her friends. Occasionally an irritable citizen phoned the police to complain about low-flying airplanes, but this body could do nothing unless there was an accident, and even then local statutes were vague.

One such flight was particularly memorable. It was Myra Elms' wedding day. She was an attractive, popular redhead with a cute nose and the right amount of freckles, properly spaced. South Central pilot Stan Roper decided that instead of attending the ceremony he would fly low over the house as the wedding party was leaving and drop masses of flowers on the happy bride and groom. It would be a nice gesture; Myra would be both pleased and surprised and she would remember his thoughtfulness for a long time.

The more he and Charlie Goldtrap talked about it, the more the plan impressed them. At the proper time Stan crawled into the front seat of an OX5 Eaglerock, surrounded himself with piles of bright cut flowers which the florist had thoughtfully tied in large bunches with "easy to undo knots," and wrapped in green waxed paper for protection. Stan and Charlie roared off from South Central Airport. The ship was skillfully maneuvered into striking distance so that when the bridal party came out of the house the Eaglerock could start its floral swoop. The crowd gathered on the front lawn and Charlie commenced his low pass—just above the trees and wires. Stan untied the first bunch, let it go, along with the green paper which he could not control, and then immediately heaved number two bouquet, plus the green paper. The Eaglerock suddenly went crazy. It lurched, dove, stood on its end, and there were strange noises and calls coming from the rear cockpit. The wax paper had smacked Charlie in the face, was pasted there by the wind, and he was simultaneously clawing at the elusive green stuff, trying to maneuver the Eaglerock blind, and yelling for help.

The wedding party was running around screaming, waving, and chasing flowers; traffic was halted, horns were blowing, and a wagon driver was having difficulty with his team. Stan fired out the remainder of his floral offerings and took over the controls until Charlie could unmask.

There were a few mild complaints from neighbors about the unusual wedding salute and a murmur from the authorities, but nothing of a serious nature. The boys continued to believe it had been a fine idea, but the next time they would leave the green paper behind.

Like all good things, the fun at South Central had to end. The Aero Corporation of Arizona was forced to liquidate in 1929. The decision was prompted by the Stock Market Crash which toppled the entire nation off its "high plateau of permanent prosperity." South Central remained open for several more years under different companies, all of whose terms were short and not too successful.

From 1931 to mid-1933, there was little aviation activity in Phoenix, except for American Airway's regular schedule. The substantial ship owners moved to Sky Harbor where a half dozen or so hung on by their teeth, watching apprehensively while their former pals gave up flying temporarily and just drifted away. For a short time Old South Central was merely an old abandoned airport; then it became a part of the city's ball park.

THE CHIDI NAAT A'I' ON THE NAVAJO RESERVATION

In the Navajo language a "chidi" is an automobile, or more loosely, any mechanical contrivance that moves by virtue of its own power and makes noise. By adding "naat a'i'" (meaning bird or something that flies) one has an airplane.

The first recorded chidi naat a'i' to land on the reservation was flown by W. P. "Bill" Cutter in 1926 when he brought a party from Albuquerque into Monument Valley and landed on Harry Goulding's racetrack. The famous photographer, Margaret Bourke White, on a *Life* magazine assignment, was the principal member of the group. Miss White's first impressions of the country were not favorable. She did not even want to unload her equipment. A day or so later, with a revised opinion, she dispatched Bill to Winslow for more film.

The second swift, raucous eagle was Scenic Airway #1, the Stinson Detroiter flown by J. Parker VanZandt who landed with a party of his eastern backers near Church Rock in the fall of 1927. Soon thereafter, John Wetherill built the first Kayenta strip at Van Zandt's urging. Wetherill's trading post offered the only possible conveniences and accommodations to luxury-resort oriented patrons in that lonely country.

Durrell Richards Collection

The Scenic Airways Stinson near Church Rock on
the Navajo Reservation in February 1927.

Later, in 1928, Charles and Anne Lindbergh flew to Canyon de
Chelly on their honeymoon. They made a successful landing on a
Navajo racetrack at the top and hiked down to visit Anne's brother
who was engaged in an archaeological dig at Big Cave in the Canyon
del Muerto.

The publicity surrounding these flights created interest in the
region but brought few travelers. Hollywood, however, got the word.
Fantastic, photogenic, and unrivaled scenery waited on the Navajo
Reservation for the producers, complete with picturesque, docile
Indians. The movie people came and their companies spent money
for supplies and comfortable accommodations for their personnel.

During 1935, E. Reesman Fryer was appointed general superintendent of the reservation and an ambitious Indian program was
started. It required numerous meetings and Fryer soon discovered
that surface travel around the sprawling reservation was extremely
difficult and time-consuming, for example, three days travel from
Gallup to Shonto for a one-day meeting. Fryer made a contract with
Bill Cutter to fly him to his various appointments. He writes, "By
perhaps a serious breach of regulations governing the purpose of

road funds I had landing strips bladed out at every major Reservation gathering place from Kayenta to Chinle." Some of these, with improvements, are still in use.

Barnstormers soon found that trips to the reservation were rewarding. Unlike the Indians around Gila Bend, the Hopis and Navajos had no fear of the chidi naat a'i', but much curiosity. Any airplane landing brought them flocking to the landing strip where they would cluster around the ship, talking quietly in their difficult language which sounds like a series of soft clucks, gentle hissing, lisps, and low grunts. A basket would be placed on the plane's floor and rings, bracelets, beads, and necklaces dumped in as exchange for trips. The Indians were satisfied with the rides and the barnstorming pilots would return home loaded with silver and turquoise.

In 1937, Reesman Fryer decided to learn to fly. Bill Cutter taught him, and then a search was begun for some surplus government aircraft. The Army donated a 1927 Stearman and the National Park Service discovered two Pitcairn Autogyros plus a pilot it no longer needed. Fryer got all three—a package deal.

One of his early projects was the Window Rock Airport and hangar. Both are still in use but now a new runway has been paved and realigned. Rough Rock, Many Farms, Oljaito, Shonto, and Leupp soon had landing strips as did Cameron and Ganado. Later Tuba City was added to the list.

And so the chidi naat a'i' came to the reservation by the combined efforts of various government agencies and a very few early pilots who were willing to risk their equipment in a remote and undeveloped land. Through their efforts a network of airports was established, linking the far-flung reservation settlements, and making possible the important and much appreciated medical evacuation flights and food and clothing lifts to isolated hogans that continue to this day.

OLD TUCSON MUNICIPAL OR MAYSE FIELD

Tucson dedicated the new Davis-Monthan field in 1927, but Charlie Mayse, southern Arizona's foremost flight instructor, charter pilot, and barnstormer, decided to keep his base of operations at the old Tucson Municipal field. While his business in early 1927 was an improvement over the previous year, it was not exactly hectic. There were a few students, and the weekend air shows put on by Charlie, with Gilbert Sykes and others doing 'chute jumps, lured paying passengers to the field. There were rodeos, fairs, and other crowd-gathering festivities at numerous towns where a reasonable, well-situated airport brought in money.

Students from the University of Arizona came out for rides and returned to take flying lessons, and Charlie's reputation as an excellent, patient, but strictly no-nonsense instructor spread. With the university group who came to the Old Municipal was one Edgar T. "Ted" Hereford. Ted's older brother, Rockwell, had graduated from M.I.T. and was taking postgraduate courses at the Harvard School of Business Administration, which he completed during 1928. That year Mr. Hereford, Sr., died and Rockwell was appointed Ted's guardian. Now and then "Rock" stopped off in Tucson to see how his 19-year-old brother was doing. During one of these visits he learned that Ted had sold his car to pay for flying lessons. Another distressing bit of news was that Ted's grades were poor because he was spending too much time at the airport. Rock wrote:

> I wanted to be broad-minded so I asked to meet Charlie [Mayse] but I really couldn't judge about this very hazardous occupation without taking some lessons myself. It ended up by Charlie taking me into the organization and [my] largely financing [his] little company so he could acquire a new Ryan Brougham like Lindbergh had so recently demonstrated.

The Mayse Air Service, with Rock Hereford as its principal financial advisor, was legally born in the late spring of 1928. The old municipal field was leased for five years at $200 per year with an option to renew for an additional five. Charlie Mayse was to have complete control of the aerial aspects of the operation.

Mayse would receive $250 per month if he handled the business by himself; if another pilot was employed to train students, the combined salaries should not exceed $300, and the assistant was to receive a bonus not to exceed 10 percent of all student payments for the time he was with the company.

The new Ryan Brougham was an immediate success. These trim little airplanes were delivered with a form of prepaid advertising that would have been impossible to purchase. Everyone wanted to ride in a ship "just like Lindy's." To reinforce this connection, Charlie immediately had "Spirit of Tucson" painted on the Ryan's burnished cowl, and a large "Mayse Air Service, Inc." on the fuselage.

Summer business was slow because most of the students were on vacation, but the company did make some plane sales. Student activity picked up in late August, and pilot Bill Kingsley was hired to teach flying and a formal ground school two nights a week. In a short time he had over twenty-five students in his class and some began flight instruction. The press kept everyone informed of the new company's charter activities. Members of the court had been transported to Ajo; businessmen flew to Mexico, Phoenix, the coast, and other spots. Weekends in Tucson there were air shows, and there had been as many as 2,000 to 2,500 at the airport to watch the aerial antics and take rides following the exhibitions.

The year 1928 closed with the young company showing a profit of $946.30, representing a 7.7 percent return on the investment or capital stock. Flight income from charter trips and passenger carrying came to $3,507 for the approximate six-month period the Ryan had been in operation; $1,716 from student training in the Waco; and $1,000 listed as "discounts on purchases" which may have been aircraft sales commissions or profit from fuel sales. A sum of $1,550 had been put into a reserve account. The salaries and bonuses which represented moneys paid to Charlie and Bill Kingsley would shock any present-day fixed base operator—$2,258.77 was the total. But in those days coffee (unlimited cups), cokes, a phone call, a streetcar or bus ride, and many other items could be bought for a nickel, and a good hamburger was only a dime.

Business during 1929 exceeded all expectations. Standard Airlines moved to the newer and larger Davis-Monthan, and all military traffic put down there, but the bulk of the increasing civilian trade still patronized Mayse Field. Along with the flying, fuel sales, storage, and maintenance, work increased.

The Mayse Air Service showed a profit of nearly $2,000 for the first two months. A good part of this money came from the sale of aircraft, both new and used, to the warring factions in Mexico's Escobar Rebellion. The planes were flown across the border at Douglas, Nogales, and sometimes Mexicali or Bisbee—all without customs difficulties and with fat profits for the dealers.

Business remained good until late in 1930 when the Depression began to pinch and competition became stiff. Licensed graduates of the Mayse Flight School free-lanced as instructors, often at cut rates, and the increased airline schedules siphoned off much of the lucrative charter business to the West Coast and Texas. The owners decided to liquidate the Mayse Air Service.

Charlie Mayse was able to sell the company's training planes. He then traded for a new ship for himself and flew off with his wife to Tegucigalpa, British Honduras, where he had secured a contract with the government to distribute new currency to banks and carry old, worn-out currency back to the capital.

The departure of Mayse and the phasing out of his field left Tucson with only one airport—Davis-Monthan.

G&G AIRLINES COMPANY, LTD.

Col. Jack Greenway was a dashing and wealthy Arizona bachelor. He served with Teddy Roosevelt in the Rough Riders during the Spanish-American War, and was the principal stockholder in the Calumet Mining Company which had properties in both Ajo and Douglas. In 1923 he met Mrs. Isabel Ferguson, a widow. They were married late that year and moved to Ajo.

Greenway's mining business required him to travel between Ajo, Phoenix, Tucson, Douglas, and Bisbee. Hours spent driving on dusty, rough roads in cars with no air conditioners led to fatigue and unhappiness, so the Colonel hired a chauffeur, Charles W. Gilpin. In addition to being a driver, Gilpin was a well-known pilot in southern Arizona and northern Mexico. The result for the Greenways was inevitable—they found themselves with an airplane and Charlie (usually called Bill) Gilpin was their pilot.

Colonel Greenway died in 1926, and now his widow had added responsibilities. In addition to her own activities she was saddled with the Colonel's mining business which required her absence from Ajo much of the time. Bill Gilpin, fearing that his flying job would evaporate, suggested that the Greenway's airplane be used for charter while she was away. Mrs. Greenway was agreeable and thus, in October 1930, Gilpin and Greenway or G&G Airlines Company, Ltd. was born. "Gilpin," as the public called it, would grow into one of the largest fixed base operations in the Southwest.

The new company began flying schedules between Los Angeles and Tijuana, carrying prohibition-parched Californians to the Mexican race tracks and gambling casinos. Bill also flew Mrs. Greenway on some of her business trips and made charter flights. During a charter flight to Mexico City in July 1932, he made a forced landing. The passengers were unhurt but Bill was killed instantly when the ship's power plant detached and struck him on the head.

Following Gilpin's death, Mrs. Greenway gave control of the airline to her godson, Walter Douglas, Jr., who had been running a flight school in California. He continued the lucrative passenger runs to the "fun spots" of Tijuana and Ensenada until December 1932, when the United States Congress repealed prohibition. Douglas then liquidated most of his fleet and removed his remaining aircraft to Tucson where he set up a fixed base operation at Davis-Monthan field. Charlie Mayse had returned from his adventure in Honduras, and he, Walter Douglas, and Dale Myers, temporarily gave the Old Pueblo three flight operators. This was too much, and Mayse moved to Douglas in 1936 to become the airport manager there and to run a flight school and charter service.

Tucson soon had three operators again when Al Hudgins of Nogales rented Charlie Mayse's old hangar at Davis-Monthan and opened a small flight school. None of the three did a booming business in the depression-stricken city but they managed to hang on. Improvements were made on the field. The runways were surfaced, a new terminal built, and Walter Douglas constructed a new hangar. When the economy began to revive and the charter business picked up, he was ready.

During 1938, the Arizona Corporation Commission issued certificates of convenience and necessity to both G&G Airlines and

Hudgins Air Service of Tucson for intrastate nonscheduled air transportation (charter). The pilots working for these organizations were required to have State Pilot's Licenses also.

Soon thereafter the First Bombardment Group finalized plans to occupy Davis-Monthan and the army expressed interest in buying Walter Douglas's hangar. Negotiations continued unsuccessfully and culminated with Douglas buying some property northwest of town, moving his building there, and opening the Gilpin Airport which soon became a showplace for general aviation.

Private pilots were not denied the use of Davis-Monthan, but as military activities increased and airline schedules grew, arrivals and departures became frustrating and the big construction program caused more difficulties. To compound the sticky situation, the military tower constantly had difficulties with the general aviation radio frequency. Except for a few of the larger twins and the carriers, all civilian ships quickly adopted Walter's fine new and convenient Gilpin Airport.

THE DAY THE LION FELL

Barnstormer Martin Jensen was involved in one of the most bizarre incidents in Arizona's aeronautical history—a plane crash with "Leo," MGM Pictures' African lion mascot.

Marty's Arizona activities began in 1923 or 1924. The following year he and his wife Peg were married in a Jenny over Yuma. Judge Smith performed the ceremony in the air and then on the ground because there was no room for a witness in the ship. Marty sat on the bride's lap and the judge in the rear cockpit.

It was in 1927 that MGM's founder, Louis B. Mayer, had asked Peter Smith, his director of publicity, to come up with a promotion that would draw national attention to the MGM trademark. Smith's idea was to fly Leo, the MGM lion, nonstop from Los Angeles to New York. Marty Jensen was chosen as the pilot.

If Leo had been present at any of the numerous pre-flight conferences he would have turned claws down on the whole crazy scheme. It was neither a suitable nor dignified junket for a mature, circus-bred African lion used to regular meals, comfortable living, and the finer things in life.

Originally the flight was scheduled to leave from Los Angeles, but there were difficulties with the Society for Prevention of Cruelty to Animals. The Los Angeles newspapers printed descriptions of Leo's comfortable cage installed in the Ryan Brougham, and explained that he would be supplied with food and water and should suffer no discomfort during the ride. The SPCA was unimpressed and threatened legal action, so Leo was spirited away to Camp Kearney near San Diego, and at 10:20 A.M. on September 16, 1927, he and Jensen took off for New York.

Pilot Martin Jensen and his B-1 Ryan Brougham. The cage, surrounded by 400 pounds of plate glass, protected Leo and made Martin feel more comfortable.

Martin Jensen climbing aboard the B-1 Ryan just before takeoff. Leo waits patiently in his cage.

The B-1 Ryan was a good airplane and its Wright 220 horse-power engine one of the finest then manufactured. Nevertheless Jensen found his ship handling poorly because, in his words, "It was too heavy for climbing." This was a considerable understatement. The Ryan was carrying 300 gallons of fuel, Leo weighed between 350 and 400 pounds, and there was an additional 400 pounds of plate glass surrounding his cage.

Jensen wobbled across Southern California, but when he reached the Arizona desert the airplane sank and refused to maintain altitude. He doubted the Ryan's ability to clear the high country that lay ahead even though the airplane engineers had assured him that by then sufficient fuel would have been consumed to lighten the aircraft.

The Ryan passed north of Phoenix and struggled through a pass in the Mazatzals. Jensen later remembered that the temperatures were very high over Arizona. Leo dozed, the unaccustomed heat and altitude making him sleepy. Marty struggled with the overloaded ship, hot air, and unfavorable currents. The forbidding Mogollon Rim was ahead and the Ryan had reached the limit of its abilities. Marty was boxed in. Knowing the results of an uncontrolled crash, he carefully maneuvererd his plane and stalled it into the top of a large oak tree. The fall was broken; the fuselage broke loose, rolled over and tumbled to the ground. Jensen had a cut over one eye; Leo was uninjured but shaken up.

Jensen crawled out of the wreckage and collected his wits. The time was 2:20 P.M., and accounting for the hour's time difference, his flight had lasted a little less than five hours, with the ground speed between 90 and 95 miles an hour.

The cage had held, and Leo, with the characteristics of the genus *Felis*, had taken care of himself during the tumble. Marty said he looked pretty disgusted but did not snarl or fuss. Some aluminum stripped from the ship made a good container, and Leo had a drink of water from a nearby creek. Marty got out his sandwiches and milk, fed Leo, and then started walking down the creek. It was not a pleasant hike. He slept under a bush that night. The next day he continued walking and finally spotted some cattle. He thought this surely meant a ranch was nearby, so he tried to follow them, but the cattle ran away. The day was additionally complicated by a cloud-burst which sent a five-foot wall of water roaring down the creek.

The following day, Sunday, Marty's shoes began to give out and he started to become weak from hunger. Monday was better. He stumbled onto a hut or line shack several miles south of Payson and explained his difficulties to some cowboys there. They gave him food and water and directed him to the nearby H-Bar Ranch where he had his first real meal in three days. The rancher took phone messages to Globe for transmittal to Jensen's wife Peg, and to MGM.

In those pre-flight plan and pre-radio days, locating a lost airplane was not easy. Peg Jensen had been frantic when her husband was reported overdue and the Ryan-Mahoney people and MGM were likewise worried. Ryan's chief test pilot and Peg set out in a Ryan to find Marty. They were faced with the problem of trying to second-guess his flight path and actions with the overloaded ship. The message from Globe caught up with them in Phoenix, and they were instructed to meet Marty at Apache Lodge at Roosevelt Lake.

Meanwhile, MGM dispatched a fast truck with a lion trainer and a receiving cage for Leo. How the crew would get their cargo from its inaccessible location to the vehicle would be decided at Payson. Marty met Peg and the Ryan representative at Roosevelt and on September 20 they arrived at Kohl's Ranch, only nine miles from the lion. While everyone was trying to figure an easy and comfortable way to rescue Leo, other worrisome complications brewed.

The Globe dogcatcher believed Leo would make a valuable addition to the town, both for educational and publicity purposes, and planned to exercise his authority as dogcatcher to capture him and bring him to Globe. The local judge quashed this scheme, stating that in his opinion the city limits of the town hardly extended the 100 or so miles to Kohl's Ranch, and that Leo was out of Globe's jurisdiction.

Martin Jensen Collection

A member of Leo's rescue party standing by the Ryan's fuselage and the intact cage. The wreckage of the plane still lies in Hell's Canyon near Payson.

A group of local cowboys claiming that finders were keepers made plans to capture Leo and hold him for a reward. A few sharp words from the Payson sheriff cooled them off. The remainder of their enthusiasm evaporated when they learned that Leo was a "fierce African lion" and not the native Arizona type.

There were fifteen in Leo's rescue party. They found him weak from his enforced fast and maggoty, but still good tempered. One of the rescuers remembered "Leo was a nice tame old boy and when the sheep dip [was put] on his sores, he just rolled over like a big old house cat." A sled was built and the cat hoisted out and onto it with an improvised crane—a large forked limb. The sled and Leo, still in his cage, were dragged to the road, then loaded aboard a truck and taken to a garage in Payson.

Leo behaved like a gentleman throughout the ordeal and never roared or fussed. After a few days' rest, food, and good care administered by the people of Payson, he was ready for the long journey back to the comforts of Hollywood. Everyone was sorry to see him leave, especially the children.

Pete Smith's idea had made banner headlines from coast to coast and all points in between, though not of the type he had envisioned. As for the good-natured, milk-drinking, sandwich-eating "ferocious" Leo, he arrived in Burbank in excellent condition and lived out his life in comfort, but with no more airplane trips. MGM later admitted they received more publicity from the episode than if the venture had gone as planned, and as a sincere expression of gratitude and appreciation, Leo was permanently incorporated into the company's insignia.

THE FIRST ALL-WOMEN'S
TRANSCONTINENTAL AIR RACE

In 1928 it seemed that everyone was learning to fly or planning to start, and by spring everyone was talking about the coming Cleveland Air Show. Unfortunately, there was more talking than actual flying, but the exaggeration was fine publicity for all concerned.

Four great races were scheduled to finish at Cleveland during Air Show Week. One of the most interesting was the first transcontinental women's derby. For years there had been many competent women pilots; now for the first time they would have an opportunity to participate in the biggest air show of the year, and compete for prizes in their own race.

For the roaring twenties, the women's derby was exceptionally well planned; judged by present standards it was a masterpiece of careless omissions with little thought given to the comfort or protection of the contestants. Race stops were inadequately policed, the ladies given scant protection from eager fans and photographers, and their ships exposed to inadvertent damage by enthusiastic crowds. The contestants were expected to attend banquets sponsored by local exchange clubs and the host cities, and this made it hard for the racers to get to bed before midnight. The scheduled six o'clock takeoffs, the long noon stops, which dragged on into mid-afternoon with frequently no opportunity to eat lunch or rest, left the women tired and edgy.

The handicapping was most casual. The ships were divided into two classes, the DW airplanes with a cubic inch displacement of up to 800 inches, and ranging from 170 to 225 horsepower, and the smaller crafts of less than 110 horsepower with a cubic inch displacement of under 500 inches. There was no regard for design or performance of the aircraft, and there was no weather service as we know it today. The race officials just "eyeballed" the skies and the girls took off. Compared to the strictly regulated Powder Puff Derbys of later years, this first race was a rather harebrained safari.

The name "Powder Puff Derby" had been coined and bestowed by Will Rogers. It was resented by earlier race boards as being derogatory and intimating that the contestants were not serious pilots. In spite of protestations, the name stuck, and the racers were popularly known as "Powder Puffers," but the expression was seldom used in their presence. As the contest gained popularity and prestige with the passing years, the old formal title, "All Women's Transcontinental Air Race" was gradually relinquished by the race boards and the yearly event became the Powder Puff Derby.

The contestants were sent off at two minute intervals, officials checked their time, and their arrivals over the line were noted by the timers at the following airport control point. Scores were based on elapsed time for that leg, and the winner of a lap was put in the last position for the following takeoff. This sequence was continued for the entire race.

On the afternoon of August 18, 1929, following a round of tiresome speeches, autographing, being mauled and photographed by an enthusiastic crowd, and posing for endless news pictures, twenty harassed contestants took off from Clover Field in Santa Monica, California. The Derby would finish at Cleveland; interim stops (control points) were at San Bernardino, Yuma, Phoenix, Douglas, Columbus, N.M., El Paso, Midland, Abilene, Fort Worth, Tulsa, Wichita, Kansas City, and East St. Louis.

There were difficulties landing at the first control point, San Bernardino, due to excessive dust raised by the first few ships. One airplane was badly damaged, there were two near misses, and some of the women landed on another field to avoid the confusion and near zero visibility. No one was injured.

Some of the pilots wished to fly directly to Phoenix from San Bernardino as the Yuma airport was reported dangerously soft and sandy unless one could remain on the concrete slab runway. Yuma had offered a leg prize, however, and the race managers stuck to their guns — they were running the show, and all pilots would land where they were told to.

Vera Dawn Walker who was flying a Curtiss Robin with a Challenger engine, one of the slowest and smallest ships in the DW Class, remembers that the Yuma airport "was an ocean of soft sand with cement slabs laid down for a runway ... very narrow and too short." To roll off the concrete was certain disaster. Herb Fahey, who was piloting the race manager and other officials, lost control of his Vega in the gusty air and slid off the runway. The ship was damaged and another Vega flown by Wiley Post had to be dispatched from Burbank to continue the trip. Amelia Earhart could not check her landing roll in time, ran off the concrete's end, and her Vega ended on its nose with a bent prop. A replacement part was immediately put on a fast ship scheduled to arrive in about two hours. One contestant overflew the field and came screaming in from the east. The small crowd had deceived her; she did not believe it was the right airport. Others who had become lost arrived from all directions; one had landed in Mexico, gotten directions and flown north to the airport. May Hazlit was so low on fuel her engine quit on final approach; she made it to the concrete but had to be pushed to the parking apron.

The contestants wilted for more than three hours in Yuma in the blistering over-100 degree temperature while waiting for Amelia's prop to arrive and be installed. They worried about Bobby Trout who had failed to land. Word finally came that she had run out of fuel and cracked up about fifteen miles south in Mexico but was uninjured.

The takeoffs commenced about 2:00 P.M. The women struggled with the unstable, heated air, downdrafts, and dust devils, and were distressed by the poor performance of their aircraft. The flight to Phoenix was long, hot, dreary, and bumpy. Vera called it "the hardest leg of the entire trip." They were happy to see the green irrigated fields west of Phoenix, and happier yet to see Sky Harbor — almost 5,000 feet of good solid airport, with a fine large hangar, and a big crowd waiting to greet them.

Boy Scouts met the contestants with pitchers of ice water and lemonade, and Scenic Airways personnel serviced the ships and rustled the baggage into waiting cars which took the weary racers to a downtown hotel for a rest.

More than three hundred Phoenicians attended the banquet that evening hosted by the National Exchange Club and the city. Governor Phillips gave the welcoming address and called the contestants "Angels," but in spite of the fun there were worries.

There was also tragedy. Marvel Crosson, one of the most experienced pilots in the race, had failed to arrive. Vera had seen Marvel's gray and blue Travel Air swinging in sweeping circles below her as she flew north of Wellton. It was too low and appeared to be in trouble so Vera turned back and circled. Nothing resembling an airplane was in sight, but she saw a white object in the bushes. Thinking it a rubbish dump, she continued on to Phoenix. There was much flat land between Wellton and Phoenix, pilots are optimists, and all felt that word of Marvel's safety would come at any minute. It would be another day before notice would reach them of Marvel's death. Engine failure and lack of a suitable landing place within range had forced her to jump. Tragically there had been insufficient altitude for her parachute to open properly. The rubbish dump Vera had seen was the crumpled parachute.

The contestants returned to Sky Harbor early the next morning to begin their flight to Douglas. They were weary from the unaccustomed heat and the strain of the first two hectic days of racing; there were rumors of sabotage (none was ever proven), concern over Marvel's safety, and unsettling bickering between the race manager and the Exchange Club officers over threatened course changes.

By 8:00 A.M. the ships were ready on the line and warming up. Vera Von Mack was first off at twelve minutes past the hour and Louise Thaden last as she had been the first to arrive in Phoenix. The time was 8:40 A.M. and already small cumuli were spotting the horizon, a warning of possible summer monsoon development.

Those with the faster ships reached Douglas with no difficulties; the slower airplanes caught the developing monsoon between Tucson and the southern city. Vern Dawn Walker ran into trouble between Tucson and Benson. She detoured, went over some clouds, lost the guiding railroad, ducked under more cumuli, skirted around another large cloud and became hopelessly lost. Near Lordsburg, New Mexico, she came out in clear weather, landed for gas at the new army field, and replotted her course to Douglas.

Near the Chiricahuas the squalls started gathering again. Vera carefully detoured around the two small storm cells, but a big one ahead was too large to avoid. She and the Robin mushed through the rain and when they broke out, the smoke plume from the Douglas smelter was right on the nose. Two more squalls were ahead, rapidly converging into a solid mass. Since the first storm had not been too bad, she decided she would try to get through this one. It was mean: Vera experienced turbulence, wind, heavy rain, and a complete loss of visibility. A dive, a stall, and something that felt like the dreaded back-slide followed. She jammed the stick forward and the Robin came out in a screaming dive—but luckily with sufficient altitude for a safe recovery of both her aircraft and wits. She was in the sunshine again, and the smelter smoke was still "right on the nose," and now much closer. A few minutes later she saw Jessie Keith Miller's damaged ship on the ground, half-hidden in some bushes. Vera made a couple of circles. There was no sign of Jessie. Thinking there might be possible injuries, she landed in a nearby pasture.

The whitefaced cattle that had been grazing there scattered and she shut down the Challenger. Almost immediately a big red bull charged at the Robin, stopped just short of hitting it, pawed mud in the air and bellowed. From Vera's story it seems the bull had a dim opinion of orange colored airplanes and lady pilots. For almost two hours he kept her trembling and caged in the cabin with a variety of strategic maneuvers. He circled the ship, bawled, bellowed, pawed more mud and pressed a wet pink nose against the windows.

The animal's owner finally drove up, got out, and waved the bull away with the remark that, "He's real friendly, just wanted to play a little."*

Vera started breathing again. Jessie Miller was with the rancher. She had landed to escape the storm and damaged her undercarriage. The obliging rancher had taken her to a telephone, and a quick call started a mechanic on his way from Cochise with tools and spare parts. He arrived about 4:00 P.M., cranked the Challenger, and fifteen minutes later Vera landed at the new Douglas International. Jessie arrived about 6:00 P.M., her landing gear repaired.

Ruth Elder had also been forced to set down because of the rain, and also among cattle. During her roll a big bull charged the ship. She opened the throttle and sloshed through the mud and downpour for a fast getaway. Opal Kunz, confused and lost in the same storm, landed in Mexico, waited for the weather to clear and, after getting directions from some friendly cowboys, flew into Douglas safely.

Seventeen racing ships took off from a slippery muddy field the next morning, and were on their way to Fort Bliss in El Paso. After spending the night in El Paso, the racers were off to Pecos where they encountered another newly cleared landing field with ankle-deep, loose dirt. There were crowds at the airport and another ship was damaged avoiding an enthusiastic spectator who ran out on the runway just as a contestant was landing.

There was another mishap on takeoff. A thoughtless observer threw away a lighted cigarette; it fell in Blanche Noyse's baggage compartment and started a fire that went unnoticed until just after

---

*During the 1920s the cattle in southeastern Arizona and west Texas acquired a reputation for violent behavior that last well into the 1940s and spread as far as the east coast. Traveling airmen were warned never to land in fields occupied by the beasts as they were notoriously short-tempered and aggressive. The bulls reportedly "attacked airplanes whether moving or parked." Arizona ranchers denied these tales with considerable amusement.

her takeoff when it began to smoke and smoulder. Blanche safely landed straight ahead on the desert—she was too low to turn back to the airport—and the blaze was extinguished.

From Pecos to Cleveland the trip was relatively easy. Vera remembers that "the weather was good, the airports wonderful and not nearly so far apart, and of course it was over flat country and an easy flight."

On August 26, fifteen contestants flew over the National Air Race grandstands at Cleveland and heard the wild cheers of the spectators. Louise Thaden won first place in the DW class, Gladys O'Donnell second, and Amelia Earhart third. Phoebe Omlie was winner in the light plane class flying a Monocoupe, second went to Edith Foltz, Jessie Keith Miller had third and Thea Rasche fourth.

Twenty pilots had started; fifteen finished. Considering the weather conditions and uncertain nature of the landing fields, it was an impressive showing by the women and their ships. The race had given them invaluable experience but it had not enriched them financially; there was only $9,850 to be divided among the finishers. This small sum and the knowledge of Marvel Crosson's tragic death made it painfully clear to the women that competitive flying—while exciting and challenging—was a hard, dangerous way to make a living.

Airmail and Arizona

In 1911, Calbraith Perry Rodgers passed through Arizona on his epic forty-nine day transcontinental flight and became, in all probability, the state's first aerial mailman.

The first airmail demonstration had been made by pilot Earle L. Ovington who carried mail on flights from an aviation meet at Nassau Boulevard, Long Island, to the post office at Mineola during the last week of September 1911. Ovington was a sworn carrier, his trips were made at scheduled times and the mail pouches carefully dropped in front of the post office. Over 4,300 pieces were successfully flown, and the postal department received a flood of requests for similar demonstrations throughout the country.

The United States Postal Service had always used unusual forms of transportation for carrying mail—coastal packets, fishing dories, dog sleds, stagecoaches, and the short-lived but romantic pony express. Not surprisingly, it became interested in airplanes soon after the Wright Brothers' historic first flight. Pioneering birdmen and "bird" builders urged the adoption of this new form of mail delivery. It was certainly no more risky or exotic than some of the earlier types of service; in addition, it was just as reliable, and according to its proponents, "so much faster."

RODGERS' AERIAL POST

The transcontinental flights of both Cal Rodgers and his eastbound competitor, Robert G. Fowler, were well-documented in local newspapers and other publications. However, very little mention was made of Rodgers's Aerial Post which was instigated to offset the horrendous repair bills for his airplane, the Vin Fiz. Picture postcards showing views of the Vin Fiz, with an insert of Cal, were made, and a large stamp in black, white, and half-tone designed. These eye-catchers showed the machine flying high in an oval medallion with the name Vin Fiz prominently displayed.

Cal's wife Mabel was appointed postmistress, and cards and letters brought to her at the Vin Fiz special train were to be flown by Cal to his next landing point for 25 cents, there stamped by her and delivered to the local post office to continue their respective journeys by more conventional and reliable forms of transportation.

The Arizona portion of Cal's journey started on October 31, when the Vin Fiz roared away from El Paso at 9:52 A.M. and headed along the tracks via Lanark and Cambray to Deming, New Mexico, where the little airplane landed at 11:33 A.M. The Deming Graphic waxed eloquent about Cal's circles over town, his flying machine and the "some thousand people who were there to greet him," but did not mention the aerial mail. Mechanical adjustments and refueling were completed; Cal greeted as many of the spectators as possible and made a "graceful takeoff at 12:55 P.M." Sometime during this short stop, W. J. Evans of Deming tore himself away from the excitement long enough to purchase a Vin Fiz adhesive from Mabel, stick it on one of his business envelopes along with the appropriate U. S. postage, and leave it with her for a partial flying trip to Oakland, California.

Cal landed at Willcox, Arizona, at 4:45 P.M. on October 31. Evans' letter must have spent the night there in its container which was probably one of Cal's larger pockets.

In Arizona, as elsewhere, the Vin Fiz Aerial Mail received little publicity. All interest was centered on the airplane and its brave pilot. The stamps had to be purchased from Mabel who was on the train, and unless Cal could find a suitable landing spot very close to the tracks, any eager stamp purchaser might miss seeing the wonderful airplane. No one but a dedicated philatelist would risk that.

Cal carried three pieces of mail across Arizona which were taken off his plane at Imperial Junction, California, carried to the post office there, and duly postmarked. They were the letter from Deming and two postcards of undetermined origin. They could have been handed to Cal or a member of his crew at any of the stops without attracting attention or comment, and stuffed in a jacket pocket. If this happened it was the first occurrence of what later became a regular activity.

When scheduled airmail commenced in Arizona, impatient senders would put an airmail stamp on an urgent letter and take it to the airport where it was handed to a member of a flight crew, stowed in his pocket, and posted at a requested stop on his run. Sometimes twenty-four hours could be saved as the missive bypassed the collection and sorting procedures at the local post offices.

MORE AIRMAIL DEMONSTRATIONS

On November 3 and 4, 1914, there was an air show at Troy, Ohio. Aviatrix Katherine Stinson carried small pouches of mail in her plane from the fairgrounds, and dropped them in front of the post office. She was the country's first sworn woman airmail carrier.

The Arizona Fair Commission had engaged Miss Stinson to perform exhibition flying and someone at the Tucson Chamber of Commerce suggested that as an additional attraction she also make aerial mail demonstration deliveries. Approval was granted in Washington, and she made regular flights from the Southern Arizona Fairgrounds at Tucson to a vacant lot near the post office where she dropped mail pouches.

Buehman Memorial Collection, Arizona Historical Society

The delivery of Arizona's first sanctioned airmail. During the first week of November 1915, Katherine Stinson flew mail from the Tucson Fairgrounds to a vacant lot opposite the post office.

Under her contract, Miss Stinson could make only one appearance a year in a state, so Tucson garnered two "firsts." It was the first Arizona city to have an aerial mail demonstration, and the first in the state to have sanctioned aerial mail service. This record stood for fifteen years, much to the frustration of other Arizona communities.

More exhibitions and longer airmail flights followed Katherine Stinson's jaunts, and in 1916 the Aero Club of Illinois proposed the formation of a company to operate regular service from Chicago to Detroit and New York. Meanwhile, the powerful Aero Club of America had plotted an aerial route from New York to San Francisco and named it the Woodrow Wilson Airway. It was eighty miles wide, encompassed the larger population centers, and faithfully followed the Union Pacific tracks west from Chicago. This airway was laid out so that it could be reached by a system of feeder lines from cities within its borders to the mail line. In a surprisingly short time it became the route of the first transcontinental airmail.

Other groups were interested in developing the southern Borderland route for airmail. One demonstration flight along this route came to a spectacular end in Arizona.

THE GILA BEND LOCKHEED

Aviation historians refer to the airplane as the Lockheed F-1A. The few Arizona flying buffs who recollect it simply call it the "Gila Bend Lockheed." Both titles are often preceded by the adjective "unfortunate" or "unlucky."

The Lougheed brothers, Malcolm and Allen, founded a small aircraft manufacturing company in the fall of 1915. As war appeared imminent, they designed and built a twin-engine hydro-airplane for navy patrol duty. It was a monster of advanced design with a long cruising range and good performance. In May 1918, the brothers flew their new creation, the F-1, to San Diego for navy trials.

Even though the ferry flight from Santa Barbara to San Diego established both a time and distance record for seaplanes, the navy turned down the F-1. The Lockheed brothers (they had adopted the new spelling for their name as well as their company) decided to convert it into a bomber for the army. Ten thousand dollars was allocated to the project in September 1918, but two months later the war was over and the army was no longer interested in bombers.

Now that the emphasis was on civilian aviation, the brothers realized there would be a need for an airplane capable of efficiently carrying transcontinental mail. Thus the ex-patrol-boat-bomber was modified for this purpose and designated the Lockheed F-1A. With a 90-mile-an-hour cruising speed and range of 1,200 miles, it could cross the country in thirty to thirty-five hours with two fuel stops.

A demonstration route was carefully planned. The plane would follow the railroad tracks and stay in the low country. The cooperative Santa Fe and Southern Pacific Railroads agreed to light smoke signals at strategic intervals to aid navigation, and arrangements were made for refueling at Deming, New Mexico, and Cairo, Illinois. The F-1A would carry a sack of mail which included a letter from the postmaster in Santa Barbara to Albert S. Burleson, Postmaster General in Washington. This would signify the start of American transcontinental airmail.

Ovar Sigmund Thorsen Meyerhoffer—"Swede"—was picked as pilot. Swede was a former race car driver, sailor, prize fighter, wing walker, stunt flyer, and one of the most capable pilots in the country. Bob Ferneau, one of Swede's students, was to be relief pilot, and the Hall Scott factory sent mechanic Leo Flint along to attend to the needs of the two, 150-horsepower Hall Scott engines.

Preparations for the flight were completed by November 16, and that afternoon the big airplane was flown to a plowed field near Goleta. This location would provide adequate space for the plane's heavily-loaded takeoff on November 20. It began to rain on November 17 and continued for the next two days. The F-1A was mired in a sea of mud and departure was postponed until November 23. The fuel dealers in Deming and Cairo were notified and the press alerted; now the problem was to extricate the 6,000-pound ship from the sea of mud. A tractor was brought in. It promptly sank in the goo. The dilemma was finally solved by a farmer and his team of eight stout horses who snaked the Lockheed out of its difficulties and dragged it to a firmer pasture.

November 23 was drizzly and damp, the forecast was unfavorable, but rather than disappoint the press and reap unfavorable publicity, the pilots decided to stick to the schedule. All 6,000-plus pounds of the F-1A broke ground from the Goleta pasture that dark, dank morning at 5:05. Strong winds, clouds, and turbulence plagued the ship over Ventura, Santa Paula, and past Sangus Junction. It took three hours to reach Colton, California, where the crew spotted a welcome smoke flare indicating the correct track to follow through the mountains. Storm clouds piled and roiled in the pass, but on the east side of the mountains it was clear except for the heavy dust picked up by the gale-force winds. The F-1A was over Yuma at 10:00 A.M., but few of the town's residents saw or heard the big airplane because of the roaring storm and the dust.

The wind had reduced the plane's speed from the normal 90 miles-an-hour to a crawling 65, necessitating a unscheduled fuel stop at Gila Bend, Arizona. The F-1A was nearing this small desert community when a valve spring broke in the right engine. Swede made a safe single-engine landing on rough terrain near Tacna. The fabric on one wing tip snagged a cactus, causing a rip, and the steel shoe on the tail skid sheared from its post.

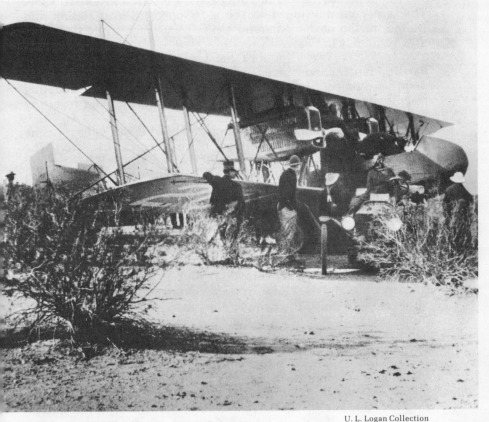

The Lockheed F 1-A being refueled at Gila Bend, November 25, 1918. By this time the pilots had begun to wonder if they were being paid to fly an airplane on the first transcontinental airmail demonstration or to construct impromptu airports.

The damaged shoe had to be repaired with welding equipment. There was no such equipment in Tacna, but nearby were the Southern Pacific tracks leading to Yuma and a well-equipped metal shop. The weary crew trudged to the abandoned railroad station and waited for the next westbound train. They successfully flagged it down and rode to Yuma.

In Yuma, Leo Flint took the broken piece to the Southern Pacific's repair shop where it was expertly welded. Later that afternoon he hitched a ride back to Tacna on another accommodating freight, and went to work reassembling the tail skid and repairing the bad engine.

The pilots spent the day resting and making the endless phone calls that are always the aftermath of an emergency landing. The following morning, they rode—again courtesy of the S.P.—back to Tacna. The weather had improved and the day was spent filling dog holes, knocking down sand hummocks, and placing planks under the heavy F-1A to raise it out of the sand. By sundown Leo had successfully tuned the engines, and the first Tacna airport was completed and ready for business. Early on November 23 the Lockheed made the first takeoff from the "Tacna Municipal Aiport" and headed along the tracks for Gila Bend.

Airplane news travels fast, and early in the morning townspeople and ranchers were watching for the big bird. The airplane was sighted flying along the tracks toward Gila Bend a few minutes before ten o'clock. It gracefully circled the town and pretty valley and was safely on the ground at 10:00, November 26—three days behind schedule. A truck arrived with gas cans, and after the fueling, the crew, with help from some of the citizens, did a bit of clearing on the runway. By two o'clock everything was ready for the takeoff. Swede gave the all clear signal; Bob Ferneau opened the throttles, and the Lockheed started to roll. The crowd was excited but well-behaved—all except one. An eager, excited young man in a flivver decided to give the people a real thrill by racing the airplane down the runway. Just as Bob was about to lift off, the car cut in front of the plane. To avoid a serious pileup, Bob aborted the takeoff and ground-looped the ship to the right. It lurched to a rough stop off the runway in the brush with a blown tire. This was not too serious as Leo had a spare wheel on board, but the prospects of maneuvering the heavy ship and changing wheels meant another frustrating delay. Moreover, the accident had put the F-1A in a poor position for takeoff. Now the ship was no longer on the solid hardpan, but on the rough, brushy desert. The crew again got to work with picks and shovels and, with help from the Gila Bend citizens, cleared an acceptable runway. By now the pilots were wondering if they were being paid to fly an airplane on the first transcontinental airmail demonstration or to construct impromptu airports. The time spent on each activity was about equal. At sundown everything was ready, but because night flying then was very dangerous except under ideal local conditions, departure was postponed until early the next day.

A crowd of Gila Bend residents, cowboys, ranchers, and a few Indians assembled at daybreak to witness the event. There were thanks and farewells, and then the crew settled into their snug open cockpits. The engines were checked and Swede gave the "Let's go!" signal. Everyone stopped breathing as both engines came to life and the heavy F-1A jounced along the short improvised runway under Bob's skillful handling. It was a good clean takeoff, but when the ship was about twenty feet in the air the right engine quit cold.

Bob had two choices and only seconds to make the decision— to his right was an arroyo and certain destruction; ahead the winding shallow river bed snaked through low sand dunes. He would attempt to knock off the landing gear on one of these dunes and make a belly landing. This might give the crew a "walk-away-from" chance.

It did not work. The nose wheel hit a dune and the F-1A upended with a jolt that caused a fuel tank to shift and crush Leo Flint. Bob scrambled down from his vertical perch and dragged Swede and Leo from the shambles that had been the front cockpit. Hot oil and spilled fuel covered both men but there was no fire.

The crowd rushed up. Someone placed the unconscious Leo on a tarp. Swede was on his feet but glassy-eyed and groggy. Bob was uninjured except for some bruises where his safety belt had held. A temporary hospital was set up in one bedroom of the U. L. Logan home, and Leo and Swede, who had collapsed from internal injuries, were moved there.

Bob had the unpleasant task of sending the necessary telegrams. When this was completed he, with a local doctor's help, made plans with the Southern Pacific Railroad to move the two injured men—first to a hospital in Phoenix and later to Los Angeles. Leo's recovery was slow and painful. He lost the use of one eye. The tough Swede bounced back to health and continued his flying, showing up in Arizona the following year with Barr's Flying Circus.

The mail sack containing the letter to the postmaster general was delivered by a slower but more reliable form of transportation.

THE U. S. AIR MAIL SERVICE

During 1917, Second Assistant Postmaster Otto Praeger had thirty-seven different temporary airmail routes under consideration as well as the transcontinental service that would be conducted by the Aero Club. The appropriation requested was $100,000, so only a few routes could be implemented. Both the military and the politicians believed that airmail service would provide excellent experience for America's military pilots, most of whom had no knowledge of cross-country flying and no experience of flying schedules.

Capt. Benjamin B. Lipsner was a non-flying member of the Aviation Service. In civilian life he was an engineer and lubrication expert. He also must have had some practical experience in cost accounting, as his presentation of an airmail route operation from New York to Washington so impressed the postmaster general, Albert S. Burleson, that the U. S. Air Mail Service was established. Personnel and aircraft would be furnished by the Air Service, and six modified JN-4Bs were allotted to the new project "for Captain Lipsner to play with" according to some journalists. A mail compartment was installed, larger fuel tanks added, and the original OX-5 engines were replaced with Hissos. Jenny was now labeled a JN-6H, and a mail carrier.

The new stamp designed for the service was an attractive carmine and white, marked 24 cents and showing an engraving of a JN-4 duded up as a mail plane. Somehow in the rush and excitement the first sheet came from the presses with the airplanes upside down. A Washington stamp dealer spied the error before the postal clerk did, paid his $24 and left with a gold mine of acrobatic Jennys. Reports indicate that one of these stamps sold for over $30,000 in May 1969.

Captain Lipsner rested poorly on the night of May 14, 1918. He fretted abut the weather and about his inexperienced cross-country pilots and shuddered when he thought of what an accident and the resulting unfavorable publicity would do to the new service.

May 15 dawned bright and sunny. President Woodrow Wilson attended the short dedication ceremonies, and two of the JN-6Hs took off from Washington bound for Philadelphia, where other pilots would continue the flight to New York. This modest route was 218 miles in length and one daily round trip would be flown except on Sundays. Considering the excitement and resulting strain, the pilots performed well. There was only one incident. A confused birdman flew in the wrong direction and had to make a forced landing. A truck rescued the mail. Captain Lipsner slept soundly that night.

On July 15, the new airmail service received formal approval from the Post Office Department, and on August 12 this body took over the entire operation, furnishing its own equipment and personnel. Performance gradually improved under Captain Lipsner's eagle eye.

The newsprint announcing the armistice was barely dry when surveying military flights began investigating Arizona. Mapping flights, photographic tours, training missions, air show teams bound for airport dedications, and a few lone eagles recorded airport sites, weather conditions, and other pertinent information. Most used the Borderland Airway but a few adventurous souls tooled along the Santa Fe Airway or Highway 66. When officials announced that "airmail delivery along the southern or fair weather route is both practicable and possible," communities in southern Arizona were jubilant.

The Post Office Department continued to develop the Aero Club's transcontinental airway, now known as the "Main Line" or "Columbia Route." The last link in the transcontinental chain, the leg between Omaha and San Francisco, was closed on September 8, 1920. The inaugural westbound flight averaged 80 miles an hour and reported no forced landings or other difficulties while carrying its 16,000 letters. It had beaten the best train time from New York to the Bay City by twenty-two hours.

On February 23, 1921, the first experimental transcontinental night airmail was flown, and regular night service was implemented on July 1, 1924. The Post Office Department, with the cooperation of the military and private enterprise, had learned much about scheduled operations, maintenance, airway lighting, and the potential uses of radio.

The military flights in Arizona continued, some along the Borderland Route and others following the Santa Fe. Tucson had a fine airport, but Phoenix was still burdened with the questionable fairgrounds and everyone was tired of hearing other people say (and having scribes write) that if "something is not done about a suitable field" the city would be dropped from the government's list of proposed airmail stops. The Post Office Department was waiting for congressional action to authorize private mail contracts. Surely this would be soon.

Eager Phoenix writers could use airmail along the Main Line. However, the Postmaster admitted it saved little time as all mail had to go to Salt Lake City by train.

CLIFFORD MAUS AND THE MEXICAN AIRMAIL

Clifford Maus, although he was in the state intermittently for little more than three years, was the first in Arizona to apply for and receive a contract from the Mexican government to carry mail, passengers, and express by air from Nogales to Mazatlán.

Exactly when or where he began flying is obscure. In those days of casual flight instruction, he was probably self-taught, and later took what would now be termed refresher courses. It would be safe to assume that his total formal dual instruction did not exceed two or three hours when he began planning his airmail enterprise.

On March 27, 1925, the *Deming Headlight* announced that Clifford Maus had purchased a Jenny that he would use on a Mexican mail contract from Nogales down the West Coast of Mexico. He took off for San Antonio in his new purchase to acquire two additional airplanes which would give him a fleet sufficient to start the schedules between Nogales and Mazatlán. He had been designated as the "official air-mail man" between Sonora and Mazatlán, and the flights would commence May 1. The signature of D. Arrias, Secretary of War for the Republic of Mexico, was affixed to the document which was in Cliff's possession.

On June 9 the Nogales *Herald* printed a small piece that hinted at a long, dreary series of frustrations and delays. "With but acceptance of one of the two propositions submitted by the Mexican Government standing in the way, an aerial mail and passenger line between Nogales, Sonora, and Mazatlán, Sinaloa, is promised the west coast." Maus was optimistic and told reporters he expected the flights to start in several weeks.

Delays continued. Early in August Maus and a partner, Paul S. Coaske, were in Tucson for meetings with the Aviation Committee of the Chamber of Commerce, and also to put the finishing touches on their Mexican plans. Maus told the committee that the Mexican government had assured a certain amount of mail on each trip from the various ports, as well as a definite rate per pound on the service. The northern terminal would be in Nogales, Arizona, and the partners planned to request an extension to Guadalajara. They further believed that it would be advantageous to start the flights at Tucson where there was a direct connection with the transcontinental Southern Pacific Railroad. The committee pricked up its ears — a transcontinental mail connection with international mail at Tucson! This wide-awake group never missed an opportunity to promote and encourage aviation progress in their city, and they promised their full support.

The partners would need three airplanes to maintain the schedules, and in a few days Coaske, who was originally from Los Angeles, would leave for that city to see aircraft manufacturers and interview interested businessmen and freight shippers. Governor Alejo Bey of Sonora had given assurance of support and cooperation, and soon Coaske would make a flight down the West Coast which would complete the final arrangements and finish the survey begun by Maus. The required three trial flights would start in September.

Things looked rosy, but finances were slim. No information had been found indicating stock sales, incorporation, or any income other than what Maus and Coaske could bring in by working the ships. It is doubtful if the permit for the trial flights would have been satisfactory collateral for a loan.

Shortage of money may have caused the cancellation of the three trial flights that the Mexican postal authorities were insisting on before drawing up the working contract. In spite of this frustration, Maus was able to put by a little cash during the winter of 1925–26. He also managed to keep his name in the local papers by dropping a wreath of carnations from 175 feet onto the grave of Ettie Lee Haraway during her funeral service, and by dickering successfully with owners of the Tucson Welding Works to be designated head of the flight department for this progressive company. Advertisements said that his "two mile a minute delivery service would save customers many valuable hours."

It was in late September 1926 that the Mexican ax fell on Maus and the three other aspiring United States transport companies. It neatly sliced all hopes for airmail and express concessions as the Secretaría de Comunicaciones y Obras Publicas felt the applicants' prices were excessive. Aerial mail saved "but hours," and the people would not pay twice or three times the regular rates when so little time was saved. A company already operating between Dallas and Laredo reported very light loads and their permit would probably soon be cancelled. The government of Mexico did not wish concession firms to go broke, hence it was preferable that the concessions not be issued.

Frustrated and disappointed, Cliff Maus disappeared from the Arizona flying scene.

THE DEVELOPMENT OF A NATIONAL AIRMAIL SYSTEM

On February 2, 1925, the Kelly Bill passed, authorizing the Postmaster General to contract for mail service in order to encourage commercial aviation. This meant that the Post Office Department would gradually relinquish all aerial mail activities as soon as the civilian contractors were judged capable of continuing the service.

Eight routes were advertised. The requirements were for stable, responsible operators, well-financed and capable. The bids were opened on October 7, 1925, and five contracts were awarded. Arizonans were disappointed again—none of the routes passed through their state.

Bob Housler's aerial survey along Highway 66 from the coast to Albuquerque in the summer of 1925 stimulated more interest in, and hopes for Arizona airmail. Meanwhile the active and always vocal group of aviation enthusiasts in Tucson was not idle. Coincident with their municipal airport dedication on November 1, 1925, was the formation of the Borderland Airway Association, organized solely for the purpose of securing a southern transcontinental airmail schedule. Thirty communities were represented.

What work was completed by this organization is not known, but the results were nil. One rather new but substantial thought presented by the Yuma delegation caused a small stir—namely, that airports should be supported by taxation and not by private funds. As the *1926 Aircraft Year Book*, reporting for 1925, listed Arizona with a total of sixty-one airports with twenty-six being classed as municipal, the state's percentage of tax-supported facilities was considerably above the national average.

There still had been no advertisements for Arizona airmail schedules. By mid-1927 it was known that the Post Office Department would relinquish the transcontinental Columbia Line to a private contractor the following year, and several companies began organizing to bid on this plum.

The electric combination of the Kelly Bill and the Air Commerce Act, plus a soaring economy, had released vast sums of capital. Technological advances, not the least of which was the proven reliability of the Wright Whirlwind engine, and the lessons learned by the Post Office Department along its Main Line, stimulated an already overconfident industry. Everyone knew that a southern airmail route was both practical and necessary, but Washington remained mute, and Arizonans waited.

In 1928, President-elect Herbert Hoover appointed Walter Folger Brown to be his Postmaster General. Brown was by education and training an attorney, and an astute and experienced politician. He knew nothing of aircraft or their operations and little about airmail, but he had the ability to apply himself and do the necessary homework. What he learned about the nation's airmail system caused him acute discomfort. It was a maze of short haul contracts, flown by young, reckless pilots in small planes.

The majority of the lines had no plans for larger, safer passenger-carrying units, and the entire system was too dependent on government mail or subsidy. Some lines actually refused to haul passengers; the uncomplaining mail paid well, much better than human cargo. Passengers demanded expensive terminals, ground transportation, and costly food. They also fussed about the cold.

The new Postmaster General dreamed of four large, well-run, adequately financed, competitive trunk lines spanning the country in fast, modern, safe aircraft hauling both passengers and mail. He attacked the problem with vigor. The original mail contracts expired November 7, 1929, and this gave him the chance to implement his sweeping plan.

On February 19, 1930, the Postmaster General requested of the House Committee on Post Office and Post Roads an amendment to the Kelly Bill (the Air Mail Bill of 1925). This amendment, tailored to meet Brown's requirements, emerged as the McNary-Watres Bill. It substituted a space-mile rate for the old pound-mile compensation, and reimbursement to the carriers would be not more than $1.25 per mile. Space not used by the mail could be filled with passengers—or shoes and ships and sealing wax. One cubic foot of space was computed to equal nine pounds of mail. Awards were to be made to the lowest responsible bidder who had operated daily schedules of at least 250 miles for a period of six months. In addition, the Postmaster General had the authority to consolidate or extend routes if in his judgment that was in the public interest.

The McNary-Watres Bill became law April 29, 1930. Shortly thereafter, Postmaster Brown began to overhaul the airmail system. He was determined that nothing should upset his basic plan of four well-financed, efficiently managed trunk lines carrying both mail and passengers from coast to coast. He realized the numerous independents operating without mail were optimistically hoping for contracts; he also knew the majority of them were underfinanced and poorly run. They were busy losing their (or their backers') shirts and did not fit into his plans.

The Old Main Line route and the route flown by Northwest Airlines presented no immediate problems, but the routes in the southern sections of the country were a mess. Two weeks after the McNary-Watres Act passed, the Postmaster General called a meeting of the operators to work on the distribution of the new contracts. No agreement could be reached and Brown was unanimously asked to umpire the hostile, suspicious group. The Postmaster General knew exactly what he wanted and he set the rules so he would get it. He stated that no transcontinental line could operate unless it was under one management, and that no line could have more than one route. This meant that only two transcontinental lines remained eligible.

Formal bids were opened August 25, 1930, and the two eligible companies—TWA and American Airways—were awarded the contracts. Now the Postmaster General had his viable transcontinental airmail lines, and Arizona would have its long-awaited airmail service.

INAUGURAL AIRMAIL DAYS IN ARIZONA

On October 15, 1930, the southern Arizona communities of Phoenix, Tucson, and Nogales happily greeted their first transcontinental airmail and passenger line after a frustrating sixteen-year wait. It was a rather interrupted service, as passengers would have an overnight stop at Dallas and a change at Atlanta to another carrier for the flights to some sections of the east. But the mail schedules from Phoenix to New York took only twenty-four hours, and this would soon be reduced to twenty. The mail sacks were taken off at Dallas and carried by National Air Transport (which serviced no passengers) to Chicago, and thence to the Atlantic seaboard.

The three southern Arizona fields had been freshly dragged and the terminals' tiny waiting rooms swept out. In Phoenix the flood lights were checked (possibly the westbound would arrive about dusk or a little later) and the hangar and terminal building spruced up. This was now occupied by Jack Thornburg and Irving Kravitz, operating their Arizona Air Service since Scenic's demise, but the waiting room and ticket office would be used by the new airline.

The previous week all of American's ships—sixteen F-10 Fokkers and ten Fords, had been sent to Dallas for installation of fireproof mail compartments and paint jobs. The mail bins would reduce the Fokkers' passenger-carrying capabilities from twelve to eight, but this would be offset by the convenience of being able to fly direct to Atlanta. Soon additional schedules would be added.

At 5:35 A.M. on October 15, 1930, American's inaugural airmail flight took off from Burbank's United Airport carrying mail pouches, eight boxes of California gardenias destined for various dignitaries along the route, and four passengers.

Promptly at 9:35 J. W. "Johnny" Martin and co-pilot F. L. Duncan landed the F-10 at Sky Harbor and taxied to the terminal building. An old stagecoach, formerly used on the San Antonio-San Diego run and known in the 1870s as the "Jackass Mail," smartly trotted up and parked under the ship's broad wing. The Phoenix postmaster climbed down to greet the passengers and crew; 240 pounds of mail were loaded; there were some short speeches; an enormous crowd cheered; the horses twitched their ears; and then the Fokker was off for Tucson Municipal (Davis-Monthan) where a mob of over 2,000 was waiting.

At Tucson, 259 pounds of mail in 13 sacks—10 pounds more than Phoenix had managed—were put in the compartment. The plane then took off for Douglas where it landed at 12:05 P.M.

The inaugural westbound flight completed its schedule the next day. Southern Arizona could now celebrate its new airmail service.

The beginning of Contract Air Mail #34 on the central Arizona route was postponed until October 25 due to delays in the completion of TWA's communications system. On this bright and sunny morning LaMar Nelson, captain on the inaugural eastbound, landed his TWA Ford on the Winslow airport at 9:20. Over 3,000 waited to greet him, the largest assembly in the state to welcome an inaugural mail flight. Eighty-five pounds, totaling about 8,000 letters, were loaded in the mail compartment. Captain Nelson was presented with an Arizona state flag and then was off to Albuquerque.

Winslow would be TWA's only Arizona stop; eastward the big ships landed at Albuquerque, Amarillo, Wichita, and then Kansas City, which marked the end of the Western Division. An early departure the next day would put the mail and passengers in New York late that afternoon. Soon the mail would ride solo with a single pilot in the Northrops for a night trip to the east coast.

Arizona now had fast mail and passenger service connections with Mexico, Central and South America, and the Virgin and Windward Islands, as well as fine domestic schedules. An early morning posting of a letter in Winslow would put it in San Francisco or Seattle the same day. The state's inaugural airmail days had been an outstanding success.

The Air
Carriers

On June 2, 1917, the Arizona Corporation Commission received its first application for a scheduled intrastate air carrier in Arizona. The application was approved, the second such awarded in the nation. The successful applicant was the Apache Aerial Transportation Company, which planned scheduled passenger service between Globe, Midland City (Miami), and Phoenix, as well as flights over the Apache Trail and Roosevelt Lake.

Apache Aerial faced difficulties from the outset. Its president, Wesley A. Hill, informed readers in central Arizona that "two new Curtiss planes have been ordered, and the factory has agreed to furnish pilots." However, the company had difficulties in getting these eight-place airplanes, as the country was at the time preparing for World War I and both machines and pilots were scarce. Apache may also have had problems in finding adequate financing, as alluded to in the *Phoenix Gazette* (September 19, 1917): "...operations of the Apache Aerial Transportation Co. [have] been temporarily suspended waiting permission from the Corporation Commission to sell stock.... The permission has been granted and the service will start soon."

When the war ended, pilots and planes were available, and the company was ready to proceed with its operations. On February 9, 1919, dedication ceremonies were held, and soon thereafter Apache Aerial launched an advertising campaign. A full-page illustrated spread described the twenty hours of train travel or the ten hours of car travel required for the trip from Phoenix to Globe, and pointed out that "the new Handley-Page type aeroplanes that are ordered will make the flight in one hour, and the twin 400-horsepower Liberty engines will give them plenty of reserve power to carry forty passengers with luggage plus twenty-five pounds of mail."

By this time routes for the new line had been extended to cover three states. There was to be an express run from Los Angeles to Phoenix, and another from Globe to El Paso with stops at Clifton, Arizona, and Deming, New Mexico. The proposed main line was to start at Los Angeles and stop at Yuma, Phoenix, and Globe, with an extension from Phoenix to Tucson and from Tucson direct to El Paso. A passenger taking this route could travel from Los Angeles to El Paso in nine hours, from Phoenix to Los Angeles in three, and from Phoenix to Globe in one.

Prospects appeared good for Apache Aerial Transportation, but like many other early aviation companies, this one failed to live up to its initial promise. Financial problems, which had plagued Apache from the start, proved insurmountable, and the scheduled flights were never begun. Nevertheless, it was the first line to be planned for Arizona, and it gave the state Corporation Commission the opportunity to cut its teeth in the air transportation busines.

THE AERO CORPORATION OF CALIFORNIA
AND STANDARD AIR LINES

In November 1926, the Aero Corporation of California was formed by Jack Frye and Paul Richter, who had been pilots in the prestigious aerial stunt team "Thirteen Black Cats" before deciding to become aircraft dealers. Aero obtained a distributorship for the new Eaglerock airplanes, and the business became an immediate success, with sales of sixty planes in the first year of operation.

In the spring of 1927, the partners ordered a Fokker and decided to start an airline to Arizona. On May 10, a representative of the Aero Corporation landed at Phoenix Municipal (Christy Road) and announced to the press that scheduled flights from Los Angeles to Fort Worth via Arizona would commence "as soon as planes are available."

That summer, Jack Frye made several goodwill flights to Phoenix and Tucson. In September, the Aero Corporation signed a freight contract with American Express Company, and on November 15 Frye made his final survey flight. On November 28, 1927, Phoenix and Tucson welcomed the Aero Corporation's Standard Air Lines, Arizona's first interstate/intrastate scheduled air carrier.

Later that fall, Aero filed an application with the Arizona Corporation Commission to carry passengers and goods between Tucson and Phoenix. The hearing was held on December 1, 1927, the first proceeding in the United States to determine whether an airline should be granted such authority. The hearing also gave the ACC the distinction of being the first state body in the country to assume regulation over interstate air traffic. The Corporation Commission approved the application, and Jack Frye received Arizona State Pilot's License #1, and his co-pilot, Paul Richter, License #2.

Standard was gradually replacing the original Fokker Universals with the newer, faster Supers, which had a cruising speed of between 118 and 120 miles an hour and a climbing ability of 950 feet a minute at sea level. It had been asking much of the 220-horsepower J5 engine installed in the earlier models to lift 4,000 pounds of airplane, passengers, baggage, freight, fuel, and other miscellaneous items from a less-than-5000-foot dirt runway in 110° temperatures. Pilots spoke of "wishing the early models over the trees" at both Phoenix Municipal and Sky Harbor.

The new Supers were seven-seaters, with temperature control and some soundproofing. Brakes, metal propellers, and inertia starters were included in their $17,500 price, which was $4,000 more than the old Universals cost. Years later, a Standard Air Lines pilot wrote "...single-engine Super Universals. One pilot, seven seats but seldom seven pasengers, no water, no toilet, no food, no nothin'." He could have truthfully added: no navigational equipment except a compass, and no radio.

The first emergency field on the Standard route was built at Desert Center, California in 1929. The gas station operator at Desert Center observed the Standard Air Lines Fokkers flying overhead on their now daily schedules. He wrote the company in Los Angeles and offered to scrape out a landing strip along the highway. He requested the required length, width, and other pertinent information which was gladly supplied. Soon a dirt runway ran parallel to the highway.

Desert Center Airport served numerous worthy purposes. It was a long flight from Phoenix to Los Angeles and the Fokkers were not equipped with toilets. Passengers appreciated the stop as a comfort station, and the pilots appreciated it as a fuel stop. Now on hot days they could leave Phoenix with a light load of gas, make safer and less spectacular departures from Sky Harbor, and replenish their tanks while having a cold drink with the gas station people.

On February 4, 1929, Standard gave Arizona and the southwest their first transcontinental plane-train connections from Los Angeles to the east coast and New York. Departure from Los Angeles was at 8:00 A.M. in the new ten-place F VII's, and arrival in Phoenix was at 1:20 P.M. The fare was $32.50. In Phoenix, passengers changed to the smaller eight-place Super Universals and landed at Tucson, continued on to Douglas, and reached El Paso about 5:30 P.M. At El Paso the travelers boarded Texas and Pacific Railroad's crack limited, the "Sunshine Special," for Chicago. Providing everything en route meshed properly, the time saved on the journey from the coast was sixteen hours.

For some time Harris M. "Pop" Hanshue, president of Western Air Express, had been eyeing Standard Air Lines. He liked its promising growth and perfect safety record, and during late 1929 and early 1930 he began buying Standard stock. By the spring of 1930 he had a controlling interest in Standard and on May 15 the final purchase agreement was signed. Standard became part of Western Air Express, and Hanshue immediately extended the line to Dallas and Fort Worth. For almost eleven months Western's central Arizona schedules had been serving Kansas City, and Hanshue felt that with the acquisition of Standard, his company was in a good position for the upcoming airmail bids.

The first five mail contracts had been due to expire on November 5, 1929. By request of the new Postmaster General, Walter Folger Brown, these were extended for six months to allow passage of the McNary-Watres Bill which, at Brown's insistence, would completely restructure the mail pay system and change the routes. There would be four transcontinental lines, two in the north and two in the south passing through Arizona. Hanshue directed his energies at the latter pair. Western Air Express would bid on both.

WESTERN AIR EXPRESS

Western Air Express was a community enterprise organized by southern Californian businessmen and civic leaders who believed that Los Angeles needed airmail service. They were irked by the publicity San Francisco received because of its status as the west coast terminus of the main transcontinental airmail route, the Columbia Line. They feared a shift of money and business activity toward the northern city unless additional aviation activity was brought to Los Angeles.

Harris M. Hanshue became president and general manager of the new company, and on July 13, 1925, Western Air Express was incorporated in Sacramento. By September 15, 1925, Western was ready for business. It submitted a bid and won Contract Air Mail (CAM) 4, the route from Los Angeles to Salt Lake City. One daily flight each way was authorized. Money was in the bank— approximately $250,000 from stock sales to enthusiastic, civic-minded southern Californians—and six new M-2 Douglas mail planes had been ordered after considerable deliberation.

The Griffith Park National Guard Airport had been used for qualifying purposes, but now Western had to find a permanent Los Angeles roost. A grain field near the Los Angeles Post Office was leased, a 4000-foot oiled runway put down, and a small hangar and an office built.

The new airline and its "airway" actually followed the Union Pacific Railroad as it snaked across the lonesome country between California and Utah. Rails were easy to follow, and the smoke from a coal- or oil-burning locomotive made a fine beacon. By present standards the ships were slow, and they flew low. In poor weather they literally hugged the tracks, and remained on the right-hand side to avoid colliding head-on with planes going in the opposite direction.

Of the original airmail contractors, Western was the fifth to start schedules. On the morning of April 17, 1926, one M-2 departed from Salt Lake City and another from Los Angeles. That afternoon the first sack of airmail from the east via Salt lake and Las Vegas was formally handed to the Los Angeles Postmaster by the Western pilot.

Western's operation was efficient, and its advertising paid off. Soon, in addition to the normal flow of business mail, the movie companies began sending their considerable correspondence back and forth by airmail, and a few passengers were induced to make the trip. Few of the mail contractors wanted to bother with passengers; Western gladly carried—and even courted—them. Two portable folding chairs could be installed in the front compartment of a plane, while still leaving sufficient room for mail sacks.

In June the Kelly Bill was amended and the mail pay was raised. At year's end the young company showed a profit of $1,029, which included fares paid by 209 passengers. Officers and directors were pleased with the results of eight months' operation. In October of 1927, Western declared a dividend—the first in this country to be issued by a company solely in the aviation business. National airmail volume had tripled, Western's revenue followed it, and the net profit after taxes was an impressive $306,974.

Officials of other less-successful lines pointed out that Western had easy routes and ideal flying weather. Western's territory may not have been as rugged as the much-publicized "hell stretch" of the Alleghenies and some of the northern runs, but it was well known for its own particular cussedness. Any pilot who has made the flight from Los Angeles to Salt Lake City via Las Vegas in a light plane will be ready to testify that it is not a pushover. The desert valleys, averaging 5,000 feet above sea level, are subject to scorching heat and violent dust storms in spring and summer. The surrounding mountains, some over 12,000 feet, attract thunderstorms in summer and heavy snow squalls the rest of the year. Severe blizzards are not unknown, and between Cedar City and Salt Lake the advance of a well-developed and fast-traveling cold front can produce an interesting combination of rain, hail, snow, blinding dust, ice, and turbulence within a few minutes' flying time.

Western's Douglas M-2 planes were rugged and admirably suited to their work. A cruising speed of 118 m.p.h. with a top speed of 140 and a rate of climb of 950 feet per minute gave the pilots some reserve performance. Their range of about 675 miles was adequate, and the wide-tread, oleo landing gear with brakes and full swivel tail wheels were well adapted to the rough airports. Flight time for an average trip was about six hours. The ships were well liked by the pilots, and admired by the company auditors.

One might question the admiration felt for them by the 208 passengers who rode on the two portable seats along with the mail in the open front compartments.

During 1928 the aviation industry changed rapidly. Eastern capital poured in, and large holding companies were formed to acquire and combine groups of small independent operators, either with or without mail contracts. These large companies were also buying engine plants, aircraft factories, and related manufacturers. The smaller operator could agree to merge with these giants or remain independent and drown in their own red ink. Western had been approached several times, but no offer had sufficient appeal to the directors and stockholders. Western had money in the bank and more rolling in. The company would continue on its own.

After failing to win the Columbia Line airmail contract offered by the government in 1926, Western decided to try for the two remaining contracts — the route from Los Angeles to Chicago by way of central Arizona, and the southern route from Los Angeles to El Paso and the east via southern Arizona.

The first step was to establish a line through central Arizona by way of Kingman, and Winslow, and then on to Albuquerque and Kansas City. This line was to be combined with a feeder system that would connect the principal population centers in the southwest and intersect the main Columbia line at strategic points. The feeder line that Hanshue envisioned would run from West Texas through Arizona to the Grand Canyon and on to Salt Lake City. To this end he began his acquisition of Standard Air Lines, and when Emery Kolb offered leases for Grand Canyon property that was suitable for an airport, his offer was immediately accepted.

Western continued to make improvements in other areas. From its beginning, the company's interest in technical advances had been outstanding. In February 1929, young Herbert Hoover, Jr., left the Guggenheim Foundation to head the company's radio engineering. Hoover assumed the responsibility of designing and installing Western's radio communications, and in cooperation with Thorp Hiscock, Boeing's communication engineer, worked on two-way radio telephones. Their sets were manufactured by Western Electric Company and installed in the aircraft by 1930. Thus the two carriers shared honors as being the first airlines in this country to use two-way radio-telephone communication.

Cooperation with competing airlines proved so valuable that Hoover and Hiscock formed Aeronautical Radio, Inc. (ARINC) as a sort of radio information clearing house. In 1930, Hoover established over thirty point-to-point radio telephone stations, thereby linking Western's various airports. The almost-instant radio communications between the terminals added safety to the schedules, and saved the company large sums of money.

Kingman would be Western's first Arizona stop. Construction of a new airport was rapidly completed, and on May 15, 1929, Kingman was "connected by air with the outer world" when the first Western plane landed at Berry Field. After being refueled and checked, the big Fokker F-10 went on to Albuquerque. Here the passengers would continue by train until Western could complete plans for an aerial route to Kansas City.

Western also opened a terminal at Holbrook on May 15. No regular scheduled stops were made there but the planes would set down on request to pick up or drop off passengers and mail. The facility was also used for unanticipated fueling and made an excellent emergency stop if the weather suddenly turned bad.

Western had cause for both celebration and concern at the close of 1929. Net profits after taxes came to $1,087,852, but the mail was still supporting the line, which now covered 2,676 miles. In spite of heavy advertising, only 21,990 passengers had ridden Western, for a revenue of just over $484,000.

In 1930 Western's routes increased to 4,716 miles—five fingers with interlocking connections. One served the Pacific coast from San Diego to Seattle. The CAM 4 from Los Angeles to Salt Lake City, and CAM 12 from Pueblo, Colorado, to Cheyenne, Wyoming, were reliable money-makers. Then there were the two longer routes that ran through Arizona, one to Kansas City, via Albuquerque, the other from Los Angeles to Dallas. Only the mail runs were making money, and it was now clear that a passenger and express line without a mail contract was doomed to financial failure. Some few independents were almost making money, providing their routes were short and the flights popular, but it was also known that the train-plane combination operated by Transcontinental Air Transport, Western's chief competitor, had lost a thumping $2,750,000 in the first eighteen months of operation. Western's deficits on the Kansas City section were substantial but not as spectacular as TAT's.

The McNary-Watres Bill became law on April 29, 1930. Shortly thereafter Postmaster General Walter Folger Brown began to overhaul the airmail system as he had planned to months before. He was determined that nothing should upset his basic plan of four well-financed, efficiently managed trunk lines carrying both mail and passengers from coast to coast. He realized the numerous independents operating without mail were optimistically hoping for contracts; he also knew the majority of them were poorly financed and run. They were busy losing their shirts and did not fit into his plans.

Brown ruled that no one carrier could have both the southern and mid-continent routes and suggested a merger—TAT and Western. Neither company wanted it, but neither could avoid it. It was, as one observer put it, a "shotgun wedding." Western's money was running low, and the new mail contracts would carry a reduced rate.

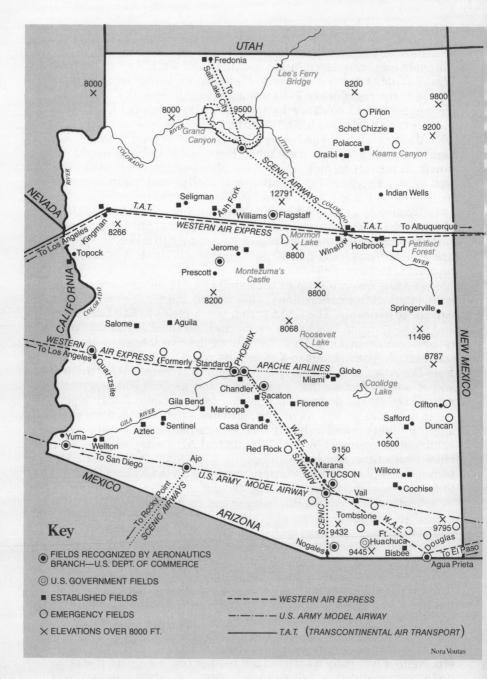

Principal airline routes in Arizona in 1930. This map is adapted from one which was published in the 1930 *Arizona Year Book*.

Further, the planned mid-continent line would bleed both passengers and the lucrative mail from their Salt Lake schedules—now their only connection with the east coast.

Pop Hanshue was over a barrel, and so were the TAT directors. Their lines were losing money and lacked the required night-flying experience that Postmaster General Brown had stipulated in the new contracts. The negotiations continued until July 16, 1930, when Western signed a tentative merger agreement with TAT. Each company would hold 47.5 percent of the stock, and Pittsburgh Aviation Industries would hold the controlling 5 percent.

Transcontinental and Western Air Express formally began operations on October 1, 1930. In the merger Western had to give up its new Alhambra Airport in Los Angeles and some equipment. Its southern route to Dallas was sold to American Airways, and about all the parent line retained were the two mail contracts, CAM 4 and CAM 12, and the mid-Continent line, which was also eventually sold.

In March 1931, the General Aviation Corporation, a subsidiary of General Motors, acquired 60,000 shares of Western stock, thereby gaining control of the line. Other holding companies bought in, and by 1934 the principal stockholders were General Aviation, AVCO (which also owned American Airways), and the National Aviation Corporation. The carriers were no longer family or local civic enterprises. They were big businesses controlled by Wall Street and eastern money.

By 1941 Western's advertising manager and some of the directors felt that there should be a name change. The "Express," which led people to believe the line was principally a cargo carrier, was dropped, and in March 1941 the company name became Western Air Lines.

Of the original airmail contractors, Western was the only operating line as of 1981 that had kept its identity. It would doubtless have pleased Pop Hanshue that, in spite of tentacles that reach east to Florida, south to Mexico, and north to Alaska, it remained a "western" airline.

TRANSCONTINENTAL AIR TRANSPORT (TAT)

On June 25, 1927, the *Arizona Republican* ran a story on the formation of a new air carrier. "Lindbergh Reveals Plans for a Passenger Air Line Which Will Cover the Nation," the headline read. That line was Transcontinental Air Transport (TAT), incorporated on May 14, 1928. In addition to Lindbergh, the Fred Harvey Company and the Pennsylvania Railroad were major investors. This was the first time that a United States railroad had invested money in an airline, and the backing of the powerful "Pennsy," plus Lindbergh's magic name, got the new enterprise off to an excellent start.

Almost a year was spent on route surveys and other preparations. The line would run through central Arizona. An airport location was sought in Winslow, and Kingman was also named as an important stop and a junction point for the San Francisco passengers. Actually, this stop was never used as a junction. The passengers for the Bay Area rode on to Los Angeles and either flew in one of Maddux Airline's Fords to the northern city or took the train.

TAT had been underwritten for $5 million and no expense or effort was spared to provide safety, comfort, and punctual schedules. The airplane offered a combined train-plane schedule (the passengers would fly during the day and sleep at night in a luxurious Pullman). The fare was expensive even by modern standards— $351.94 from Los Angeles and New York. This included a lower berth for the two nights on the trains, but no meals.

Coincident with the company's humming airport building program, new radio stations were installed at Columbus, Ohio; Indianapolis, Indiana; Waynoka, Oklahoma; Clovis and Albuquerque, New Mexico; Winslow and Kingman, Arizona; and Glendale, California, which had been selected as the line's western terminus. The Santa Fe and Pennsylvania Railroads' weather observations were taken at locations where TAT or the U. S. Weather Bureau had no facilities. In the west, Santa Fe personnel took observations at Ludlow, Parker, Needles, Prescott, Seligman, Flagstaff, Grand Canyon, Adamana, and Gallup; TAT observers were at Kingman, Las Vegas, and Winslow. The U. S. Weather Bureau in Phoenix was the only such government service then in Arizona, and by the end of October they furnished two daily balloon reports.

By midsummer 1929 all preparations were complete. On July 7, Colonel Lindbergh, sitting in the California governor's office in Los Angeles, pressed a small button which flashed an instantaneous signal across the country to a large bell in the Pennsylvania Station in New York. When the bell rang, a white satin ribbon stretched in front of the new Pennsylvania Railroad's "Airway Limited" gate was cut, signifying the beginning of TAT's formal schedules.

Arizona now had three major carriers for transcontinental travel working in cooperation with the railroads. TAT led the pack with its offerings of elegance and comfort, if not speed. Most of the Fords used on the new line's regular schedules were the high-powered 5-ATs. Sliding windows could be opened for fresh air, and earplugs and cotton were offered to the travelers as a substitute for soundproofing. The first meals served aloft were advertised; these complimentary delicacies catered by the Harvey system marked the end of the sandwich-apple-orange era. A typical menu was cold chicken, tongue, ham, a dainty salad, sandwiches, and the dependable coffee-tea-or-milk. Gold flatware was used and playing cards were available, as were current newspapers. Outside of assisting the captain now and then, the copilot had nothing to do except pamper

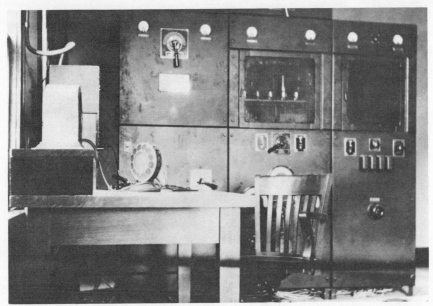

W. E. Davis Collection

The TAT radio station at Kingman. Facilities like this were the forerunners of modern communications stations.

the passengers. There were trial screenings of movies en route, but they were not successful. Fickering movies in a noisy, vibrating Ford wallowing in the rough air could easily upset the stomachs of apprehensive passengers.

During July and August, 1,787 passengers used the service. Travel on the eastern division, because of the heavy traffic between the larger centers of population, was almost double that on the western division. No actual counts of Arizona traffic have been found, but it was light. The main reason was that the journeys from the two large cities, Tucson and Phoenix, to the TAT terminals in Winslow and Kingman were long and harrowing.

During late August and September 1929 the monsoons gathered energy in the Gulf of California, moved out of their usual area of activity, and spread into eastern Arizona and western New Mexico. The wet, warm, unstable air was forced up by the high country, causing heavy thunderstorms, snow squalls, and hail storms, but between the showers bright blue sky showed, luring pilots into believing the weather was clearing.

On September 3, TAT's westbound flight, the "City of San Francisco" was overdue at Winslow. The airport personnel tried to hide their concern. The pilots were veterans on this route, and it

A TAT Ford tri-motor at the Winslow Airport in 1929 or 1930.

seemed reasonable to allow a little time for them to do some dodging and detouring before hitting the panic button. Also, in bad weather the big ships sometimes flew a course father south to keep over lower country.

Showers peppered the horizon in all quadrants. Hours dragged by, the plane did not appear, and concern gave way to despair.

The following morning, the *Winslow Mail* announced "City of San Francisco Lost in Storms." The first account mentioned six passengers on board; this was later amended to five. All TAT schedules between Winslow and Clovis were canceled—the ships would be searching for the lost aircraft—and the nine waiting passengers were courteously ushered onto Santa Fe trains.

Winslow was designated as search headquarters and arrangements were quickly made to have fuel, food, and other necessities at the airport to supply the expected airplanes. By noon, thirty volunteer ships had been fueled, some twice, and all were flying. A $10,000 reward was posted for the pilot who spotted the downed airliner.

The exhaustive search continued until September 6, when pilot George K. Rice, flying Western's flight 107 from Los Angeles to Albuquerque, spied the wreckage on a south slop of Mt. Taylor near the 10,000 foot level. At first he and his copilot thought it was a patch of snow. They took their Fokker down to within 1,000 feet of the crumpled liner. A wing was torn off, and the fuselage had skidded and burned. It was clearly an unsurvivable accident. Rice reported that there were no roads or trails to the location and rescue parties would have to go in on foot or horseback.

The more than 100 pilots and observers in the 60 search airplanes had no accidents or forced landings during their passes over the rugged country. This was fortunate, as many were totally unfamiliar with mountain flying and new to the locale, and often under such conditions the original tragedy is compounded by mishaps of the searchers. The $10,000 reward was split among Rice, his copilot, and the courier.*

MADDUX AIR LINES

Henry Ford was a cautious, conservative aircraft manufacturer who was unusually safety conscious for his era. His early models were thoroughly tested hauling company freight and mail before carrying any passengers. His statement that there was never a fatal accident caused by a Ford's structural failure was based on his company's care and attention to design and engineering.

When the early tri-motors, the 4-ATs, were ready for the market, all Ford car agencies were set up as aircraft dealers. Jack Maddux, president and owner of the successful Lincoln-Ford distributorship in Los Angeles, was so enthused over the new airplanes that he ordered one for his own use. He then realized that he could not possibly do enough flying to justify the $37,500 that the plane, with his dealer's discount, had cost.

The stock market was booming, and flying was growing in popularity. Lindbergh and some prominent associates were discussing an air carrier of "national scope," and Maddux decided that the time was right for him to sell some stock and begin his own air operation. He took the plunge, and Maddux Air Lines was incorporated on September 2, 1927.

Jack made cursory attempts to sell stock in his new venture, but with meager results. Then his first big Ford flew into town on July 27. This was the first trimotor Ford to be delivered to the west coast, and its ferry flight brought the new owner more publicity than he could have purchased. The plane's landing at Williams, Arizona, on July 26, 1927, made banner headlines throughout the southwest and even elsewhere. Almost out of both daylight and fuel, the huge ship had set down at the Williams ball park. A successful takeoff ensued the following morning after the Ford had been lightened by off-loading all but two of the passengers, and a section of the ball park's left field fence had been removed.The ship's excellent performance from high altitude, improvised airport, plus its comfort, luxury, and range (the flight to Los Angeles from Williams was nonstop), impressed the timid investors. Money poured in. Daily

---

*A courier was a steward. Western hired men rather than women to wait on the passengers, believing they would be more useful in an emergency.

Photo courtesy of Harrah's Automobile Collection, Reno, Nevada

The cockpit of a restored Ford tri-motor. Modern brakes have replaced
the original Johnson bar.

schedules were planned from Los Angeles to both San Francisco
and San Diego; later routes would include Imperial Valley and
Phoenix.

Maddux began its Phoenix-Los Angeles daily schedules on
February 23, 1929, bringing two planeloads of celebrities to the
opening of the luxurious Phoenix Biltmore. The three-day dedication was a great success and the new airline gained much favorable
publicity.

Maddux's published schedules showed daily flights between
Phoenix and Los Angeles. The westbound flight departed Sky Harbor at 7:30 A.M. and arrived in Los Angeles at 10:45 A.M. Its opposite
took off from Los Angeles at 11:45 A.M. and arrived at Sky Harbor at
4:45 P.M. San Diego passengers made connections at Calexico, and
those headed for San Francisco caught the northbound plane out of
Los Angeles at 11:30 A.M. With the winter season starting and the
great interest created by the new Biltmore Hotel, Maddux hoped for
lucrative runs on the Arizona segment.

The new line tried various other route combinations—a spur line during the summer to the Monterey Peninsula, and flag stops in the San Joaquin Valley, but the "Race Track Specials" to Agua Caliente were the money makers. During the season, four flights daily each way kept the bank account bolstered. In March the San Bernardino, Palm Springs, Imperial, and Calexico loop commenced operation (one could also gamble and drink in Mexicali). The following month the schedule was revised to include Phoenix, San Diego, and Agua Caliente from Los Angeles. Palm Springs was dropped in the hot season.

In July when TAT began its plane-train luxury schedules from Los Angeles to New York, passengers ticketed from San Francisco were carried to Los Angeles by Maddux Fords. There was no extra charge for the flight. It was about this time that the Arizona schedules stopped and Maddux concentrated its efforts in California. The company's safety and technical record was good, but its load factors, while impressive for that time, were not sufficient to get the organization out of the red ink. It had again been proven that in most cases passengers alone could not support a first-class airline operation.

Maddux and TAT merged on November 16, 1929, and the line became TAT-Maddux. Meanwhile rumors came from Washington regarding the new Postmaster General's plans for the airmail. As if this were not enough to worry air carriers, the Depression had crippled the economy. In late summer of 1929 TAT had cut its fares; the reduced rates were $176.43 from Columbus to Los Angeles with a lower berth included, and passengers could be carried between Winslow and Kingman for $15. From Winslow to the coast was $33; from Kingman, $18. Scheduled air passenger travel for the year showed a 300 percent increase nationally in spite of the economic crisis, but the line's heavy losses continued.

On January 25, 1930, an amendment to the Air Commerce Regulations set 500 feet as an aircraft's minimum altitude except when taking off or landing. Line pilots now would have to be very discreet when they "highwayed" it. The controversial McNary-Watres Act passed in April, and the next month the Post Office Department ordered two passenger seats installed in each mail plane operating on daylight schedules.

Arizona still had no airmail, and now the service would be further delayed by the Postmaster General's merger order welding TAT-Maddux and Western Air Express. A preliminary agreement was signed in July, and the new company officially commenced operations on October 1, 1930, under the name Transcontinental and Western Air. The long unwieldy name was shortened to TWA. Again the flying wits got into action—unofficially TWA would be "Teenie Weenie Airlines."

TRANSCONTINENTAL AND WESTERN AIR (TWA)

On August 25, 1930, Postmaster General Brown awarded the contract for the central airmail route to newly formed Transcontinental and Western Air. In October Arizona finally got its long-awaited airmail service.

Both trimotor Fokkers and Fords were used for passenger and mail schedules. Beginning October 30, 1930, TWA made the entire trip, coast to coast, by air in thirty-six hours with a night layover at Kansas City.

Safety improvements continued, one of the most notable being the lighting of the 185-mile stretch between Kingman and Winslow, paid for by TWA. In addition to lighted airports and emergency fields, there were twenty-seven assorted guiding beacons en route, including the one on Bill Williams Mountain, said to be the "highest in the world."

On a clear southwestern night this illuminated airway was an impressive and beautiful sight to see from either an airplane or an advantageous bit of high country. The glittering, pulsating light swept up and down over the rugged mountains and, with perspective, merged into a continuous shimmering cord that came alive and stretched to infinity. There were pilots who preferred to postpone a trip until almost sundown to "fly the light lines." Navigating was easier and it was impossible to get lost on a fine evening.

The problem of uneconomical equipment continued to plague the carriers. All the airlines in use were too slow, had inadequate range, and burned up money faster than they flew. Early in 1932, Jack Frye, now vice-president of TWA, went to visit Donald Douglas of the Douglas Aircraft Company and told him what his line needed: an all-metal trimotor capable of carrying at least twelve passengers and two pilots at 150 miles an hour, and with a 1000-mile range.

During July 1933, a prototype, the DC-1, was tested. Research and development continued and the finished product, labeled the DC-2, was the plane which would revolutionize the air transportation industry.

The DC-2 was called the world's most researched aircraft. Pilots were invited to fly it and offer criticism on cockpit layout. Engineers and executive were asked to ride in it and comment on the arrangement of accessories, the soundproofing, comfort and appointments. By routing the stresses around the fuselage and not through it, most vibration was eliminated, and with its excellent design and variable pitch propellers, the DC-2 obtained a cruise speed of 175 m.p.h. carrying a crew of three and fourteen passengers.

TWA ordered twenty-five of the planes at $65,000 each. American and four other domestic carriers also placed orders, as did some foreign airlines. In all, 300 DC-2s were built.

The carriers received an unpleasant surprise shortly after they placed their orders for the new planes. A congressional committee was convened on September 28, 1933, to investigate the nation's airmail system. Charges of illegal favoritism had been made against former Postmaster General Walter Folger Brown and now the records were made public of the 1930 "Spoils Conference" at which Brown had awarded the airmail contracts. Evidence of discrimination and collusion mounted, and the radio and press worked the country up to a fever pitch of indignation.

This negative publicity brought a presidential order on February 9, 1934, canceling all domestic airmail contracts as of February 20 of the month. The army would take over on "limited schedules" which omitted Arizona. The results were disastrous. Five pilots were killed and six injured in the first week's operation. The weather was unusually vicious, the army men inadequately trained for the type of flying required, and their equipment unsuitable for the chore.

All airmail was grounded on March 10 for one week while the military received additional training and became familiar with higher-grade equipment. Following this their airmail schedules resumed but were restricted to daylight flights. The service performed creditably, but twelve pilots in all were killed.

On April 30, 1934, the former airmail contractors were given a second chance. Bids were submitted, but with minor name changes to save faces in Washington. TWA would continue, but as TWA, Inc. American Airways, bidding as American Airlines, also won its original route.

On May 16, 1934, the first DC-2 flew on the schedules, but August 1 was TWA's big day. Its overnight limited, the "Sky Chief," introduced overnight transcontinental trips from Los Angeles to New York in a mere 16 hours; the westbound flights consumed only 120 minutes more. Both runs were planned at night for the hurried business executive. Now he could board late in the afternoon, spend a short time aloft in a restful living-room environment and arrive refreshed for a day's business.

Planned stage lengths were 750 miles, so neither Winslow nor Kingman ever saw these new beauties except when one landed because of poor weather. Eastbound stops were Albuquerque, Kansas City, Chicago, and Pittsburgh. Westbound schedules omitted the latter city. Arizona travelers had to be satisfied with the slow Fords and their "milk run" schedules which lasted twenty hours.

In 1934 the carriers flew more than 48,700,000 miles; thirty-eight persons had been killed and ten aircraft destroyed. The following year public confidence waned. During the first half of 1935 six airplanes were lost, eleven people killed, and many more injured. Economic conditions had improved but air travel lagged.

On May 6, 1935, Senator Bronson Cutting and five others were killed when a TWA DC-2 hit a small hill near Kirksville, Missouri. A congressional investigation of the accident and of air safety in general followed. It lasted two months and produced over 700 pages of testimony, most of it highly critical of the Bureau of Air Commerce's parsimonious budgets for the operation and maintenance of navigational aids.

Requests were made for more reliable radio navigation systems, more frequent weather reports, additional beacons, and better maintained emergency fields. As a result, the Air Commerce budget was increased in 1937, and almost doubled the following year. It would continue to expand annually until a full complement of navigational aids was implemented.

By summer of 1935 TWA's through-flights were making a swing over the Grand Canyon, and the "Sky Master" and "Sky Queen" (Flights 3 and 2) stopped at Winslow, connecting with Grand Canyon Air Lines to accommodate those who wished to take side excursions and see the famous gorge.

With the delivery of TWA's new Douglas "Sky Sleepers," the express runs omitted the Grand Canyon overflights and the Winslow stops. However, when Boulder Dam was completed and tourist activity increased, CAM 34 was amended to include schedules from Los Angeles to Boulder and Winslow. In November of that year TWA, Inc., came to Phoenix with daily shuttles that connected with the company's spur line from Boulder to San Francisco via Fresno. A TWA DC-2 spent each night in the Sky Harbor hangar and was towed by the line crew to the terminal every morning in time for the 11:15 departure.

TWA continued to grow, and its passenger routes stretched farther and farther away from the original CAM 34. On May 15, 1950, the company changed its name from Transcontinental and Western Air to Trans World Airlines.

As of the 1980s, TWA's routes stretched across the continent and spanned oceans. The line no longer put down at Winslow and Kingman. These communities were serviced by the regionals and commuters, our second and third level carriers which completed a balanced transportation system, as it was economically impossible to operate the mammoth, sophisticated aircraft over short hauls. The majors' big jets passed over north central Arizona unseen by groundlings except for their contrails, but now and then a gray-bearded ancient mariner of the old airways would look up at one, chuckle and say, "There goes Teenie Weenie Airlines."

Ed Betts Collection

A TWA DC-2 over the Grand Canyon in 1935.

AMERICAN AIRWAYS

American Airways, Inc., the last of the early great domestic air carriers to form, was a manufactured or assembled airline. The original structure was put together by the sprawling, powerful Aviation Corporation of America (AVCO), and its final polishing touches were the work of Postmaster General Walter Folger Brown. He whipped the company into shape to make it eligible to bid on (and receive) the southern transcontinental airmail contract.

In January 1930, American Airways was formed as a subsidiary of AVCO. American's president began the difficult task of consolidating and paring routes flown by the numerous small air carriers owned by AVCO. The reorganization was completed to the satisfaction of the Postmaster, and on August 25, 1930, American Airways was awarded the contract for the southern trancontinental airmail route.

In early summer 1932, American's light line through Arizona and its emergency field system were completed. These had been paid for by the company, though they had a gentlemen's agreement with the impoverished CAA which promised to reimburse them when the money was available. Fiscal year budgets for air navigation facilities had been $7,944,000 in 1931; the following year saw an increase of only $1 million—not sufficient to provide improvements. Sadly, the budget would remain substantially the same in 1933: $7,553,500 plus a $500,000 allocation for "Emergency Construction."

President Franklin D. Roosevelt announced the New Deal. At this time the thirty-four carriers with mail contracts were flying routes along 27,062 miles of airways; most had placed orders for or had already accepted new equipment. Neither financiers nor airlines executives slept well, but surprisingly the scheduled trunks showed an increase of over 36 percent rate of passenger growth. This would drop to an alarming rate of 8.3 percent in 1934 and then pick up again. During 1930 the lines' average stage lengths had been 221 miles; by 1934 these had stretched to over 400 miles.

The company began negotiating with the Douglas Aircraft Corporation for the larger, faster, more efficient DC-3s, and the sleeper versions, the DSTs. On June 25, 1936, American's first DC-3 was in service. The early "3s" cruised at 180 miles an hour and were powered by two Wright 1200 horsepower engines. Later models carried two Twin Row Pratt & Whitney Wasps, and at 75 percent of horsepower their speed ranged from about 195 to 207 miles an hour.

By 1934 most airlines were flying by instrument, and about half their airborne time was during darkness. Pilots still complained about the unreliability of navigational aids and the paucity of lighted emergency fields, but with the New Deal came changes— more stringent air regulations and the announcement of an airport development plan. The latter, in cooperation with the Civil Works Program, would provide needed employment and also improve landing facilities. In 1937 the Bureau of Air Commerce budget was increased and would continue its upward spiral until the country had proper airways facilities, and trained personnel to operate and maintain them.

The twenty-one active mail contractors broke the million passenger mark in 1936—the first time this had been done—and flew 63,777,226 miles. In 1937 the Los Angeles and Oakland Air Route Traffic Control Centers were activated. Also, an extensive program of modification and modernization of the navigation facilities commenced. What doubtless gave the pilots the most satisfaction was the planned conversion of the four-course radio ranges to simultaneous voice and broadcast capabilities. This meant that pilots would have adequate communications at all times.

What made the airline executives and stockholders the happiest were the 1935 figures which showed for the first time that non-mail revenues could exceed mail income. Walter Folger Brown's dream had been realized. Passenger business continued to increase, and both the Tucson and Phoenix terminals were enlarged.

Walter Douglas Collection

American's DC-3 at Tucson's Davis-Monthan Airport after the big snow of 1937.

As navigational improvements continued and the network of ground radio stations expanded, general aviation pilots were encouraged to file flight plans. These were known as "PXs." The pilot gave the radio operator his name, the ship's make, color, and point of departure and destination, with approximate times. He then took off. If the trip was during daylight, navigation was by pilotage; if at night the pilot followed the light line, and the bright beacons, with their red code lights spaced every ten or fifteen miles, guided him. About every fourth or fifth beacon carried a green code that indicated a lighted emergency field. If the plane had a range receiver, the pilot could also follow the radio but few small aircraft carried receivers then — they were expensive, heavy, and not too dependable.

Pilots were required to report when passing a station. If the plane was not radio-equipped, the accepted procedure was to fly low and sufficiently close to the airport radio shack to be identified. Thus, if the operator had received no call at the proper time, he or his assistant stood at the building's door knowing the signal would be visual. At night the rule was to blink the aircraft's navigation lights and "jazz" its engine. Daylight allowed a bit more latitude, particularly for the acrobatic enthusiasts to emphasize their skill with a slow roll or two. Stories circulated of observers being chased into their radio shacks or forced to lie down by over-zealous birdmen. When composure returned, the visitor's time over was put on the wire to alert the next victim.

The early radio station operators encouraged the use of flight plans and furnished valuable services not included in the "book," such as fuel and hot coffee for those who landed for a chat. The operators also phoned hangars to alert the line crew, they called pilots' homes or offices, requested taxi service, made hotel reservations, and sometimes airline reservations. These extracurricular favors stopped when the government decided they were not running a free travel service but operating a continuously busier airway communications system.

Public confidence was building again, and by mid-1937 a passenger's aerial life expectancy on a scheduled carrier had almost doubled since the casual days of 1929. By 1938, the percentage of fatalities per hundred million passengers flown was down to 4.46 on the domestic scheduled flights.

AIRLINES AT THE GRAND CANYON

Following the liquidation of Scenic Airways in late 1930, Red Butte Airport at the Grand Canyon was abandoned. The thought of this lovely field with its almost-new hangar and quarters, all in prime condition, was too much for Jack Thornburgh. He and Irving Kravitz made a great team, and a Canyon operation would take up the slack when their Phoenix business evaporated with the summer heat.

Jack's dream of a Grand Canyon airline became a reality on November 29, 1930, when he purchased Red Butte from the United Aviation Corporation. Early in 1931, G. E. "Roxy" Ruckstell became interested and bought into the project. It was Roxy's money that enabled the new company to purchase new aircraft suitable for its operation. On April 29, 1931, Grand Canyon Air Lines, Inc., drew its first legal breath with the blessings of the Arizona Corporation Commission.

The move to the Canyon was made in the spring of 1931. A new Tri-Motor Bach was the mainstay of the new operation's fleet. The first flight was made on May 6; Thornburgh took a Fred Harvey representative for a ride. The following day a couple from Oakland and a lady from Cincinnati enjoyed a Canyon trip, and Grand Canyon Air earned $30.

The new line did reasonably well. There were numerous charter trips to Oraibi, Cedar City, Las Vegas, Phoenix, plus the usual local sightseeing rides. The operation prospered until the onset of cool weather; Thornburgh and Kravitz returned to Phoenix in January and February to pick up their student instruction again. They would go back to the Canyon in the spring.

In April 1932, Grand Canyon Air Lines submitted an application to the Secretary of Commerce for a certificate allowing it to operate an interstate air transportation service from the South Rim to Cedar City, Utah, via the North Rim, Fredonia, and Zion Park. As the Utah Parks Company and Fred Harvey held the contracts for transportation of passengers, mail, and goods at Zion and Grand Canyon, it was necessary to get a sublease from them. The agreement was to run for five years and the old bugaboo prohibiting passenger solicitations that had hampered Scenic was omitted.

In 1934, Thornburgh left to fly for TWA, but Ruckstell and Kravitz remained optimistic about their operation. On July 30, 1934, Grand Canyon Air Lines commenced schedules to Winslow, connecting with TWA's flights to take tourists for an overnight stay at the Canyon which included an afternoon and morning of sightseeing.

A year later, TWA and Grand Canyon Air lines signed an interline agreement. It was the first in Arizona executed between a major trunk line and what would now be called a third-level carrier whose major income was from scienic flights. Now, for a mutually agreed upon cash sum, the Grand Canyon Air Lines pilots would be flying a TWA Ford Tri-Motor on the Red Butte-Winslow schedule. In addition, Grand Canyon would be included in the major line's advertising and enjoy the complete cooperation of its sales personnel.

The year 1935 was a good one for Grand Canyon Air Lines. It flew numerous passengers over the Canyon, the Navajo and Hopi reservations, and on various charter flights to more distant spots. Park officials continued to use the service, and there was a close and excellent relationship between the airline personnel, park employees, the Harveys, and the influential Kolb brothers.

Roxy Ruckstell was now at work on expansion plans, and on June 4, 1936, Grand Canyon Air Lines submitted an application to the Department of Commerce for scheduled service between Boulder City, Nevada, and the Grand Canyon with stops at Pierce Ferry. This was granted on June 28, and Grand Canyon Air Lines became Grand Canyon Boulder Dam Tours.

Grand Canyon Boulder Dam Tours

Boulder Dam was completed in 1936 and now the new and still raw looking Boulder City had a lovely blue lake forming in its front yard. Tourists came in swarms to see the "biggest dam in the world," to take tours through the modern power station, and to go boat riding or flying over the immense and increasing body of water.

Before starting scheduled passenger service to Boulder City, the always safety-conscious Roxy, with the help of Scenic's former ramrod, Kit Kintner, began an airport building program. Roxy decreed that there must be an emergency field available at all times

A Grand Canyon Airlines publicity photo. The caption read: "To the muffled throb of skin-covered drums, the Hopis performed their Eagle Dance today with a big tri-motor plane as the backdrop...."

along the route, one which could be reached from an altitude of 1,000 feet. This was a large order for that remote and unpopulated section of Arizona. An airport of sorts was bladed off at Tuweep, another near Hillside where the trail from Supai Canyon came to the rim's top, and one close to Frazier Wells. The facility at Pierce Ferry was Kit's masterpiece. It took him three days to get a bulldozer the ninety miles across rough country from the nearest town so work could be started. A small waiting room, radio shack, and two good gravel runways, plus a boat dock and a trail from the river, completed the airfield. This gave sightseers various options. They could fly from Las Vegas or Boulder to Red Butte, or take a boat ride around the lake and up the river to Pierce Ferry, then ride one of the Tri-Motor Fords to the Grand Canyon. Westbound choices were the same, and from Red Butte there were trips to the North Rim, and flights connecting with TWA and with the Santa Fe Railroad at Winslow.

In spite of an excellent safety record, good operating practices, and advertising, the airplanes did not make money. Roxy said that the boats "about broke even," but former pilots say that Ruckstell "lost his shirt" on the Boulder Dam Tours. The company was soon out of business.

Grand Canyon Airlines

The demise of Grand Canyon Boulder Dam Tours did not leave the Grand Canyon without a flight operator. During 1938, Walter Douglas of Tucson started Grand Canyon Airlines, Inc. as a subsidiary of his G & G Airlines Company Ltd. He ran it, with a break for World War II, until 1957, when he sold his interest to the Hudgins brothers.

Meanwhile, the newly formed Arizona Department of Aeronautics, headed by James Vercellino, decided that a modern airport closer to Grand Canyon Village was needed. Senator Barry Goldwater played a key role in the successful effort to acquire property near Tusayan, which was the only practical site. On October 20, 1967, the new Grand Canyon Airport with its 6,800 foot paved runway, lights, and beacon, was dedicated.

Surely one of the happiest participants in the ceremony was Emery Kolb. This attractive and efficient facility, owned and managed by the State of Arizona and constructed with both federal and state funds, occupied portions of the site originally chosen by Emery for his 1925 landing field.

The old Red Butte location, always loved but often blasphemed by frustrated pilots, once again became a cattle ranch.

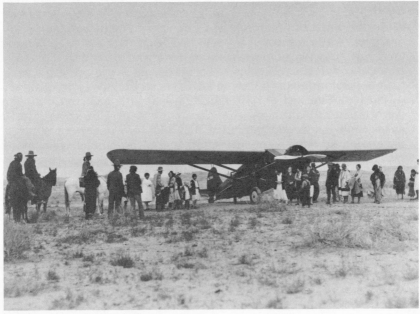

Irving Kravitz Collection

A Grand Canyon-Boulder Dam Tours Travel Air 6000 at Kayenta in the late 1930s.

8

Coming
of Age

The barnstormers and Army fliers in their sputtering biplanes explored Arizona's mountains and deserts and blazed two important aerial highways, the Borderland and the Santa Fe. On their heels came the airlines, carrying passengers and mail at speeds undreamed of a few short years before. The Santa Fe Airway became the LA-A (Los Angeles-Amarillo) Airway and the Borderland Airway the LA-EP (Los Angeles-El Paso) Airway as the primitive navigational technique of following railroads and highways was slowly discarded. The airlines lit these routes with beacons, and the Aeronautics Branch of the Department of Commerce built emergency fields and perfected and put into operation a radio-navigation system. Soon thereafter, the government began taking over the operation of the nation's aerial routes, designating them with colors and numbers and controlling traffic along them. Aviation was coming of age.

FLYING THE LIGHT LINE ON GREEN 4

A generous appropriation for fiscal year 1932 allowed the Department of Commerce to complete the air navigation facilities on the LA-A (Los Angeles-Amarillo) Airway which had been started by Western Air Express and further developed by TWA. Soon, in addition to the revolving airport beacons, auxiliary beacons with course lights—some coded, others uncoded—would glitter and blink every ten or fifteen miles along the route. These did not run in a straight line but were staggered and often marked obstructions.

The LA-A or (later) Green 4 Airway was the first of Arizona's transcontinental routes to be bought and paid for by the government. Following its purchase, developments continued until its accessories were the most sophisticated in the southwest. Between Los Angeles and Albuquerque it serviced no major cities, but it harbored some famous "weather factories"—Bill Williams Mountain and San Francisco Peaks in Arizona and Mt. Taylor in New Mexico. The distances between its airfields were distressingly long, but it was still the most direct route between southern California and the eastern seaboard, had superb scenery, and boasted what must have been the most spectacular light line in the country. It also had several dedicated men along its way who donated their time, energy, and sometimes ill-afforded money to the advancement of aviation in this section of the west.

Kingman

Despite Kingman's location on Highway 66 and on the important LA-A Airway, local aviation activity developed slowly. The city's first aircraft owner was R. L. "Bob" Manship who, in early 1928, had a private license and flew an OX5. Prior to this, George L. Steinke, flying from Minnesota to California, landed his OX5 Travel Air at the Hall Street field. He was interested in flying and mining, and Kingman appeared to have possibilities for both. His visits continued until he finally settled there permanently and contributed greatly to aviation in Mohave County and northwestern Arizona.

The beginning of scheduled passenger service by Western Air Express and TAT had a galvanizing effect on aviation activity in Kingman. The two competing lines embarked on a hasty airport-building program. Western won the race with Berry Field, but TAT's Port Kingman was a more ambitious and technically modern facility. It was the first of TAT's chain of fields in the west and was dedicated on July 4, 1929. Western Air Express almost suffered a total eclipse when the first TAT flight landed on July 8 with Charles Lindbergh at the controls.

Meanwhile, George Steinke continued his Kingman visits. His local mining properties were thriving, and he decided to relocate there permanently. TAT had merged with Western to become TWA, Berry Field was deserted, and all flight activity was at the new Port Kingman. On November 9, 1933, Steinke signed an agreement with the Port's manager, Emmet Baker, which gave him permission to build his own hangar for a ground rental of $10 a month and to conduct commercial operations. Steinke now owned a big Fairchild 71 which was used for barnstorming trips and for charter flights.

When World War II began in Europe and the United States started its military buildup, the army eyed Kingman as a possible site for an air base. This stirred the interest of numerous Arizona contractors and resulted in charter trips from Tucson and Phoenix and additional business for Steinke. The government established a flexible gunnery school at Kingman at the site of the present Kingman Municipal Airport. The first training ships, thirteen AT-6s, arrived on December 18, 1942.

After the new base received its full complement of trainees it was found that the traffic pattern conflicted with the flights in and out of Port Kingman. The Port was closed, but civilian pilots carrying passengers on emergency flights or those engaged in "essential wartime work" could use the military field. By July, 1945, Army activities were winding down, and Port Kingman was able to open again. George Steinke was chosen by the city as the airport's manager.

With peace, Kingman witnessed undreamed of aeronautical activity. The closed Army airfield was chosen by the War Assets Administration to become the country's largest storage depot for military aircraft. People from all over the country flocked to Kingman to examine and purchase the many surplus types available. Some were bought for their new owners' pleasure and use, others for speculation or specialized flight chores such as photography and fire fighting.

On August 3, 1948, the Kingman Army Air Field became the property of Mohave County. Old Port Kingman would be closed. George Steinke was the only one to submit an application for management of the new facility.

During the early 1950s, Steinke became involved in an unusual aerial money-making operation. Tucked in the recesses of the Grand Canyon just below Pierce Ferry is an ancient and rich guano mine, remote and inaccessible. Its owner, a Californian named King, had a contract with a Kern County helicopter operator to haul the stuff out for $20 a ton. When the contract came up for renewal the helicopter's owner raised the price to $30. King felt this was more than he could afford. He advertised for bids. George inspected his aging but faithful Fairchild 71 and decided he could do the job at the $20 a ton rate. A small strip along the riverbed to accomodate the F-71 was needed. When the little riverside canyon strip was completed George hauled out the guano in his 4000 Travel Air and the Fairchild 71. When asked about the tiny new moonshaped airport, the stoic Steinke merely said, "not so bad if the weather's reasonable and the river not too high."

The mine had been operated with permission of President Harry Truman, and when his administration ended in 1953 so did the operation's authorization. The Parks Department ruled that scenic preservation was more important than guano.

Williams and Flagstaff

From Kingman, the LA-A (Green 4) Airway stretched east over lonesome high ranching country toward Williams and Flagstaff, passing over emergency fields at Seligman and Ash Fork. Both Williams and Flagstaff were supported by lumber interests, scattered ranchers, the Santa Fe Railroad, and a minimal amount of tourism. The financial debacle of late 1929 aided none of these enterprises, and when Scenic Airways disappeared, aviation activities evaporated. Both communities were on the LA-A Airway but were never considered a part of the "system;" hence, no government assistance bolstered their airport coffers.

During the 1930s, Williams gained its first resident pilot, Hubert A. Clark, but in spite of his efforts, the city's airport deteriorated. Occasionally pilots flew in from Prescott, but this generated little aeronautical interest. Not until the government began the Civilian Pilot Training Programs in 1939 would there be a rebirth of aviation interest in Williams.*

Flagstaff also had problems attracting any aerial traffic. Pilots refused to take their new modern production aircraft into marginal facilities and risk potential damage. Koch Field was located eight miles northeast of San Francisco Peak; plagued by heavy winds, it offered no ground transportation, and was used infrequently by visiting pilots. Whatever lured passengers to other communities seemed to be lacking at Flagstaff, which received only an occasional visit by ships from Clemenceau, Prescott, or Phoenix. When the Civilian Pilot Training Programs began, an effort was made to rehabilitate the field. The effort was unsuccessful, and Koch, like other "unguarded" airports, closed for the war's duration.

In the late spring of 1946, Challenger Airlines Incorporated made a survey flight to Flagstaff in its new 18 Beechcraft. The line was considering the city as a potential stop on its new Salt Lake-Phoenix thrice-weekly schedules. Even with only three passengers and two pilots on board, the Beechcraft required three circles of the "Koch bowl" to attain sufficient altitude for a reasonable on-course departure to Salt Lake. This so impressed the new line's chief pilot, that he reported Flagstaff "undesirable for scheduled operations."

---

*The Civilian Pilot Training Program (CPTP) was a federally funded program started in 1939. Its purpose was to introduce thousands of young people to aviation training. Fifty-hour courses were given at approved flight schools and the government picked up the bill. It was hoped that this training would improve the performance of Air Service recruits, though military overtones were avoided. Following Pearl Harbor the CPTP became the War Training Service (WTS) and was greatly expanded.

When the Federal Airport Aid Programs commenced in 1947–48, the Flagstaff city fathers, led by city manager Clarence "Maggie" Pulliam, decided that it was time to do something about a new airport. After careful consideration they decided to abandon Koch. With government assistance, city funds, and a small amount furnished by the new Arizona Department of Aeronautics, work started on a new facility, whose runway was 6,300 feet long, paved, and lighted and which had a blacktop ramp, parking area, a stone administration building, and a stout metal hangar.

Business picked up in a hurry. Pulliam Airport, as the new facility was later named, was a handy fuel and lunch stop between Los Angeles and the east. Its location eliminated some of the erratic guests that plagued Koch and had contributed to its dangerous reputation and ultimate rejection.

NASA Comes to Flagstaff

On October 10, 1969, the much maligned Koch Field had another opportunity to achieve aeronautical fame. The numerous cinder bowls and craters in the vicinity were chosen by NASA as an ideal location for a simulated moon walk by the Apollo astronauts. The selected site was about three miles north of the field, and a few small additional craters were blasted in the cinders to provide a perfect setting for the required exercises. News media arriving in airplanes were advised to land at Koch, where transportation would be waiting. On the day of the simulation, both Flagstaff and Winslow reported forty knot surface winds with heavy gusts. No airplanes put down at Koch. The planes carrying the press representatives landed at Pulliam, and the following delays and transportation foul-ups were monumental. However, the "moon walk" itself was satisfactory, and the TV shots were better than expected. Newsreel men arrived in time to see the astronauts emerge from their van and enter the simulated lunar module, which swayed in the vicious gusts despite protective sandbagging. Technicians, scientists, security guards, reporters, photographers, and a sprinkling of curious townspeople stood or crouched in the lee of cars and trucks as the astronauts struggled out of their module and completed assigned tasks in the whistling wind. Vans loaded with technical equipment, pickups, and even jeeps teetered in the gale.

Five years later, Flagstaff weather again frustrated NASA. The February 7, 1973 *Arizona Republic* reported:

> Following their successful trip to the moon in Apollo 17 the astronauts, Eugene Cernan, Ronald Evans and Dr. Harrison (Jack) Schmitt went on a national tour. On their agenda was a stop at Flagstaff to visit the U.S. Geological Survey Center of Astrogeology. A welcoming crowd at Pulliam listened as their ship made four attempts to land and then headed for San Diego.

To quote Jack McCauley, chief of the branch for astrogeologic studies, "We managed to get to and from the moon very easily, but we still cannot control Flagstaff weather." A waiting official added, "If they had been five minutes earlier they could have made it."

THE SD-EP AIRWAY BECOMES AIRWAY RED 9

The original Army Model Airway swung south from Los Angeles to San Diego, then turned eastward to El Centro and Yuma, and then southeast to Tucson. A newer airway forked near Wellton, its northern branch leading directly to Phoenix. This was known as the direct route and was eventually designated the SD-EP.P (San Diego-El Paso via Phoenix) Airway. The southern branch, via Tacna, Agua Caliente, Hassayampa, Gila Bend, and Maricopa, became the SD-EP (San Diego-El Paso) Airway. The two joined near Casa Grande to continue on southeast to Tucson. Gradually, airplanes flying from southern California to Phoenix began to use the direct route from Los Angeles via Blythe, and when Standard Airlines schedules commenced they also went direct. The CAA recognized this as a "Private Airway," but it caused Yuma's prominence to wane.

Both the Reclamation Service and the city wanted a better facility and the present site of the Yuma MCAS-Yuma International Airport was surveyed in 1925. A small tin hangar went up, some concrete pads were laid down for a north-south runway, and all was in order for the first Powder Puff Derby during the summer of 1929.

During the 1930s there was little air travel between Phoenix and Yuma. The latter was closer to San Diego for trade, and the long disagreeable hot ride to Phoenix, coupled with some apprehensions about the highway and lack of intermediate airports, acted as a deterrent.

Yumans felt that their city was doing well aeronautically but were somewhat disgruntled that the Los Angeles-Phoenix route snared most of the traffic. American Airways had a small station at Yuma, but it was seldom used. The lines' few flights from Phoenix to San Diego overflew the city. It was not the boomtown it would become during and following the war, but business and population were increasing.

In March 1941, the Yuma City Supervisors attempted to interest the military in their airport site. It was excellent: level ground, no obstructions for miles, and no nearby population to bother. The experts believed the location was too close to the Mexican border. Additionally, all their funds were spent. The city tried again but the best response they could get was, "We will keep you in mind."

Following Pearl Harbor that promise was kept. By December 19, 1941, the site was selected for an Army Flight School which would also offer gunnery instruction, and events moved so fast that

Yuman heads swam in the hustle and bustle. Under the Desert Training Programs, strips were bladed at Horn and Hyder, plus another dirt airport at Montezuma. Also added to the program were the Gila Bend Air Base with its auxiliaries and gunnery ranges, Luke Air Field and Marana with its sub-fields.

During the mid-1940s the SD-EP Airway became Airway Red 9. Pilots flying east from San Diego followed it to Gila Bend, turned north on Red 15 until it crossed Green 5 from Los Angeles to Phoenix. A right hand turn onto Green 5 led straight into Sky Harbor. Those wishing to go directly to Tucson continued east on Red 9 until it crossed the southeast leg of the Phoenix range near Coolidge, and then proceeded southeast on Green 5.

When World War II ended, Yuma's population, swollen by the huge air base, its satellites, and the nearby desert training camps, rapidly shriveled. In 1949, the Army decided to close its big airfield, and the city's population sank again to its pre-war level of 9,000. Now the community's only shred of distinction was its reputation as one of the hottest spots in the United States.

Two local pilots, Woody Jongeward and Bob Woodhouse, decided to give Yuma a publicity boost. A pair of California pilots had recently established an endurance record for light aircraft, 1008 hours airborne, and garnered headlines for their home town of Fullerton in the process. Bob and Woody believed they could better this record and win fame for Yuma and all Arizona.

A borrowed Aeronca Sedan was to be used for the flight. After extensive modification it was christened "The City of Yuma—The City With a Future," and was readied for practice hops. Refueling was tricky. A powerful Buick with a wooden platform behind the driver's seat roared along the runway at speeds between sixty-five and eight-five miles an hour while the "City of Yuma" swooped down and wavered directly overhead. Cans of gasoline, oil, and other necessities were exchanged.

The first official flight was a disappointment as it lasted only seventy-four hours. The second flight lasted twice as long but mechanical troubles forced a second early landing. The engine received a thorough going-over, and on August 24, 1949, "City" soared away on its third and final attempt to break the record.

The plane droned around Yuma, ventured into California, and paid Phoenix a visit with its refueling car faithfully tagging along. The exchange of gas, oil, and food between the car and the plane never failed to excite the expectant airport crowds.

On October 5, the Fullerton record fell. Five days later, after a magneto failure, the plane landed before a crowd of 12,000. The weary crew had flown the Aeronca 89,920 miles in 1,124 hours, and more importantly (in their estimation), had gained much favorable publicity for Yuma.

E. D. Newcomer Collection (Courtesy *Arizona Republic*)

Sealed cans of gasoline, oil, and food are passed to the crew of the airborne "City of Yuma" during its record-breaking endurance flight in 1949. This photograph was taken at Phoenix Sky Harbor.

Irving Kravitz Collection

Phoenix Sky Harbor in the spring of 1930. The paucity of airplanes on the flight line is indicative of the Depression's effect on general aviation in Arizona.

PHOENIX SKY HARBOR

The year 1930 was an unhappy one for Scenic Airways' Phoenix Sky Harbor. The field's new owners, under the aegis of Acme Investment Company, were ranchers and investors. They had no desire to run an airport; thus Charlie Goldtrap, the former operator of South-Central, was invited to become "nominal manager." He and his partner Ed Lee moved in with their Monocoupes and a Monoprep. These, plus a new Aeronca and a few privately owned units, helped to fill the void left by Scenic's departure.

The Depression continued to inflict deep wounds on the aviation industry. Pilots changed jobs, airlines changed schedules and cut fares, and operators switched bases so rapidly that it was impossible to keep any accurate records. However, people still frequented the fields. For the unemployed any airport promised an economical and rewarding place to spend a few hours. There was always the chance of seeing a celebrity—or an accident. A coke cost only a nickel and most airports had penny candy or gum machines. One could spend a frugal afternoon with exciting possibilities, the ultimate being an invitation for a free ride.

Charlie Goldtrap found a berth with American Airlines and Ed Lee went into a business which he hoped would be more lucrative than running an aircraft operation, so again Acme was without a manager. The company wanted a stable and reliable fellow who would not be tearing off to air races, to the airlines, or to start another flying school, and Carl Knier fit the desired pattern. With a wife and small daughter, he was unable to afford the luxury of instability, and he was a well-known pilot and hard worker.

Knier had the privilege of operating his own business at Sky Harbor. He had free hangar space for two ships, made 2¢ per gallon on all gas sold (exclusive of airline fuel), all profits on general aviation oil sold, and split the hangar rentals and transient parking fees. In return he was required to keep the aging, wheezing, Nash Quad in condition to haul the field drag, and to furnish all labor for field maintenance and building upkeep except for the airline terminal. Acme paid for the airport lights and $10 a month towards hangar illumination—Kneir paid for any overage.

Between the 1932 election and the inauguration of President Franklin D. Roosevelt the following March, a second wave of depression and panic hit the country. More banks closed, concerns that had survived the debacle of 1929 found themselves in bankruptcy, and Arizona, which claimed the three C's (cattle, copper and cotton) as its business backbone, was in worse condition than many other sections of the country. The heavily mortgaged ranches were taken over by the banks or were forced to shut down. Mines and smelters closed, throwing additional unemployed workers into an over-crowded labor pool. Liquidation was an empty word—no one had the money to buy even a bargain. Carl Knier's old friends and customers vanished, leaving him at Sky Harbor with his little Monoprep, three or four students, and five or six airplanes to watch over. Transients averaged two or three a week.

A first sight of Sky Harbor (often referred to as "the farm") in May 1933 inspired neither confidence nor admiration. The pavement and streetcars on Washington Street ended at 16th Street, and Airline Way degenerated to a rough trail at the entrance to the terminal. Eastward it petered out into a maze of chuckholes and tire tracks. Some of the cottonwoods had died from lack of water; others were near death, and not a blade of grass relieved the barren expanse. No airplanes were flying, but in the neat hangar five or six rested in lonely elegance.

There was a new operator at Sky Harbor during the spring of 1933. Paul Odneal bought an almost new J6-5 Spartan and opened Copperclad Airways. He gave Carl Knier some competition, but as the Spartan rented for $12 an hour solo or dual, while Knier's Monoprep rented for half that price, Odneal was at some disadvantage. For an Arizona trainer the Spartan was unusually well equipped, having a compass, air speed indicator, rate of climb and turn and bank instruments, a clock with a sweep-second hand, and navigation and panel lights. In the manner of flight instruction during the early 1930s, the turn and bank, rate of climb and airspeed were carefully covered with tape—they were not to be trusted, and novices were warned to place no confidence in these treacherous gauges. Hours (or possibly several years) later the then experienced pilot would be taught to fly all over again on instruments, with the promise that now these formerly unreliable indicators could safely take him through the worst weather.

Economic conditions improved, and by 1934 there were sometimes two or three students shooting the interminable "touch-and-goes." Both Knier and Odneal decided that more than two students in the pattern constituted "saturation" and the third trainee was ordered to go to the "practice area," which was actually any location away from the field. Neither owner wanted a mid-air collision.

A small flying club was organized, mostly consisting of Odneal's students, and then expanded to include anyone at Sky Harbor with a student permit or higher rank. This original Phoenix Flying Club, later named the Phoenix Aviation Club, Incorporated, eventually had more than 100 members from all over the state and continued until it was disbanded shortly after the beginning of World War II.

Acme Investment Company had purchased Sky Harbor as an investment, and its operation of the premises was an exercise in applied economy. Every Monday morning an accountant arrived to collect the accrued money and balance the books. He also sadly listened to requests for such necessities as washroom supplies, paint for the peeling hangar, parts for the decrepit Nash Quad truck which pulled the field drag, a new hangar roof, and other required services or supplies. He was able to offer little assistance. Acme was badgering the city to buy the facility, but the municipality was reluctant. The company's veiled threats about plowing the airfield up and farming it fell on deaf ears.

Airline pilots and transients made disparaging remarks about any municipality which would tolerate such a shoddy facility. Actually, Sky Harbor was an average airport for a community of Phoenix's size and was better than many.

The hot, Depression summers seemed to wear on forever. Each afternoon the west hangar doors were closed to within a few inches, the east doors opened, and three hoses trickled water on the concrete floor. With even a tiny westerly breeze this generated a cooling system of sorts, and customers and friends with unrefrigerated offices downtown spent the scalding afternoons swapping stories in chairs near the east doors. It was known as the "coolest un-air-cooled spot in town." The real reason for the seeping hoses (to provide humidity for the "wooden-winged" airplanes) was overlooked.

On many afternoons, even during the normally busy winter season, there was nothing to do. The line boys painted a badminton court near the east end of the hangar floor, and by shifting only one or two ships enjoyed some fine games. Winslow, with a still larger hangar and no permanent tenants, had a full-sized indoor tennis court—one-upmanship on Sky Harbor and cause for some bragging.

Afternoons the high cumuli puffed and swelled around the valley, and by mid- or late afternoon a great golden cloud of dust might roar over the city, making driving or flying impossible. Visibility would be reduced to zero, and the wind blew in oven-hot gusts. By three o'clock all ships were safely stored inside the hangar. The wooden north wall was false, to permit a further addition, and it was affected by pressure changes. it huffed, puffed, and swayed during these outbreaks and the five or six stored aircraft were placed in the middle or against the south brick wall as a precaution. Often these dusters were followed by a driving rain which reduced the entire field and all its dirt access roads to a sticky morass. Cars sank in mudholes and occasionally an unfortunate pilot became mired on the field if he strayed from the hardpan in the center. The sporadically cooperative Quad could extract the smaller craft from such difficulties, but an airliner was beyond its capabilities. When one of these became stuck, the Quad, the American Airlines pickup, and any other available vehicles flocked to the stranded Douglas with ropes, shovels, crowbars and large boards. Disgusted pilots and a frustrated line crew wondered what ailed Phoenix for offering such a miserable facility.

Occasionally, excitement came from other quarters. Washington delighted in surprises—amendments to the Air Traffic Rules. The regional CAA offices were notified, and when these offices found time, they forwarded rules to field inspectors and occasionally to a few of the better known operators.

One new amendment became effective December 1, 1931. It required counterclockwise (left-hand) turns around landing fields. When local conditions prevented this, special markings were to be displayed; for example, a letter "R" in the field's center was to be illuminated if the airport had lights. Minimum flight altitude over open country was set at 500 feet; over assemblies of people and settled communities, 1,000 feet or safe gliding distance to open country in case of engine failure.

On January 1, 1934, the government issued Bulletin No. 7, a controversial piece of literature that was both admired and hated by General Aviation pilots. It clarified the old regulations, added some new ones, and stipulated that written tests were to be given to all new trainee applicants. Pilots were now to be classified as either commercial or private. The commercial category was further broken down into commercials, limited commercials, and industrials, with weight and type classifications, such as single or multi-engine and land or sea. Air transport pilot ratings had been in effect since 1932; now instrument rating standards were added to these.

A shocking new rule in Bulletin Number 7 was that there would be no acrobatics over settled areas, and that when a pilot was performing these maneuvers he had to wear a parachute, as did any other occupant. Further, no acrobatics with paid passengers were permitted, and all these evolutions had to be concluded at or above 1,500 feet from the ground. The new regulations contained one bright spot: the unlicensed pleasure pilots were still at liberty, providing their aircraft were registered and properly marked with identifying numbers. They could not carry mail, engage in any interstate commercial activities, or use federal facilities, but there were few of the latter in Arizona.

The real blow in the thirty-six page bulletin was to the pride and pocketbooks of the owners of licensed aircraft. Many had flown and maintained their ships for years with little professional help and had achieved a reasonable safety record. They could see no reason for flying 100 miles so that some inspector could look over their pride and joy. Furthermore, there were stories circulating about these young, inexperienced, officious government employees who "cut holes in the fabric and found all manner of imaginary ailments." An inspector might even criticize some of the owners' improvements, such as rigging changes or the installation of a larger (or smaller) engine. They were rumored to have disapproved spar splices, and one raised a loud roar about a push rod that had been installed following a forced landing at Wittmann. The rod, rescued from an old car engine, was modified and put in place by the garage owner and the pilot. A reliable piece of merchandise, it had functioned perfectly for over 100 hours, so why all the fuss even though the part was not "approved" and therefore illegal?

Some owners simply washed their hands of regulations and moved their ships to smaller outlying fields where they continued to operate as they saw fit. They did not engage in commercial flying, interstate commerce, or use any federal facilities. The new regulations did not apply, and they further disclaimed any state authority. Gradually age, poor maintenance, the owners' changed interests, and neglect eliminated these planes. They were disassembled and stored in barns, where they waited, forgotten, for some twenty or more years, to be ferreted out later by antique enthusiasts who would rebuild them properly and fly them with pride.

It was now a violation not to make proper reports, to equip a plane with a type of engine or propeller not specified in its license, or to remodel either engine or aircraft structure and fly same without it first being rated as airworthy by the Secretary of Commerce. Operating with passengers in excess of the authorized number was forbidden, as was flying in excess of authorized load. Also, general aviation pilots had their first introduction to the mysteries of weight and balance. Everyone knew that a horse or a vehicle loaded improperly or too heavily did not get along well, and the same rule applied to airplanes. The earlier procedure had been to eyeball the people and baggage, put them where they would fit, with some consideration for weight distribution, and then take off. Now all these items had to be mathematically figured, put in their proper places, and sometimes something had to be left behind. A pilot's judgment was no longer trusted.

The itinerant inspectors' arrival dates were posted on the airport bulletin boards at Phoenix and Tucson as soon as they were received. The days were carefully noted by the acrobatic set so they could make decorous arrivals at both fields. The usual screaming dives, slow rolls, and wild slips were omitted.

License applicants would be out early, spruced up (some even wore ties), and provided with parachutes, even though they were likely to be uncertain of the proper method of donning them. The runways would be freshly graded, hangars and offices carefully swept. After these preparations both Davis-Monthan and Sky Harbor appeared to be model operations, but the inspectors were not fooled. They knew that the minute they left conditions would regress to their normal state, but they hoped that the regression would be slowed somewhat by the impact of their visit.

Since the almost total collapse of general aviation in Arizona in the Depression, the itinerant inspectors had seldom visited the state. The major operators, Walter Douglas and Charlie Mayse in Tucson, and Carl Knier and Paul Odneal in Phoenix, controlled their students and renters to some extent, but not the private owners. These pilots had good intentions but were still constant violators of all regulations. Then there was the troublesome unlicensed group. They buzzed tall buildings which made ideal points for loops, and attempted slow rolls. They buzzed farmhouses, hazed livestock and rustled trees near friends' houses. All experienced birdmen considered it their privilege to do snap or slow rolls on the downwind leg and to have dogfights over the airport. American Airlines complained, as did irate citizens, including the manager of the Phoenix Country Club. He did not appreciate pilots (these included some club members), who landed on the 18th fairway, fetching up almost on the green and occasionally just missing the clubhouse terrace. There were unconfirmed stories of a plane missing the swimming pool by about three feet. Arizona, and particularly Phoenix, was getting a very bad reputation. Something had to be done.

Word came that an inspector would be sent over from Los Angeles. A few days later Jimmy Payton neatly landed his Fleet with the Department of Commerce insignia on its fuselage at Sky Harbor. His two-month tenure was marred by only one incident. A couple of men in a decrepit Jenny landed at an outlying strip and drove to Sky Harbor to request a waiver for an air show, billed as "the only one of its kind in the world." They proposed to bulldog a steer with one of the team doing the flying and his intrepid partner hanging from the undercarriage. Payton wanted no part of the hare-brained scheme and refused the waiver. The two pilots were verbally abusive and said they would put on the act anyway, waiver or not. The Jenny and its operators were unlicensed, and Payton lacked jurisdiction. Following this meeting, the owners contracted for more advertising, sold tickets and prepared for the show, meanwhile announcing around town that the inspector could not stop them as he did not fly well enough to land his Fleet at the fairgrounds and hinder their act as threatened.

On the appointed morning Jimmy Payton took off for the fairgrounds, landed, and parked his Fleet so that the infield was blocked. The grandstand was crowded, Jenny came fluttering overhead, circled, and disappeared to the north. The steer did not make an appearance. A disappointed audience drifted away after Payton announced there would be no show, giving the reasons for his decision.

A Third Municipal Airport for Phoenix

Early in 1935, the Phoenix government announced that it was purchasing Sky Harbor. The city would now have a real municipal airport. The in-limbo stepchild owned and operated the Acme Investment Company and leased to Maricopa County was to be transformed into a respectable, permanent facility.

On June 13 the county lease on Sky Harbor was cancelled, and on July 18 Ordinance #2082, approved by the City Commission, was formally signed by Major Joseph S. Jenckes; a warranty deed was accepted from Acme Investment Company which legally, under a declared emergency, turned Sky Habor into a municipal airport for $35,300 cash.

All agreed that Carl Knier should continue to manage Sky Harbor, and terms were set forth for the three year contract. Today they appear harsh and unrealistic, but in 1935 they were deemed better than those many airport managers lived with. The city agreed to furnish water, local telephone service, electricity for the hangar and office not to exceed $10 a month, all field lights, a compressor, fire extinguishers, lighting fixtures, a tractor, grader and drag, and labor for all major improvements. It reserved the right to contract with, and sell fuel to, all scheduled airlines. Knier was responsible for all electricity overage, and all long distance calls. He was to furnish labor for routine maintenance and to purchase all fuel and oil for his own use and retail sales. He was to pay the city $100 a month for hangar rental plus 2¢ per gallon for all gasoline sold. In turn, he kept all profits on oil and the surplus on fuel plus hangar rentals and tie-down fees. He furnished adequate line service personnel and a watchman, was charged with enforcing the CAA regulations, and had the privilege of operating his own flying business as long as it did not conflict with management of the airport.

Word came from Los Angeles that a resident inspector would be based in Phoenix to service Region 9. This was considered a fair warning to all violators to mend their ways. A few weeks later a black and orange Kinner Playboy with Department of Commerce markings circled the field. The Playboy was a low wing, two-place cabin craft, beautifully faired, with a spatted landing gear which cleared the ground by approximately two inches. It appeared to be a cross between a very noisy, furious beetle, an equally angry bird with its legs extended, and a pursuit plane with an enclosed cockpit. The new inspector's landing was excellent, but his roll-out was embarrassing. A metal spat caught one of Sky Harbor's numerous rocks, resulting in a slow 360° ground loop. No damage was done, but taxiing was impossible until the rock was removed. It was a frustrating and certainly unimpressive arrival for Edward V. Pettis, Arizona's first resident CAA representative.

Pettis' arrival and the city's acquisition of Sky Harbor elevated the community's aeronautical prestige. The mayor and the city were congratulated for their foresight and wisdom by the postal authorities and the press. Sky Harbor was cleaned up and elaborate plans made for its formal dedication in November. A chain link fence between American Airlines' terminal and the hangar apron went up. This would keep all unauthorized cars from the runway.

Dedication Day, November 11, 1935, was an outstanding success, and the new airport ownership, a rising economy, and the word that federal aid for Sky Harbor would soon be received gave aviation still another boost. A few more ships berthed in the hangar. Inspector Pettis, against some opposition, began to bring order to the facility. More students began taking flying lessons though a school still might be one pilot with one aircraft.

The year 1936 promised to be a good one for Arizona aviation, but the high hopes were tragically dashed. That year four crashes led to fatalities, one of them involving a group of well known Phoenix businessmen and flight school operator Paul Odneal. The headlines following this accident were lurid. Four dead, four wrenching funerals — the combination had a stunning effect on all Arizona flying. Student business ceased. American Airlines reported that their boardings fell sharply, and numerous agitated wives argued for the sale of family airplanes.

In February, 1937, the Phoenix City Council guaranteed $10,000 to secure a $100,000 Works Progress Administration loan to oil Sky Harbor. In April, *Aviation* reported that the state had 106 pilots. Of these, 32 were transport, 6 limited commercial (the industrial class had been discontinued), 64 held private tickets and 4 had amateur licenses. Arizona was listed as having 44 airports, with Winslow, Yuma, Phoenix, Tucson, Nogales and Douglas receiving WPA assistance for improvements.

After the shock of the 1936 accidents had dissipated, student and transient business increased and occasionally a charter flight broke the monotony. American Airlines even complained about the increased traffic. The company's officials wanted the pesky students to go elsewhere to practice their figure 8's and stop using the nearby Wilson School and the Sky Harbor hangar for pylons. Following these complaints everyone practicing flight maneuvers was ordered to an open area south of the Salt River, and word went out in no uncertain terms that no one was to interfere with the airlines. They were to have the right of way over all students and private pilots regardless of what the regulations stated.

On January 7, 1938, the Arizona Corporation Commission cracked down on unlicensed pilots and their aircraft, specifically ruling that no individual, company, or corporation could engage in the aerial transportation of persons or property for hire or reward, including sightseeing and student instruction, without first registering with the Commission and receiving a permit issued by that body to conduct such activities. Furthermore, no permits would be granted to unofficial operators unless their airplanes had a valid airworthiness certificate from the federal Bureau of Air Commerce. There was no mention of pleasure or business flying or required pilot certificates. The ruling theoretically grounded the outlaws and their ships but its effects were minimal. Any Bureau of Commerce Flight Inspector had the authority to ground unlicensed aircraft, as did any agent of the Commission. The ACC was somewhat short of agents, and as Inspector Pettis had departed, Arizona was without federal representation. No visiting inspector would have had the time or knowledge to ferret out the many small, scattered fields and the miscreants simply holed up for a few months, avoiding Sky Harbor, Tucson Municipal, or any airport where the conspicuously marked orange and black CAA visiting aircraft would park.

More Improvements for Sky Harbor

Newspaper editorials, aviation-slanted or otherwise, and politicians all agreed that the Depression was over. Aeronautical activity almost equaled the boom times of 1928 and 1929; and with additional federal aid available, the city reassessed Sky Harbor. It did not meet the standards required of a metropolitan airport. Each fiscal year since 1935, Carl Knier had, as required, submitted a budget, and each year the City Auditor had slashed his request, leaving the airport chronically short of supplies.

The fiscal pain inflicted by the City was alleviated somewhat by the increasing hangar and tie-down fees, by more air carrier schedules, and by soaring fuel and oil sales. More company aircraft were stopping. These were mostly four- or five-place cabin jobs—Stinsons, Wacos, a few Howards and the various oil company Lockheed 10s and 12s. They drank up gallons of gas and considerable oil. All had what were then called "full panels," indicating a directional gyro and horizon along with a primary group; some had two radios and a few boasted one of the new radio direction indicators with a left-right needle. They could be considered the parent of the later ADFs and their sophisticated progeny. These conveniences were developed for the military and air carriers and, like other avionic goodies, were at first too heavy and expensive for smaller general aviation ships. However, in a remarkably short period of time they were scaled down in both weight and cost, and by the 1950s many two-place trainers were better equipped than the airliners of the 1930s.

There were no more badminton games. The hangar was too crowded and no one had time for such foolishness.

A New Law With Teeth

On June 23, 1938, the controversial Civil Aeronautics Act was signed into law, to become effective August 22 of that year. The act created a five member Civil Aeronautics Authority and a three member Air Safety Board. Airports were to be included in the federal airway system. This meant that any facility accepting federal airport aid was off limits to unlicensed airmen and aircraft.

Arizona was shifted to the 6th region, headquartered in Los Angeles, and in September a new inspector, Carroll Doak, flew into Phoenix. The local pilots thought that someone should feel out the new man, and a couple of experimenters decided a good dogfight over the airport would be appropriate. Doak let them know in a rather unpleasant tone that this time they were forgiven but subsequent offenses would result in a violation, a stiff fine, and possible confiscation of their licenses. From now on all pilots were to fly right or stay on the ground.

The $7 million airways modernization begun in July 1937, was finished, and now the country had 25,500 miles of federal airways, complete with modern navigational aids. The national airport system, however, was a mess, as the government had insufficient funds to cope with aviation's growth. Arizona had seven good airports—Kingman and Winslow along Green 4; and in the south-central section Yuma, Phoenix, Prescott, Tucson and Douglas. All would have been classified as air carrier if such a category had then been established. The CAA emergency (now known as intermediate) fields were of doubtful value as they were usually remote and rough. All were almost too small for the new transports. Many smaller communities had abandoned their airports during the Depression. These had literally gone to seed or back to the cattle and deer, and it was wise to telephone before planning to use any of them.

With the slight improvement in the economic situation, many of the smaller communities started airport upgradings on their own. Usually this meant dragging the field, mending fences, and in a few instances installing a gas pump. Sometimes it also included building a small hangar if a local owner based his ship there. Included in this informal program were Gila Bend, St. Johns, Holbrook, Flagstaff, Globe-Midland, Ajo, Buckeye, and Bisbee. Tucson was adequately supplied with Davis-Monthan which was still "joint use," the new municipal field, and Walter Douglas's excellent Gilpin Airport, which was under construction.

During 1939 Sky Harbor Air Service applied for an approved flight school. With approval would come lowered insurance rates, which were needed because of the growing number of aircraft on the line. Also the designation was a prerequisite to get a contract for the new Civilian Pilot Training Program which Congress would pass within the year. Inspector Doak said a school manual had to be submitted, but neither he nor anyone else knew what was required. However, Walter Douglas in Tucson had recently gotten approval — the first approved Arizona flying school since Scenic Airways' demise — and generously lent his manual. It was copied, sent off to Washington, and likewise approved. A half year or so later, when Southwest Airways Incorporated opened its Civilian Pilot Training Program, Sky Harbor lent Southwest its manual to be copied. The offering came sailing back from Washington with a curt note that it was "unacceptable." The tome was slightly changed, resubmitted, and found satisfactory. Now Arizona had three approved flight schools. During the next two years many more would be added to the list, all with training manuals slavishly copied from either Douglas' or Sky Harbor's and happily accepted by Washington.

THE FIRST AERIAL BROADCAST IN ARIZONA

During the 1930s a new type of barnstormer appeared. The behemoths of the mid-1920s: the Tri-Motor Fords, Fokkers, and Boeings, made obsolete by the efficient DC-2s and 3s, were snapped up by Latin American lines, by mining companies, a few specialized local carriers, and the new breed of barnstormers. The latter employed a manager or advance man who traveled by car, arriving well ahead of the ship and making arrangements for advertising, finances, and accommodations with the local airport managers and the CAA. Such an outfit visited Phoenix in 1938 and during its stay carried hundreds of passengers.

Perhaps inspired by the success of this visiting barnstormer, Robert A. "Bob" Gosnell hit upon a novel advertising idea for the restaurant he was about to open in Phoenix. Why not sponsor a live broadcast from an airplane over the city? It would be a first for Phoenix, and it just so happened that there was a suitable and unusual antique aircraft in town—George Prescott's Stinson. Arrangements were made with KTAR Radio, which, sniffing publicity, may have offered the air time at a reduced price. Andy Anderson would be the technician in charge with Howard Pyle, Arizona's favorite announcer, on the microphone. To eliminate undesirable noise (the Stinsons were soundproofed to some extent) the program would be transmitted from the ship to the station by shortwave, and from there rebroadcast to the public on the regular channel.

On the morning of the big event, a large crowd assembled around the ship. Some of the Stinson's seats were removed. No one was sure what a piano which was to be taken aboard weighed, but after it was carefully examined the consensus was that there was too much weight for the floor. Some stout planks were brought up and positioned, again by eyeball, in the correct spot to properly balance the aircraft, and the little instrument was maneuvered into place. Cables were strung, the mike tested and, for additional noise suppression, placed inside the piano. The pilot crawled in and everything was ready.

Francis Beck, Gosnell's fine piano player, was unhappily viewing the nine-year-old, fabric-covered Stinson. Beck had never been in an airplane and had no desire to go up in this one. His reluctance was further compounded by a roaring hangover and a splitting headache. The Stinson's cabin with half its seats removed, the piano perched on the planks, the wires and cables strung along the floor, did nothing to quiet his jangling nerves.

The radio technician and his helpers were ready. Gosnell shoved Beck on board, climbed in after him, and closed the door. Pilot Charlie Hirst started the engines and the Stinson waddled westward to takeoff position. In minutes it was winging over town, broadcasting the first live airborne musical program to thousands of Arizona listeners.

At the piano, Beck trembled and sweated but bravely continued to bang on the instrument as though his dexterity alone held the Stinson aloft. Pyle in the KTAR studio happily relayed the music, his advertising pitch, and more music. On the airplane one of the wooden planks holding the piano cracked. A terrified Beck continued playing. Charlie was uneasy about the piano's weight. Beck, further unnerved by the creaking floor, played louder.

Now the excitement began in earnest. A big-footed radio assistant tripped over a wire, and midpoint in the broadcast the Stinson went off the air. The plane continued to circle over town and Beck played on, unaware of the technical difficulties. All on board were sure that the act was a huge success and Gosnell beamed brightly.

Meanwhile, phones were ringing all over the valley. The switchboards at the police station, the sheriff's office, and KTAR were jammed. Listeners were certain the big airliner had crashed in the middle of the broadcast, and wanted to know where its smoking ruins were located. Sky Harbor's phones jangled too. No one there knew what had happened, but the airport reported that the Stinson was a half-mile out on final approach and that everything looked normal.

Gosnell was heartbroken when he learned the news. He believed his last advertising dollars had been wasted and that the opening night of the restaurant would be a failure. He was dead wrong. Many congratulated him for the clever and exciting act, and opening night was an unqualified success.

PRELUDE TO WAR

The delayed Civilian Pilot Training Program started in the late fall of 1939 and thirty new trainees arrived at Sky Harbor. Germany invaded Poland; Great Britain and France retaliated by declaring war on Germany, and with each belligerent action more students wanted to learn to fly. Most were sure the United States would be at war soon, and flying was more appealing than the infantry. Sky Harbor rapidly became the busiest airport in Arizona.

On May 16, 1940, the Selective Service Act passed, and when this legislation was digested there was another rush of students, more urgent than their predecessors.

Twenty-eight men and two women graduated from the first Phoenix CPTP class, and Sky Harbor Air Service was allotted forty-five trainees for the next group. More instructors had to be hired, and when told to expect a larger student quota for the following class, Knier put his foot down. According to all previous directives, operators had been told to keep their non-CPTP business. The school was up to its viable capacity and he had obligations to non-government trainees and charter customers. Both office and hangar space were crowded and the airport was at a saturation stage now.

The government's WPA airport program accelerated to a pace that could not have been imagined a few years earlier. In the west and northward from El Paso to the Canadian border, old fields were enlarged and improved, and communities formerly harboring messy, marginal dirt strips sported lovely new paved facilities. Already fine airports were treated to longer runways and improved taxiways and ramps. A base was built at Alamagordo; the tiny airport at Hot Springs, New Mexico, was improved, as were fields at Albuquerque, Santa Fe, Pueblo, Colorado Springs, Denver, Cheyenne and on north to Canada. Often new air bases supplemented municipal airports, as was the case at Farmington, Alamosa, Grand Junction and Montrose, to mention a few. Arizona general aviation pilots were delighted. Now they could fly just about anywhere in the southwest and be assured of a good airport and reliable service.

Word went out that this was the nation's "second line of defense" against any attacks from the Pacific. In Arizona, TWA's
Winslow Airport received a new triangular runway and the Ferry
Command moved in to set up a refueling facility. Prescott and
Nogales had their lumpy grass runways changed to smooth pavement, and at Willcox the smooth dirt field bordering the town's west
edge was ignored and a large new paved triangle built about four
miles west of the community.

Phoenix's expansion plans were duly approved in Washington
and with generous amounts of WPA money Sky Harbor's big building program commenced. Simultaneously the city made a contract
with the Army on a joint lease and the military erected temporary
buildings for the Ferry Command personnel who would remain
until they moved to Coolidge in 1944. Sky Harbor got a control
tower.

Beginning December 1, 1941, all United States pilots and aircraft were required to be federally certified. This was the end of
unlicensed ships in Arizona and several other states that, because of
faulty regulatory legislation or lack of enforceable laws, had allowed
them to continue operations locally if they remained within their
state or did not enter a federal airway system. Following a fourteen-
year struggle, Arizona and the nation had effective aerial laws and
reasonable order.

Sundays were usually relaxed days at Sky Harbor. The CPTP
trainees did not fly unless they were behind schedule, and the bulk
of the activity consisted of rental to students building up their time,
to those already certified who took friends for short hops, or to the
usual passenger-carriers. In mid-morning of Sunday, December 7,
1941, the local Associated Press representative raced into the Sky
Harbor office and announced that the Japanese had bombed Pearl
Harbor. The radio was turned on and the tragic messages poured in.
Pilots and non-pilots jammed the office, remained for a while, then
hurried home.

Early the next morning government directives showered in. All
civilian pilots were grounded until they could establish evidences of
citizenship—meaning birth certificates. Later, acceptable substi-
tutes for these documents would be permitted. On December 10, Air
Defense Identification Zones (ADIZ's) were established, protecting
American boundaries for varying distances up to 150 miles inland.
No flights were allowed in these areas without a flight plan, and
these were denied to civilians except in cases of emergency. All
aircraft owners and operators with schools in the ADIZ's, those with
military contracts and CTP programs were advised to make arrangements to move inland. In Phoenix, general aviation pilots and
CPTP trainees were grounded for only a day or so, long enough for
Doak to receive the proper forms and get the sheriff's people to the

field to fingerprint everyone who worked at any airport, from the now required gate guards to those holding airmen's certificates.

An Executive Order of December 13 authorized the Secretary of Commerce to "exercise his control and jurisdiction over civil aviation in accordance with requirements for the successful prosecution of the war as may be required by the Secretary of War."

Directives fluttered like snowflakes in a blizzard. All operative airports were required to have 24-hour guards. All civilian aircraft in an ADIZ had to prepare to vacate the zone or be made inoperative and hangared. All civilian airplanes outside an ADIZ must be kept under a 24-hour guard or likewise made inoperative. This order caused some confusion. A few owners in the smaller cities merely removed the propeller. Doak did not believe this fulfilled the law's intent and suggested removing one or more wings. Aircraft parked or left at an unguarded facility had to have a local sheriff or other law enforcement officer with them at all times. Air carriers were required to have all window shades drawn when flying near military installations or in an ADIZ. The pilots at Luke were ordered to fly escort with the schedules; this caused considerable consternation among the passengers. The practice was soon abandoned and the military pilots turned their attention to the general aviation ships by flying around them to look the situation over.

In Arizona, the 4th Interceptor Command and Luke Air Base ruled the skies.

GREEN 5 CONTINUED

From Phoenix, the eastbound pilot picked up Green 5 at Casa Grande, flew southeast to Tucson and on via Benson and Douglas to New Mexico and the east (later, as airplane range increased, pilots bypassed Douglas and flew a more direct route by way of Cochise and Rodeo).

In the late 1920s and early 1930s the towns in the Phoenix-Tucson corridor stuck out like the proverbial sore thumb. Small circles of bright green crops surrounded each settlement; from the air the dun-colored desert appeared to be constantly encroaching on the irrigated fields. The reverse was actually happening, and the desert shrank as the cultivated areas expanded.

The local airport building program followed these fine lush farms almost to Tucson and extended east to Queen Creek and west to Casa Grande. Chandler, Casa Grande, and Florence all dedicated small municipal airports during 1928 and 1929. Following the Depression, some closed. In 1939 and 1940 the military, attracted by southern Arizona's excellent flying weather, built Williams and Luke Air Bases, Marana for a basic training field, and the present Coolidge-Florence Municipal as an auxiliary for Williams. The generous scattering of other auxiliaries also stretched to near

Tucson. With peace came a second explosion of airports. Both Chandler and Coolidge built smooth strips; later, with state and Federal government aid, these were paved, lighted, and equipped with Unicoms.*

The 1968 *AOPA Airport Directory* listed over twenty private or quasi-private strips in this corridor built by ranchers, aerial applicators, and a few by hopeful airpark developers. Added to this were municipal airports and military satellite fields, some active, others abandoned. The State Aeronautical Chart for the same year, which depicts airports with blue circles, bore more resemblance to a modernistic painting of grape bunches than to a navigation aid. To quote a livid and exasperated visitor who was trying to locate a farmer friend's strip in the region, "the whole country is paved with airports."

A NEW TUCSON MUNICIPAL AIRPORT

Both 1938 and 1939 were confusing years for the city of Tucson and its flight operators. Everyone realized the days of Davis-Monthan as a joint use facility were numbered. Tucson started negotiation for property for a new municipal field and in 1940 completed arrangements for the purchase of 4,000 acres two miles south of the old Mayse Field. Of this, 2,500 acres would be reserved for the new facility and the balance sold or leased for industrial development.

On September 11, 1941, a city resolution assured the government of land titles for further expansion of the new Tucson Municipal. The CAA planned to spend $223,000 on it, principally for runway extensions. In return, the city agreed to maintain the field, protect all approaches, and assume liability for defending any damage suits. A few service structures went up; from appearances, most were of the ten year life expectancy type that flourished during those uncertain times.

Walter Douglas was awarded thirty students and Hudgins Air Service ten when the Civilian Pilot Training Program began in 1939. Both schools trained these first groups at Davis-Monthan and then moved to Douglas' new Gilpin Airport. Hudgins again moved, this time to the new Municipal for one more allotment of ten.

The gigantic new expansion program for Davis-Monthan was announced in the *Air Service News Letter* of November 1, 1940. Total cost would be $1,386,212. A large housing development was erected

---

*Unicom is a radio advisory frequency reserved for conversations between aircraft and aircraft ground stations not on the regular airways circuit. Airports not having a control tower often have a Unicom and the communications are handled by an airport official, not a federal employee.

and the WPA paved all access roads and extended the runways in stages, strengthening the latter to accept the larger, heavier military aircraft. To civilians the three long ribbons of black asphalt were impressive, but the longest was a frightening sight to pilots accustomed to 3,000 feet or less. Its 8,000 feet of shining pavement stretched to the horizon.

When the new Municipal was barely completed, Davis-Monthan became an all-military field except for American Airlines and those having prior permission or an emergency. By 1941 all three airports were considered crowded, and traffic continued to increase. Gradually some of the general aviation aircraft—whose pilots dreaded mixing with the students training at Gilpin, the larger twins, and pilots with business on the south side of the city—shifted to Municipal. No one complained about lack of patronage.

DOUGLAS INTERNATIONAL BECOMES DOUGLAS MUNICIPAL

The aviation boom of the late 1930s rubbed off on southern Arizona and extended into northern Sonora. Charlie Mayse's business at Douglas International increased and the field was always busy. The transient trade lessened but was supplemented by local students and sales in Arizona and Sonora.

American Airlines pilots on the Tucson-Douglas milk run complained about the Douglas field conditions. The smelter smoke caused poor visibility at times, there was no instrument approach, the runways were too short and the approaches were poor, the field was overcrowded. This was doubtless due to Mayse's CPT Program which started in early 1940. The sky was full of small Taylorcrafts darting about.

Douglas, like many other communities, learned that a completed airport is an obsolete airport—or a building permit for future expansion. This was impossible at Douglas International, as growth was blocked on all four sides by the Mexican border, the city, "D" Mountain, and the highway. During 1941, with the sponsorship of both the city and Cochise County, the site of the present Bisbee-Douglas International Airport was chosen. Work started on this new commercial field in February 1942, when the WPA built two 3,000 foot runways. The Army moved in, acquired additional property, and completed a huge training base with barracks, a hospital, the usual complement of buildings, and several auxiliary fields.

With the introduction of the Visual Omni Ranges (VOR's) and the decommissioning of the low frequency radio stations, Green 5, like its gaily colored counterparts, disappeared and was replaced by Victor 16 (V16) which almost followed its predecessor route from Tucson to El Paso. A new airway, V66, which traverses a very ancient trail, starts at San Diego, turns southeast at Gila Bend, passes near Maricopa Wells, and continues to Tucson and thence to Douglas. Here it bears northeast to join V16 at Animas and continues to El Paso del Norte.

Douglas Municipal has never been closed. Its international designation was lost, and it became Douglas Municipal when American Airlines moved to the new larger field after the military training programs closed. In January 1976, Douglas Municipal was entered into the National Register of Historic Places, the official schedule of the nation's cultural property that is considered worthy of preservation and continued use. It is the first Arizona airport so honored.

IMPROVED CONNECTIONS

By the mid-1940s, Arizona was criss-crossed by a network of federally funded and operated airways. These important aerial highways connected many of the state's cities and towns and linked them with other regions of the country.

Because of their geographic location, other Arizona communities were not directly affected by the government airways. This did not mean that they were devoid of aerial activity, only that their aeronautical development followed a somewhat different pattern. The powerful influence of the army and the airlines was felt less strongly in these towns; consequently, the push for aviation came from within, from people interested in flying as sport or as an aid to local business.

Aviation growth in these towns, while not as dynamic as in some more strategically located communities, was just as important. It helped draw together areas of the state separated by distance and geographical barriers, and led to the development of a balanced, state-wide transportation network.

Parker

Even before Arizona could boast of a dozen men capable of managing a flying machine, the state could brag about the only woman in the United States licensed to operate a ferry boat. She captained the "Nellie T," often referred to as the "Arizona Navy," which hauled people, horses, and cars across the Colorado between Parker and Earp, California.

Nellie Trent was about five years old when her family migrated to Arizona. She grew up in the Phoenix area, taught school there, and married Joe Bush in 1912. Joe had an itch to go pioneering, and three years later Nellie reluctantly accompanied him to Parker, where they bought an interest in the ferry. It was the start of a full and successful life for both. Considering that she did not want to pioneer and had never heard of the Women's Lib movement, Nellie chalked up an impressive record of firsts for her sex in the state.

In 1926, a barnstormer landed on Parker's main street with an ailing engine. He spent the following three weeks overhauling the OX5 and working on the Jenny that carried it. Nellie got ideas about owning an airplane, but at the moment she was occupied with other duties. The Bushes had started an electric light and ice plant, a water company, and had opened a drugstore. Nellie also ran the ferry back and forth across the Colorado, took care of their young son, Joe Jr., and in her spare time studied law and served as Parker's justice of the peace. Now and then "Fat" Dunnegan flew up from Blythe in his OX5 Lincoln Page to take the Indians and any other paying passengers for rides. This kept Nellie's interest in owning an airplane alive.

Nellie decided in 1928 that she and her husband really needed a ship and went to the coast for flying lessons. Her instructor was Lee Williams, the race flyer, and the two families became good friends. Lee flew to Parker frequently on weekends so Joe and Nellie could continue their flight training. Nellie also took some lessons from G & G Airlines in Tucson when she had the opportunity. Building the Parker hotel may have delayed the airplane purchase, or it may have been Nellie's other activities. She was appointed U. S. Commissioner, was the second woman to serve in the Arizona House of Representatives, and then was elected to the Arizona Senate, the first woman to hold this position.

During the eary 1930s, Nellie was instrumental in acquiring land for Parker Municipal Field. She and her husband then bought a new Waco, earned their licenses, and used the plane to commute to Phoenix and Tucson. They joined the Phoenix Flying Club and flew in for meetings when the trips could be combined with business activities. On November 3, 1935, they extended an invitation to the club to be their guests for the formal dedication of the Parker Airport.

Another well-known Arizona pilot who played a key role in Parker's aeronautical development was Cliff Davis. He learned to fly during the 1920s in Prescott, where he supported himself by taking charter flights, hauling local passengers on weekends, and occasionally giving lessons until the dam construction began at Parker. Both the Parker field and the one at Cross Roads were adequate for his plane, and he began concentrating his activities there. In 1936, he moved to Parker permanently. There were numerous emergency flights for parts, personnel transportation, and for ambulance cases to Riverside, California. Cliff was always ready and would be at either airport in a matter of minutes. Joe Bush also felt more comfortable when Cliff rode with Nellie on her numerous trips. It was not that Joe doubted her competence, but in those days it was important to know how to repair a balky engine, and Cliff was an able mechanic as well as excellent pilot. With Nellie, Cliff was responsible for early improvements on the Parker field. When the dam was completed his charter business ceased, so he started flight schools at both Blythe and Parker. When the Civilian Pilot Training Program started, Cliff moved to Phoenix to take the new tests for Rated Flight Instructor status. He then went to work for Southwest Airways on its primary program, and a year later was chief pilot for its Sky Harbor program, which by that time included secondary, instrument, cross-country and Link Trainer courses. After the Southwest program shut down, he continued to teach students at Sky Harbor during the 1950s and 1960s and as of 1981 was still flying 100 hours a month, solidifying his reputation as one of the state's foremost instructor/pilots.

Ajo

The Border Patrol and the Corps of Engineers' photographic ships moved out of Ajo in the early 1920s. With them went the small service buildings, the tank cars of gasoline, and some of the town's prestige. The improved ball park and the little strip north of town were still available for landings. The little field was soon abandoned and another strip bladed out nearby but further to the north. This was the site directly adjacent to the slag pile, and both were owned by Phelps Dodge. Now and then a road grader wandered over the runway, making a few swipes to remove encroaching brush, but the site was a natural — its solid surface repelled all but the most persistent growth and therefore required little attention.

It was probably during late 1929 when the Ajo District Chamber of Commerce negotiated with the Bureau of Land Management for 160 acres five miles north of the city for a new airport. The enterprise was backed by Phelps Dodge and work must have been completed prior to January, 1930, as the *Aero Digest* of that month announced that Ajo had been named by the Customs Service as a second port of entry along the Arizona-Mexico border.

The year 1930 was a busy one for Ajo's new field. Word spread rapidly about the handy port of entry. In early January, Charlie Gilpin of G & G Airlines landed in a ten-passenger Bach with passengers en route to Puerto Peñasco for fishing. The next month a southbound Scenic Airways ship nosed up in the mud. A wrecking car summoned from town righted the Fairchild 71. It was gassed and the party was on its way with just over a thirty minute delay. It was an easy ninety mile hop from Phoenix to Ajo and a similar distance from there to Puerto Peñasco if the pilot flew a straight line — maybe ten miles more if he elected to "highway it." It took two and one-half hours elapsed time as opposed to almost two days of rough road travel. Occasionally the air travelers did not win. During the first week of April a charter pilot was forced by a failing engine to land fourteen miles short of his destination. No injuries were reported, but it took him and his two passengers more than two days to walk through the desert to Puerto Peñasco and help.

Ajo's airport was officially dedicated on April 12, 1930. It quickly became a popular refueling strip for those flying between San Diego and Tucson, as it was almost on a direct line. In addition to excellent service, the site offered a reliable if non-standard beacon. The smelter stack's towering smoke plume could be seen for miles.

During the national airport building program in late 1938 and early 1939, Pima County leased some land from the government and the present municipal field was begun with federal assistance.

World War II brought changes. The military moved into the area and built the Gila Bend Army Air Base. Ajo's airport received lengthened paved runways, a wooden control tower, and a covey of barracks with a maze of paved roads. Later a radar with its forest of antennas was installed on a low mesa southwest of the airport. At night the complex resembled a small lit-up city. Ajo acted as an auxiliary for Gila Bend, which in turn was an auxiliary for both Luke and Williams fields.

With the cessation of hostilities the Ajo Base was deeded back to Pima County. It ceased to be an auxiliary field, but Gila Bend continued as headquarters for the gunnery ranges used by fliers from both Luke and Williams Air Force Bases. Civilian flying up and down the Ajo-Gila Bend corridor was allowed with prior permission, which meant a phone or radio call to Gila Bend or Luke. Gila Bend furnished the final clearance which, if the ranges were "hot," was to remain one mile east of the highway and 600 feet above ground level. These transits in no way interfered with the gunnery practice. The fighters swooped down from the east and crossed the highway at about 200 feet (and thus under the civilians), dropped their missiles on the targets which were about a mile west of the highway and in line with the airport scoring towers, made a steep climbing turn to the east over the highway traffic and positioned themselves for another run. Everyone hoped that all concerned had good depth perception. There were never any reported conflicts. General aviation pilots called it "threading the needle" and other unprintable expressions. The military term for the little exercise is unrecorded.

Safford and The Gila Valley

Safford and its satellite communities were more fortunate than many parts of Arizona, being blessed with a reasonably stable farming economy, a good water supply, public-minded and aviation-conscious citizens, and frequent visits from Charlie Mayse, all of which kept aeronautical interest alive and thriving. Thus it was announced early in June 1928 during the Republican Aerial Pictorial Survey that the Safford Board of Supervisors had purchased 160 acres so that the community could have an airport. On August 19, 1928, the facility was officially dedicated as Wickersham Field.

During the mid-1930s the Safford "Cloudbusters Flying Club" was formed. The club members went on flights to nearby towns for breakfasts, to airport dedications, and elsewhere. Safford hummed and buzzed with airplanes and airplane talk, and by the late 1930s Wickersham Field was a busy place.

Its traffic included numerous visits from the local CAA Inspectors, E. V. Pettis and later Carroll Doak. Both men liked the Safford pilots but not their modus operandi. Everyone seemed to believe he was an experienced aircraft mechanic and a seasoned pilot. If accidents were a criteria, most of the local flyers were seasoned. Enthusiasm was high, but any degree of law and order was a myth. Formal flight instruction was intermittent. Charlie Mayse dropped in occassionally to promote sales and give a little instruction and much good advice. Earl Pylant, who had a small operation in Phoenix, came in and out at rare intervals. Inspector Pettis knew that private pilots instructed their friends (which was legal if no compensation changed hands), and he suspected, but could not prove, that the more advanced students were teaching for free. He did not so much blame the Gila Valley enthusiasts as he did circumstances, but was ready and willing to pin a violation on any unwary, lawless soul he could catch.

It was not difficult for two watchful students to observe Pettis' conspicuous black and orange Kinner Playboy sitting on the field or flying over the valley. Numerous good spots to set down offered an opportunity for the trainee to hop out, leaving his trainer to fly back to Wickersham solo—clean and legal. Everyone was polite and cooperative, always promising to abide by the rules, and they were not to be compared with a certain defiant and lawless group around Phoenix. However, Pettis's disposition was always short when he returned from the Gila country, and occasionally he complained of ulcers.

About 1936 two Safford pilots, Johnny Hicks and Gerry Rhodes, bought plans for a Pietenpol Air Camper designed to be powered with a Model A Ford engine. The would-be airplane builders found a used LeBlond 65 horsepower engine which packed more power and weighed less than a converted Ford motor. This would give the Camper increased load capacity and improve its performance. As for its effect on the plane's center of gravity, that was figured and eyeballed, and the trial flight would uncover any discrepancies.

Inspector Pettis, returning from his Safford trips, grudgingly admitted the mens' workmanship was good, but the idea of the frail little home-built craft—"an accident going somewhere to happen"—gave him chills and aggravated his ulcer.

Early in April 1937, Gerry Rhodes, with his twenty hours of experience, successfully test-hopped the little ship. It flew wonderfully and, with its 65 hp LeBlond, showed excellent performance that exceeded its owners' expectations. Now it had to be registered, have a number, and become a legal, though unlicensed aircraft, so Hicks and Rhodes flew in to Sky Harbor to confer with Pettis and make application for an identification number. There was nothing Pettis could do except urge the owners to be cautious and law-abiding, but he could pray that a bolt of lightning might strike the little rascal some dark night while it was tied down at Wickersham. The application papers were properly completed and left with Pettis for forwarding to Los Angeles and then Washington for a number assignment. Mr. Pettis had not personally approved of their efforts but he had been cooperative and very civil.

The numberless Pietenpol continued to fly and please its owner-builders. A few inquiries were made as to why no numbers had been assigned and the word was always that the papers were in process. The Bureau of Air Commerce had a heavy work load and a small budget.

Later in the fall of 1937, Inspector Pettis left for active duty with the Air Corps, and for the following half year Arizona saw only occasional visiting CAA officials who had no time to visit Safford. Before the arrival of the state's new inspector, Carroll Doak,the usual rumors flew. "He's a tough inspector, crabby and unreasonable." "He's a grand chap, easy to get along with, an ex-military man and a fine pilot." "He can't fly a kite."

As it turned out, Doak had less patience with unlicensed pilots and unlicensed aircraft than Pettis, and he zeroed in on the undesirable Pietenpol as his first target. He declared that that "homemade trap" would kill someone and he let it be known that he wanted it out of his territory. Moreover, the owners had continued to fly it without any identification, which was strictly illegal. Sharp words were exchanged by Doak and the owners. Hicks, being the impatient type, wrote to Santa Monica to question why the application for a number and registration had not been processed. The reply stated that the assigned number and registration data had been mailed to and received at Phoenix. Doak had simply held it with no action, and now he was in trouble. Some verbal fisticuffs ensued. Hicks and Rhodes left with the Pietenpol's registration and identification number for their ship, again with Doak's prediction that utter ruin and death awaited anyone foolish enough to fly the aircraft.

The home-made Pietenpol continued to soar and sputter over the valley and neighboring towns, but its flying days were numbered. The implementation of a new federal regulation on December 1, 1941, which stated that all pilots and aircraft must be federally certified, left "Piety" in limbo. With the outbreak of hostilities on December 7, Doak ordered the little plane disassembled. Compliance was acknowledged and several months later the controversial aircraft was sold to the Gila College as a required adjunct to their equipment for an approved ground school. The diminutive bird ended its days as a strictly legal but groundbased trainer.

The planners of both the government colored airways and their successors, the Omni or Victor Airways, ignored Safford and its Gila Valley satellite communities. However, some years later, when the high altitude jet airways were implemented, J-181 just grazed the thin high air above Safford Municipal's northeast border. For those not so fortunate as to have one of these official aerial highways to follow, the method inherited from Charlie Mayse, Cliff Davis, and other adventuresome souls was used. To quote from Mayse's directions, "Just take off and p'int her nose where you wanta go. You'll end up there sometime."

The Strip Country

The 37th Parallel marks the dividing line between Arizona and Utah. For over 400 miles the wayward Colorado on its journey to the sea has carved the massive Marble and Glen canyons on its southern course, and then with a right-angle turn westward has labored on its masterpiece, the Grand Canyon of the Colorado. The huge gorges hinder surface travel to and from the large northwestern rectangle of the state, and this desolate but beautiful country known as the "Strip" belongs economically, socially, and geographically—but not politically—to Utah.

Airplanes have been sputtering into and out of this region since the 1920s, but before World War II, few general aviation pilots ventured a flight from the Phoenix area direct to Salt Lake City. After he passed Ash Fork and Airway Green 4, no weather reports or reliable airports were available to the traveler until he reached Milford, Utah. The seasonal Grand Canyon field was not very popular; it and Fredonia were also some thirty miles off course, and the airport at Cedar City, Utah, was too small for a four-place ship if loaded. Radio communications were poor. Stories circulated about vicious downdrafts over the Canyon, and it was easier and safer to go around by Las Vegas. Residents of the strip, because of its proximity to Las Vegas and Salt Lake City, did their trading at those cities and seldom visited Phoenix. The remote land and its people were unknown to most in central Arizona.

Very early on the morning of February 16, 1944, an Army bomber was in trouble over the desolate and darkened strip. Somehow the ship, on its way to Las Vegas from Hill Air Base in Ogden, Utah, had gotten off course. It was lost and practically out of fuel. Jumping was an unattractive thought when the canyons of the Colorado and the spires and cliffs of Bryce and Zion Parks were both in the vicinity, and the earth below was a flat black blotter. The pilot circled once or twice, and suddenly all the lights in both Fredonia and Kanab were blinking. Now the crew could at least bail out near civilization and help, but what about those rumors that Fredonia had an airfield? With his last few gallons of fuel the pilot buzzed the town and the lights began concentrating in one spot. Meanwhile, five crew members had jumped. Suddenly below the ship was a long landing strip, illuminated by practically all the cars in town. The big bomber made a successful arrival and promptly sank in the soft dirt surface. As soon as daylight came citizens went on a search for the five jumpers. All were safely wrapped in their parachutes; only one had suffered an injury, a broken ankle. They were all taken to town, fed and allowed to rest. One more problem remained after refueling, and that was getting the big ship unstuck. A large truck was carefully backed up to the bomber's nose late that afternoon and then driven back and forth the length of the field to pack the soil. Takeoff was scheduled for daylight when the ground would be frozen solid, and the bomber's getaway was successfully accomplished. A thankful letter written by the captain and signed "gratefully yours" by each crew member came a few days later. The quick cooperation of the Fredonia and Kanab people had possible saved some lives and certainly some valuable property.

When an Omni was installed at Bryce Canyon and later another at Cedar City, there were a few less lost pilots to worry about. But by that time everyone was using the direct route to Salt Lake City. Those who had been most vocal concerning the wild canyon downdrafts and the horrible country admitted that the new way was superior.

For a time, uranium prospectors kept the Fredonia and Kanab airports active. In the late 1950s, Glen Canyon Dam plans brought more airplanes to the strip; the majority landed at Kanab. Contractors, their representatives, and suppliers flew in and out. It was not unusual to see twenty or thirty ships on the field, and on the project's bid-opening day a control tower would have been an asset.

Fredonia and the Arizona Strip made national headlines in the fall of 1964. Senator Barry Goldwater, a native Arizonan and the Republican candidate for President, chose to adhere to the pattern he had followed during his previous state campaigns. His opening speech would be in Prescott and the closing ceremony at Fredonia.

The scheduling of the speech at Fredonia caused some problems. The senator's chartered Boeing 727 would have to land at Kanab where the runway's length and wheel weight capability were questionable. In addition, the small airport would have to host a fleet of smaller aircraft carrying members of the press and the rest of the campaign entourage.

The party arrived at Kanab almost two hours late and the time element precluded the brief ride to Fredonia. The closing speech was given at the Kanab Airport before one of the largest crowds and largest collections of aircraft ever congregated on the Strip.

A New Name for an Old Flyway, Victor 190

The beginnings of the present direct route from Phoenix to Albuquerque, Airway Victor 190, are as clouded as its early reputation. The first airmen to use it were two intrepid Air Service lieutenants, John Macready and Oakley Kelly. The first general aviation pilot along its path was probably Bill Cutter from Albuquerque, as the records of early barnstormers in St. Johns and Springerville indicate they came south from Holbrook along the road.

Tales of Arizona's mountains, many exaggerated by retelling, did nothing to enhance the route's reputation. The Indians were peaceful, but the mountain lions were not. There were stories of unfortunate grounded flyers whose sad remains were carried out in baskets following what must have been a good meal for a hungry cat. Since the first Powder Puff Derby everyone knew that all southwestern bulls despised airplanes and would immediately attack a ship or its stranded pilot. The entire country was said to be plagued with horrible electrical storms accompanied by hailstones as large and hard as baseballs. The winds reportedly almost competed with the west Texas types, and everyone knew that in some locations wind socks were not practical—a good breeze could shred one in ten minutes. A stout logging chain provided the answer, and when the links began snapping off it was time to call in all solo students.

These tall tales did little to encourage air traffic in the area. By the mid-1930s there were few regions of the state that had not been covered by some type of airborne equipment. Balloons, barnstormers, airline surveys, the military, and fearless owners of small aircraft had soared, roared, sputtered and put-putted over almost the entire state, but the country south of Springerville and east of Highway 60 was still virtually unknown to pilots.

Even before the Los Angeles-Amarillo airway was bought by the government the carriers used it through central Arizona. Smaller craft veered northeast at Holbrook and clung to the Santa Fe tracks to Gallup, Grants, and then direct to Albuquerque. Later when TWA began its Phoenix-Albuquerque schedules, the DC-2s and 3s flew the non-radio airway to Winslow and then along Airway Green 4 to New Mexico. In spite of the wonderful new sectional charts, pilots got lost on the shorter direct route from Phoenix, particularly in the high, wide valley east of St. Johns. Eastbound travelers found themselves in either Belen or Magdalena, New Mexico; westbound, they might end up anywhere between Safford, Clifton, or Lordsburg if they mistook the Escudilla for Baldy Peak. General advice to pilots flying into the region was, "if you are lost, or think you are, head north to the Santa Fe and follow that."

Because of the Depression, the airports at St. Johns, Springerville and Globe-Miami had closed. Cautious eastbound pilots flew from Phoenix to Winslow and then along the Santa Fe into New Mexico. Some paddled around by way of Tucson, El Paso, and on to Amarillo. Braver souls whose aircraft had the necessary range flew direct, hoping to find better weather by avoiding Mt. Taylor. Open fields near Show Low, St. Johns, and the farms at Fence Lake comforted them. Telephones were miles apart and gasoline supplies dubious. An experienced pilot with a long range, high performance ship might try it. Otherwise, the long way around was best.

A pilot flying the direct route to Albuquerque took off from Sky Harbor and headed northeast, over Roosevelt Lake and the Apache Reservation, before reaching the first real settlement along the way, Show Low. Following World War II, a local pilot, B. Y. "Pete" Peterson, scraped out a short landing strip on a bed of almost level cinders two miles northeast of town. He used it to give lessons and also began twice-daily passenger runs to Phoenix. As Show Low gained popularity as a summer resort, Pete's business picked up and he added a runway and made additional improvements to the Show Low Airport. The runway was stretched, a short cross strip added, and a Unicom installed. Show Low was also designated as a weather reporting station, much to the delight of all general aviation pilots. Now, for the first time, reliable reports from this critical region were available on the circuit. No longer did pilots have to phone the sheriff or the local telephone operators to see if a flight to Albuquerque was feasible.

Leaving Show Low behind, the Albuquerque-bound pilot arrived over the communities of St. Johns and Springerville. St. Johns had developed a good landing field, but like hundreds of others around the state, it had been abandoned during the Depression. During the early 1940s the field was rejuvenated, much to the relief of those who used the route. Now they could stop and refuel without swinging to the north.

Following the renaissance of the St. Johns airport, travel increased along this route, and the new Highway 60 brought more visitors to the territory. Some of the residents of Springerville felt their town deserved a good airport. The final selection was one of the old sites formerly used by the early barnstormers on a mesa, some two miles west of downtown. With advice from the CAA, two runways were aligned. The county road grader came in and loosened the generous rock crop so that the unyielding surface was workable without heavy machinery, and then the entire community swung into action. Several "Rock Picking Days" were scheduled, and people swarmed out with trucks, wheelbarrows, picks, shovels, and carts to clear the two runways. Kids, dogs and horses followed; and each noon the women arrived with hot lunches. Those who helped with the project were issued honorary work certificates, and over 500 of these treasured pieces of paper were presented. Now the communities had a good dirt airport with two runways of about 4,500 feet each.

With the renewed activities of the airports at St. Johns and Springerville, aerial traffic along the direct route from Phoenix to Albuquerque gained additional popularity. It also gained some disgruntled pilots who realized the need for weather reporting and a navigational radio range along the way, preferably at St. Johns. Government agencies were approached and the bad weather conditions along Green 4 were explained. The conditions along the direct flyway twenty to thirty miles south were usually superior and the requested navigational facility would increase safety. Replies were the usual government brush-offs—"Traffic does not warrant the expense;" "Fly to Winslow and go along Green 4 ... everyone else does;" "The airlines do not care about it."

This was discouraging, but after the war, changes occurred rapidly. By October 15, 1950, over 250 Omni ranges were operative and the first Omni Airway was commissioned. It linked a chain of significant midwest and eastern cities into a controlled Visual Omni Airways. Gradually VOR's appeared at Albuquerque, Grants, Zuni, Winslow, Prescott, Needles and Phoenix, and later one was installed at St. Johns.

Now the new Airway, Victor 190, was open for business, and about a mile south of the old dirt road that meandered northwest from Quemado and snaked around the Little Salt Lake (a favorite checkpoint), and about twenty nautical miles west of that tiny settlement, sat the new St. Johns VOR. Now any confused or distressed pilot could fly to the new St. John's Omni turn to a heading of 280 degrees for some 12 miles and be over the paved St. John's Municipal Airport.

Prescott

Following the spectacular performance by the lady aerialist in spangled tights in 1890, aerial activity in Prescott was scant. The city did not have the population to attract the big-name air shows, and its mountainous location acted as an additional deterrent.

The first heavier-than-air machine was shipped into town for the fair of 1915. The tiny airplane was exhibited at the fairground, and while attendants held firmly to its wings, the pilot revved up the motor to an ear-splitting crescendo. His helpers let go of the impatient machine, it rose about fifty feet and flew around the half-mile track for a few laps.

In 1926, the Chamber of Commerce decided Prescott needed a real municipal airport. With the passage of the Air Commerce Act there was sure to be an increase in aeronautical activity, and while the target range field at nearby Fort Whipple was considered satisfactory by visiting pilots, it was not a proper facility for a growing city.

Unusual foresight and planning went into the selection of the site. Two runways were bladed off and some of the eager airport committee members grubbed out the worst of the dog holes and hummocks. A 100-foot circle graced the runways' intersection, and as an added touch of courtesy, a generous supply of manila rope and all the discarded Ford axles in town were on hand to provide tie-down facilities. Two outhouses were hastily constructed, and the Prescott Municipal field, without benefit of a master plan, survey, or studies, much less any state or federal aid, was open for business. The city, the volunteer workers, and the pilots were all happy, and a brief dedication ceremony was held on July 4, 1926. In August, 1929, the field was formally rededicated as the Ernest A. Love Airport.

Activity was reasonably brisk at first but the second wave of the Depression which swept the country in late 1932 and early 1933 almost washed the new airport away. Few transients stopped in for fuel; the little activity remaining was supported by two local pilots who hung on and hoped for better days. By late 1933, things looked a little brighter and a Prescott delegation visited the Copperclad Airways office at Phoenix Sky Harbor to see if instructor Paul Odneal would consider coming to their city one day a week to give flying lessons if they could guarantee him eight or ten hours of instruction. Mondays were always slow in Phoenix and Odneal believed the idea was worth a try. On his first trip more trainees turned out than were expected.

Love Field had worsened during the Depression. Only the three hangars remained. The telephone had been removed from its three-sided booth and the two outhouses had suffered complete demolition. However, pilots George Voller and Cliff Davis greeted Odneal, a 50-gallon drum of fuel waited for use, and the eager students were ready.

More students enrolled for the Monday classes, and by late summer of 1934, the Prescott Flying Club formed. The members obtained an old boxcar, removed its wheels, carted it to the airport, and with a neat coat of white and red paint a sort of informal administration building was established at Love Field. Old pieces of furniture scrounged from various members were painted, a wood stove installed, and an elderly couple moved in to oversee the activities. Two more outhouses went up, the telephone booth was repaired and a new floor and instrument added, and now pilots had a snug place to wait and communicate with the town. Soon a fuel pit appeared and Love Field was again a properly equipped and operating airport.

The phone booth quickly acquired a quiet but permanent tenant — a large bull snake — who spent his days stretched along two of the inner walls, bent in a 90° angle to take advantage of the sun's warmth filtering through the thin timbers. Strangers' reactions were sudden and noisy if no one had forewarned them of his presence and harmless nature. He or one of his twin brothers returned each summer for several years to spend the season guarding the phone company's equipment. He was borrowed several times for the Prescott Smoki ceremonies and carefully returned the following morning.

Gradually more transients stopped by, and the boxcar terminal building was again repainted and improved. A second wind sock had been installed on the little knoll to the east of the long runway, and the concrete circle at the intersection was dug up and the ground leveled. Love Field's improvements continued under the WPA Airport Expansion Plan. Two runways received pavement and with continued urging from the navy, a Weather Bureau communications station moved in. The field acquired inside plumbing and inside phones, and the bull snake moved to a quiet hangar. The old LA-A Airway, now Green 4, was realigned and Prescott received a radio station and an instrument approach.

After the disaster at Pearl Harbor, when all the flight schools along the West Coast were ordered out of the new ADIZ (Aircraft Defense Identification Zone), large CPTP and WTS programs moved to Love Field where they remained for the duration.

Following World War II Prescott and its airport continued to grow. Subdivisions mushroomed as people decided Prescott was a good place to live, and Love Field kept pace with more hangars, shops, and tiedowns. In 1977, Embry-Riddle Air University acquired the Prescott College plant and opened a branch of their eastern approved flight school, one of the oldest and largest such institutions in the country.

As for the bullsnake who so zealously guarded the telephone company's property, his descendants are still around and occasionally seen in quiet spots. Once a year they receive some public recognition. Armfuls are rounded up for the Smoki Ceremonials. Disguised as rattlesnakes, they play a prominent role in the dances, following which they are returned to their original airport habitat where they occasionally act as caretakers for a quiet hangar.

The Verde Valley

Marcus Rawlins was born in Texas, probably about 1893. He liked machinery, learned to drive a car when he was very young, and also took a few flying lessons, doubtless from itinerant barnstormers. An eye injury received when he was about nineteen ended his active flying, but not his interest in aviation. In 1923, he decided to move to Salt Lake City, and while en route he stopped for the night in Verde Valley. He never made it to Utah; he liked the pretty valley and believed it had a promising future for him and the airplane business which would in time bring him the title of "Mr. Aviation" for that small section of Arizona. Meanwhile, to earn some money, he went to work in the copper mine at Jerome.

In his spare time, Marcus studied local weather conditions, assisted by a few books and a Texas ranch boy's insight. He firmly believed that the only practical aerial route from the coast through central Arizona was through Needles, Prescott, the Verde Valley and direct to Winslow or Holbrook. When the forbidding Mogollon Rim was socked in, snow and turbulence raged around the San Francisco Peaks while the Verde Valley basked in sunshine. True, it sometimes stormed there, but ceilings were generally above 1,500 feet and the sky above navigable.

The Western Air Express, TAT, and TWA planners eschewed Marcus's ideas and recommendations. Although they would not admit it, the air carriers were still dependent on the railroads and would be tied to their steel apron strings for several more years.

Money in the Verde Valley was plentiful due to the Phelps Dodge and United Verde Extension mining interests. Already a small building boom had started; easterners were buying ranches around the valley's perimeter and building permanent homes. By 1927, Marcus, with his records, studies, and enthusiasm, had convinced the heads of UVX (United Verde Extension) that the valley should have an airport. Land for the project adjacent to Clemenceau, a small company town named after the French premier, was donated. The drab little settlement consisted of tiny unpainted houses surrounded by a large fence. Some said the fence was to keep the wild burros out of the kitchen gardens; others claimed it was to confine the wild miners on Saturday nights. The airport property was directly southwest of the three-strand wire barrier.

Marcus grubbed out and built the original airport by hand. The new facility was named the Verde Valley Airport and the first plane landed there in 1927. Marcus continued to slave on his airport during all his spare hours, and in a year the 1,050 foot landing patch had grown to a 2,000 foot runway. A shorter strip of some 1,200 feet now crossed it at right angles. The small hangar was almost completed and a new wind sock, furnished by an oil company, fluttered from its ridgepole.

A small group of enthusiastic local pilots as well as visitors from Phoenix kept the new field busy. Small weekend air shows with a local parachutist were staged. Since both the mines and smelter were active, the valley did not know a depression was in progress, and crowds flocked to the field for rides.

In 1931, W. A. "Bill" Clark, the young owner of United Verde Extension mining company, began making plans for a Nogales-Salt Lake City airline. He designated the field at Clemenceau as a stopping point and joined forces with Marcus Rawlins. Three million dollars were budgeted for the enterprise and six Stinson R-3s were ordered. The plans came to a sudden and tragic halt on April 15, 1932, when Clark and pilot Jack Lynch were killed in a crash two miles north of Cottonwood.

The combined effects of the accident and the Depression, which had finally caught up with the copper companies, caused local aviation activity to vanish. Marcus was forced to open an auto repair and appliance shop at the airport. He kept the runways graded, and fuel, a phone, and transportation to town waited for any stray pilot, but there was little business.

During 1934, the Copperclad Airways ships from Phoenix visited Verde Valley, the Prescott people came more often, and in the first nine months of 1935 twenty-five transients signed the airport register. It was an auspicious new beginning, and the next few years would bring further developments and changes in the quiet valley and its aviation activities.

Many local ranchers became interested in flying and had landing strips bladed out on their property. Soon the Verde Valley had more airports per capita than any other location in the state, and possibly the country. Marcus continued to improve his field. The runways were kept dragged and as free of rocks as possible, but with all their scraping and rolling a new crop of stones surfaced after every rain. The ramp and concrete warm-up pad were enlarged, and now the facility was capable of taking anything up to and including a DC-3 under most conditions.

On March 15, 1942, flight operations at Clemenceau were ordered suspended by the CAA and the War Department. Marcus continued his mechanical services until July and then left for Prescott to manage the maintenance for the Stinson Flying Service's CPTP and later WTS programs. Clemenceau reopened December 2, 1942, when a CPTP class moved there from Williams. Marcus returned to supervise maintenance and field operations. During this time his dream of a direct airway from Needles to Prescott, overflying the Verde Valley, became a reality with the realignment of Airway Green 4.

Following the war, Clemenceau buzzed with students training under the new GI program. Various federal, state, and local grants enabled the airport managers to enlarge and improve the field, and these improvements still continue.

Marcus Rawlins died in 1972, satisfied with the aeronautical progress in his beloved Verde Valley.

ARIZONA AVIATION COMES OF AGE

The wonderful new DC-3s were dependable; and with improved weather service, more sophisticated communications, and better-trained pilots, the carriers had little use for the emergency airports. Along Airway Red 9, when the government completed its wartime airport building program between Yuma, Gila Bend, and

Tucson, the military auxiliary facilities were so close together that a DC-3 (and possibly one of the huge newer DC-4s) could have experienced complete failure of all engines and had a fair chance of coming safely to earth on a paved runway.

On Green 5 eastward from Blythe, Quartzsite was the first auxiliary to be closed. It was followed by Sacaton, then Hassayampa; Red Rock was abandoned shortly after nearby Marana was opened. Smith's Field at Tonopah was maintained until the mid-1960s when its lights were removed, but it was adopted by local general pilots and the crop dusters. Salome lost its illumination in the late 1950s.

During the war, service pilots guardedly hinted of a new military VHF (Very High Frequency) airway between Los Angeles and Denver. It was all very hush-hush, but they prophesied that some day the restrictive four course, static plagued low-frequency ranges with their split and swinging beams would be replaced with this new efficient system. One only had to tune in the "coffee grinder" (frequency selector), identify the station, set the course to be flown on an indicator—any desired track from 001 to 360 degrees was possible—then keep the indicator needle centered and that track would be followed either to or from the station.

It all sounded wonderful, but general aviation had more pressing worries. From 1942 to 1945, only military aircraft had been manufactured in this country. The old prewar civilian aircraft were wearing out. Their engines, radios and accessories were feeble. Meanwhile, owners scrounged, fixed, patched, and traded to keep them flying until the wonderful new models would come on the market along with some desirable surplus military planes that were suitable, with modifications, for general aviation use.

By June 1, 1952, the country had 45,000 miles of the promised new VHF Victor Airways and 70,000 miles of the old low frequency routes in operation. There were delays and arguments in Washington. The military wanted its Tactical Air Navigation (TACAN) system, and some civilian representatives desired their VOR (Visual Omni Ranges) and DME (Distance Measuring Equipment) systems. The argument wore on until August 30, 1956, and was resolved by merging the two into the new "common system"— VORTAC, as it is known today. Four years before this, the decommission of the maligned low frequency ranges had begun in the east and the work was gradually progressing westward.

The first Air Route Traffic Control Center had been commissioned at Chicago on July 1, 1936. Los Angeles was soon added, and many more centers opened during World War II. Phoenix became the 35th city to receive the designation, which came April 19, 1959.

During the mid-1950s, studies were made of how to manage the proliferating civil and military air traffic, which the experts claimed had far outstripped the capabilities of the existing control system.

Then, on June 30, 1957, a TWA Super Constellation and a United Airlines DC-7 collided over the Grand Canyon. There were no survivors. A national uproar ensued, followed by more investigations and studies, which ultimately resulted in the new Federal Aviation Act of August 23, 1958.

The new legislation repealed the former Acts of 1926 and 1939, including miscellaneous interim mandates relevant to both civil and military aviation. The new Federal Aviation Agency would regulate and control America's navigable air space under a common system. The Civil Aeronautics Board (CAB) retained most of its responsibilities, including economic control of the air carriers and accident investigations.

So far as the run-of-the-mill general aviation pilot was concerned, the new Act had little impact. The amounts allocated to airways modernization, the grants-in-aid to airports and those for facilities and equipment were all equal to or greater than the 1958 sums. Better control and more airports would result, and whether the individual flier operated under the CAB or FAA was of little consequence. Such pilots had simple but expensive desires—namely, for more sophisticated radar service, better traffic control, additional control towers, improved weather services, and a complement of good airports.

A Department of Transportation for Arizona

Following World War II, general aviation activity in Arizona exploded. Civilians who had curtailed their flying for four long years eagerly snapped up surplus military airplanes and new production models. Hordes of discharged service pilots opened various operations, and generous government loans became available for individuals, young companies, and municipalities that needed new or updated aviation facilities. It soon became apparent that the state needed expert aeronautical advice and guidance.

In 1950, the Arizona Aviation Authority was formed. Six years later a reorganization created the State Department of Aeronautics, with James Vercellino as its director. The new department was responsible for the acquisition, construction, and operation of the state's new Grand Canyon Airport, and for regulating flying schools, flying clubs, and aircraft dealers. It was also charged with assisting counties and municipalities with technical advice and funding for airport development and improvement, developing a state aircraft registration and taxation system, directing the use of aircraft for emergencies, promoting air education, and assisting in the development of intrastate scheduled air carriers.

Changes were also occurring at the national level. A new federal Airport Development Aid Program increased the states' grants. In 1964 the total for the United States was in excess of $75 million.

By 1979 this amount had grown to over $147 million, with Arizona receiving over $1 million in airport aid.

The Arizona Department of Transportation was born July 1, 1974, as a consolidation of the State Highway Department, Motor Vehicle Department, State Highway Patrol, and Aeronautics Department. A 1979 department study showed that Arizona had 97 public and 99 private airports, and well over 5,000 resident flying machines. These included general aviation ships, crop dusters, gliders, and 45 hot air balloons.

One of these ballons is based in Prescott, where its bright colors and modern amenities attract considerable attention. Even so, it cannot compete with the exhausted, dingy object that magically inflated into a huge, gleaming, snow-white globe and soared over Prescott's plaza on that festive morning of July 4, 1890, carrying the brave lady aeronaut in her spangled tights.

Aviation is anything but static. Its progress and growth continue and accelerate. Figures written today can be erroneous by next week — or tomorrow. As astronaut John Glenn said on February 20, 1962, "our efforts today and what we've done so far are but small building blocks on a very high pyramid to come."

Sources

Interviews and Personal Correspondence

Adams, Henry
Albright, Sydney
Allard, D. C.
Anderson, L. D.
Baker, W. F.
Ballard, Walter
Barr, Alfred T.
Bean, Harold
Beard, Melba
Beaver, Marion
Beck, Paul
Bethancourt, Arthur
Betts, Edward
Bettwy, William
Boardman, Theresa
Brooksby, Alfred
Carpenter, Paul
Christofferson, Merrill
Clark, Hubert A.
Clarke, D. B.
Clay, Eugene O.
Connelly, Jack
Crocker, Emery
Crowl, Marjorie
Curlee, Art
Cutter, Mrs. William P.
Davis, Cliff
Davis, W. E.
Denny, Natalie
Doherty, Ralph

D'Olive, Charles A.
Dwiggens, Don
Epstein, Richard A.
Fryer, E. Reesman
Gardner, Gail
Garrison, Ersel
Gillespie, Bernard
Gilpin, Frank
Giragi, Columbus
Givens, Edward
Goldwater, Barry
Gosnell, Robert
Graham, E. C.
Grant, Darwin
Goulding, Harry
Guerin, Alfred M.
Harrison, Michael
Hathaway, Lucinda
Hathaway, Steve
Hayes, Carl D. W.
Hayward, Lealand
Henderson, Randall T.
Hereford, Rockwell
Hickerson, Carl
Hicks, John
Hirst, Charles
Housler, Gil
Hovart, Col. (ret.) William
Howard, Jack
Jensen, Martin

Johnson, Connor
Jones, Everett Sr.
Johnson, Walter
Kennedy, Robert
Kintner, James
Kitchell, James
Knee, Chester
Knier, Carl
Kolb, Emery
Kravitz, Irving
Langford, R. P.
Larkins, William
Larson, Norman
Lawrence, Harry
Lewis, Farrell
Lewis, Mary
Lindamen, Paul
Lisitzky, C. E.
Logan, Mrs. U. L.
Macready, Col. (ret.) John A.
Marsh, W. D.
Marshall, Natalie
Mayse, Charlie
Mayse, Lola
McEvoy, Albert
McKinney, Frederick A.
McSparron, Inja
Mellis, Tony
Metcalf, Thomas
Moore, A. Lee

Morgan, Allen
Morgan, Charles
Morgan, Thomas Jr.
Mounts, W. W.
Murillo, George
Murphy, Floyd
Murphy, James
Myrick, David F.
Neilson, Willis
Nelson, Carlyle LaMar
Odneal, Paul
Olsen, Ivan
Osborn, H. B.
Owenby, Harold
Packhard, Gene
Packhard, William
Parks, Harry
Parks, Laura
Peterson, B. Y.
Pettis, Edward V.
Phillips, Jack
Pirtle, Ira Jr.
Pradeau, Albert
Rankin, J. G.
Rawlins, Marcus

Reed, Thomas
Reinhold, Robert
Richards, Durell S.
Richardson, Keith
Richardson, Moselle
Ridgeway, Rider
Rockwell, John A.
Rodgers, George Z.
Roper, Stan
Russell, Idora
Schmitt, Mrs. Joseph
Scott, Denham
Schackelford, J. Gordon
Sherman, Benjamin
Smith, Leo
Smith, Pete
Snyder, George
Spain, Larry
Spain, Madeline
Steinke, George
Stephens, Glen
Stilwell, Floyd
Stockton, Henderson
Sykes, Gilbert
Taylor, Lloyd

Taylor, Neil S.
Thaden, Louise
Thomasson, Edward
Todd, Arthur
Uhl, Betty R.
VanDoren, George
Vaughn, Col. (ret.) Ralph G.
Vercellino, James
Volpi, Harry
Walker, Vera Dawn
Waterman, Waldo
Way, Thomas E. (Spike)
Wharton, William H.
Whelan, Bernard
Willard, Charles
Williams, Jack M.
Wilson, Ben
Wilson, Esther
Wilson, Newton
Wilson, T. M.
Wolfe, Paul
Wright, Ethel
Zimmer, Hugo

Newspapers

Ajo Copper News
Arizona Daily Star (Tucson)
Arizona Gazette (Phoenix 1892–1928)
Phoenix Evening Gazette (1928–present)
Arizona Republican (Phoenix 1910–1930)
Arizona Republic (Phoenix 1930–present)
Bisbee Daily Review
Brewery Gulch Gazette (Bisbee)
Coconino Sun (Flagstaff)
Courtland Arizonian
Deming Headlight (Deming, New Mexico)
Detroit Free Press
Douglas Daily Dispatch
Douglas International

Douglas Vidette
El Observador (Hermosillo, Sonora, Mexico)
El Paso Times
Graham County Guardian (Safford)
Mohave Miner (Kingman)
New York Times
Nogales Daily Herald
Nogales Oasis
Phoenix Herald
Prescott Courier
Salome Sun
Tempe News
Voz de Sonora (Hermosillo, Sonora, Mexico)
Williams News
Winslow Daily Mail
Yuma Morning Sun

Books

Broman, Charles H. *The Story of the Tucson Airport 1948–1966.* Tucson: privately published, 1966.

Davis, Joe, ed. *Flying Saucers Have Arrived.* New York: World Publishing Company, 1970.

Dollfuss, Charles, and Bouche, Henri. *Histoire de l'aeronautiques.* Paris: Société National Entreprises de Presses, 1942.

Emme, Eugene M., ed. *Aeronautics and Astronautics.* Washington, D.C.: NASA, 1960.

Hatfield, D. D. *Aeroplane Scrap Book.* Los Angeles: Northrop Institute of Aeronautics, 1971.

Josephy, Alvin M., ed. *The American Heritage History of Flight.* New York: Simon & Schuster, 1962.

Juptner, Joseph P. *U.S. Civil Aircraft, Volume 1.* Fallbrook, California: Aero Publishers, 1962.

Larkins, William. *The Ford Story.* Wichita: Robert E. Longe Co., 1958.

Marshall, James. *Santa Fe: The Railroad That Built An Empire.* New York: Random House, 1945.

McNitt, Frank. *Indian Traders.* Norman: University of Oklahoma Press, 1962.

Mingos, Howard. *Birth of An Industry.* New York: W. B. Conkey, 1930.

Scammerhorn, Howard. *Balloons to Jets.* Chicago: H. Regnery Co., 1957.

Smith, Henry L. *Airways.* New York: Russell and Russell, 1969.

Speakman, Frank and Frank C. Alexander. *History of the Albuquerque, New Mexico Airport 1928–1942.* Albuquerque: privately published, 1965.

Stanton, Robert D. *Down the Colorado.* Norman: University of Oklahoma Press, 1965.

Vallee, Jacques & Janine. *Challenge to Science: The UFO Enigma.* Chicago: H. Regnery Co., 1966.

Magazines

Clark, Nancy Tisdale. "Demise of Demon Rum," *Journal of Arizona History,* Vol. 18, No. 1 (Spring 1977).

Halstead, A. Stevens Jr. "Pioneer Flights," *Branding Iron,* 74 (Sept. 1965).

Harris, Sherwood. "Coast to Coast in Twelve Crashes," *American Heritage,* Vol. 4, No. 6 (October 1964).

Hobgood, Claire. "Imperial Junction As I Knew It," *Branding Iron,* 74 (Sept. 1965).

White, S. S. "Ballooning the American Way," *Air Force Magazine,* May 1968.

Aero Digest (various issues).

Air Service News Letter, Maxwell Air Force Base, Alabama (various issues).

Aviation Week and Space Technology (various issues).

Western Flying (various issues).

Exchangite Volume 8, October 1929.

Museums, Agencies, and Historical Societies

Air Force Historical Foundation, Bolling Air Force Base, Washington, D.C.

Arizona Department of Transportation, Phoenix, Arizona

Arizona Chapter of the Air Force Association

Arizona Historical Foundation Collection, Tempe, Arizona

Arizona Corporation Commission Microfilms, Phoenix, Arizona

Arizona Pioneers Historical Society, Tucson, Arizona

Arizona State Parks Board, Phoenix, Arizona

Davis-Monthan Air Force Base Archives, Tucson, Arizona

Luke Air Force Base Archives, Arizona

Maricopa Historical Society, Maricopa, Arizona

Maxwell Air Force Base Archives, Alabama

Mohave Pioneers Historical Society, Kingman, Arizona

Northern Arizona Museum, Flagstaff, Arizona

Phoenix State Archives, Phoenix, Arizona

Postal History Museum, Tucson, Arizona

United States Department of State, Civil Archives Division, Washington, D.C.

Williams Air Force Base Archives, Arizona

Index